THE ROAD TO WAR

DUTY & DRILL, COURAGE & CAPTURE

A HISTORICAL NOVEL BASED ON THE DIARY AND NOTES OF CAPTAIN WILLIAM C. FRODSHAM, JR.

BY

STEVEN BURGAUER

IUNIVERSE, INC.
NEW YORK   BLOOMINGTON

THE ROAD TO WAR
DUTY & DRILL, COURAGE & CAPTURE

iUniverse books may be ordered through booksellers or by contacting:

iUniverse
1663 Liberty Drive
Bloomington, IN 47403
www.iuniverse.com
1-800-Authors (1-800-288-4677)

Because of the dynamic nature of the Internet, any Web addresses or links contained in this book may have changed since publication and may no longer be valid.

ISBN: 978-1-4502-1880-1 (sc)
ISBN: 978-1-4502-1882-5 (dj)
ISBN: 978-1-4502-1881-8 (ebk)

Library of Congress Control Number: 2010903734

Printed in the United States of America

iUniverse rev. date: 3/25/2010

TO THOSE WHO WALK THE WALLS

THAT WE MIGHT BE FREE AND SAFE

ACKNOWLEDGMENTS

Even if an author is, in the final analysis, solely responsible for the finished product we call a book, such an undertaking is rarely written in a vacuum. I depend on an entire support network to bring such a large project to fruition. Let me acknowledge some of those people.

The Frodsham family of course. They not only allowed me unfettered access to Captain Frodsham's memoirs but also to his (unpublished) autobiography as well as correspondence he had with former comrades in arms. His daughter Victoria, especially, was of invaluable help, not only in initially spearheading the project but also in having enough confidence in me to complete it on time and in a manner acceptable to the family.

Significant contributions were made by my several readers, who read the first draft with love and care and made many positive suggestions. Margaret Burgauer, my mom, who knew Bill and Dottie well. Debra Burgauer, my wife and chief editor. Kate Rose Burgauer, my daughter, an exceptionally talented writer in her own right. My friend and neighbor, George Springs, brave soldier, veteran of the Korean War. James Duffy, historian and longtime friend.

I want to especially thank Robert DeGise, Ed.D., a former Marine who fought in the Pacific and was wounded at the battle for Iwo Jima during World War II. I want to thank him not only for his service but also for his valuable insights into Captain Frodsham's character and training.

Finally, I want to thank Bob Meismer, a talented graphic artist associated with the Peoria Public Library. Captain Frodsham did a free-hand sketch of the hedgerow battlefield in France where he was wounded in action and subsequently captured by superior German forces on 13 June 1944. I wanted to include the Captain's sketch in this book. But the years had not been kind to the ink or to the paper he drew it on. Bob did a masterful job of reproducing the original map using modern techniques. It now appears herein on page 240 of the manuscript, as well as on the cover

AUTHOR'S INTRODUCTION

When I was a boy, I lived across the lane from this man. He was different from my father. This man had a gun. He had been in the war. My father had not.

My parents were very close to this man and to his wife. The wife was at my family's house nearly every day, visiting with my mother. Her name was Dottie. His name was Bill. I called them Mr. and Mrs. Frodsham, occasionally Mr. and Mrs. F.

Bill and Dottie had two kids, both much younger than me. I was maybe fourteen at the time. When I was a bit older, I met their oldest son. His name was Dennis but he went by Buz. Dennis was married, going to college at the time, perhaps graduate school. He and his wife lived with Mr. and Mrs. Frodsham for a while. The house seemed crowded.

Sometimes, when Mr. and Mrs. F went out, I would baby-sit for the two younger kids, a boy, Christopher, and a girl, Victoria. The kids were fun, and I liked them. Apparently, my parents did too, as they soon became godparents to these kids from across the street. I wasn't sure what being a godparent meant, but it sounded important.

Fast forward now, half a decade. I'm done with college, getting married. The families are still close. Vicki is a flower girl in our wedding. At rehearsal dinner, Christopher, now twelve, is sipping on a beer, slowly getting drunk. My father is playing the piano, something he loved to do. Everyone is smiling.

Now married, I moved away from home. In time, Bill and Dottie leave the area as well, move east, relocate in the Carolinas. I lived my life, lost track of theirs.

Flash forward now, three decades. I have had a career in investment brokering, retired, now teaching economics part time, writing science fiction most of the time.

Suddenly comes a question. That little girl Vicki, now a full-grown woman with children of her own, contacts me. It is the sixty-fifth anniversary of D-Day, both her parents are dead, and she has in her hand her father's memoirs recounting his experiences in World War II. She knows that I am a writer. She would like to see her father's memoirs published. Could I give her any advice how to make that dream a reality?

Next thing I know, I'm deeply involved in the project. Rather than just a dry recitation of facts and events, I have written it as a "novel." I put the word in quotation marks because novels are generally fiction. This is not. This is real.

But in some sense it *is* fiction. To avoid making this account read like a Russian novel, filled with countless unpronounceable names and enough characters to fill a small telephone book, I have simplified matters a great deal, changing names to protect identities, eliminating characters that add little to the story, constructing others as composites of several people spliced together as one. Historical characters, such as General Eisenhower remain intact, blisters and all.

So as to not make this account an unreadable textbook, I have limited the use of maps and the like. But, inevitably, a reader may want to summon a Google map of southern England or the Normandy coast to help follow along. There are countless online sources of maps. I only mention Google, as I referred to it often.

Writing this book entailed much research. I don't know from guns or grenades. Wikipedia was an incredible aid to me in this regard.

William had a remarkable memory. Written so many years after the fact, I would say William possessed a stunning clarity in his recollection of events. I, myself, at a much younger age cannot lay claim to remembering so many details from my twenties. Even so, William had at least some of his "facts" wrong.

For instance, he reports in his text that he returned to the United States after the war onboard the U.S.S. *Lafayette*. He specifically mentions that the *Lafayette* was formerly an Italian luxury liner by the name of the *Conte Grande* before the United States military commandeered it to carry troops. — Not possible.

The *Lafayette* began life as a French-built luxury liner called the *Normandie*. The *Normandie* was seized in New York by the United States after the fall of France. It was to be converted into a high-speed troopship but caught fire and sank. It was later raised again at great expense and floated to the Brooklyn Naval Shipyard for repair but never returned to service and was later sold for scrap.

The *Conte Grande*, on the other hand, was indeed captured from the Italians. It did indeed become a troopship. But it was renamed the U.S.S. *Monticello*, not the *Lafayette*.

So which story is correct? I suspect William came home on the *Monticello*, as the *Lafayette* was still in a Brooklyn shipyard at the time of his return.

I found several such "problems" in Mr. Frodsham's account. In each case, I had to go with my best guess as to the actual facts. Any mistakes in this regard are entirely mine.

Thus, I call this work a "novel." It is somewhat fictionalized and somewhat improvised. William reveals very little about himself in his account. He doesn't reveal whether or not he misses home, whether he is lonely, whether he is scared. So I have tried to ferret out his feelings the best I could. Again, any mistakes in this regard are entirely mine.

But even with these admitted shortcomings, what remains is still an amazing story of youthful valor. A young man — patriotic, athletic, daring, willing to take risks — enlists in the Army to defend the country he loves so dearly. His leadership skills and acumen with guns and field artillery is quickly recognized by his superiors, and he is encouraged to become an officer.

William trains hard, leads his men into battle, makes snap decisions, is wounded, captured by the enemy, slapped into solitary confinement, sent to a prisoner-of-war camp on the Eastern Front, starved to within a few inches of his life.

Yet, he returns home after the war a hero and what does he do? — promptly enlists in the Army Reserve.

A classic American story. I think you will like it.

Respectfully,
Steven Burgauer
June 6, 2010
D-Day plus 66 years

LIEUTENANT WILLIAM C. FRODSHAM, JR.
Marazion, Cornwall, England, Spring 1944

(reprinted with permission by the Estate of Captain William C. Frodsham, Jr.)

PREFACE

For more than fifty years I tried unsuccessfully to forget the events of World War II. Finally, in 1994, shortly before the fiftieth anniversary of the Normandy assault, I started communicating with old buddies and joined my Division Association.

Realizing that there might be some historical value to be gained from my writing because our Army is so different now, I thought putting my experiences down on paper might perhaps be appreciated.

When I decided to tell the story of my time on active duty in the Army, I felt holding it to a minimum of detail and avoiding the excessive use of adjectives would limit over-emphasis of the good times and the trials and tribulations which popped up all too frequently.

What has developed is a narrative that will give you the flavor of things as they were and some of the actions I lived through. I have chosen to describe but a few of the many battles I experienced during my relatively short time in combat, only a small part of the total. For instance, there is scant mention of the frequent bombarding by heavy mortars and artillery, or the murderous fighting in the hedgerows.

Each hedgerow was a new scrap. Often, we could knock out a machine gun, kill a few Germans and gain another three to four hundred feet of France. The Germans would retreat, often to a hedgerow with prepared positions. They would have holes dug through the hedgerow near the ends for their machine guns to fire through, as well as many holes all along for their riflemen. Concentrating fire into the corners often temporarily eliminated a machine gun, and a frontal attack was the only way to get at them. Flanking moves often found the flankers

STEVEN BURGAUER

getting lost, because the fields were odd-shaped, with no order apparent. Very confusing.

No sooner would we take such a hedgerow by force, than horrendous enemy bombardments by heavy mortar or artillery would zero-in on us. The shells would fall on us with disastrous results, as we had no time to dig in to protect ourselves before they hit.

The Germans had more — and heavier — mortars than we did. My Rifle Platoon was not equipped with any mortars at all. What mortars the Company had were light, 60 mm mortars, and they were deployed at the CO's discretion.

The enemy's MG 42 was the best machine gun in the world, firing at a cyclic rate of twelve hundred rounds per minute versus our heavy machine gun which fired at a rate of only six hundred rounds per minute. The Company I was attached to had two sections of light machine guns as well as three sections of 60 mm mortars and two .50 calibre machine guns. The heavy machine guns and 80 mm mortars were in H Company.

Further, a German squad had at least four Schmeisser machine-pistols with a high rate of fire. They sounded like pieces of cloth being ripped, hence the nickname B-r-r-rp, or Burp gun.

In my forty-man platoon I had three bazooka teams, as well as three B.A.R. (Browning Automatic Rifle) teams, one of each in each squad. The rest of us were armed with M1 rifles and, in my case, a carbine, plus all the grenades we could carry.

If your bazooka men were good, and still had ammunition, maybe a machine gun would be destroyed. But not all bazooka men were that good, and ammo had to be used wisely. They were, primarily, an anti-tank weapon, but light. The German Panzerfaust was far superior and was designed to be operated by only one man, not a team.

A word about the Germans. They — at least the ones I faced — were very, very good, tough soldiers.

I have avoided expressing my feelings in detail, particularly about the carnage, with men being hit or blown apart and dieing, in favor of milder descriptions. The thing that still sticks in my memory is the smell of large amounts of freshly spilled blood. It is a funny smell, but not an unpleasant one, a sweetish-thick smell that could be sickening. I was always afraid, but quickly became wily, crafty and often bold.

There is just a little mention of the tremendous courage of my men. They were the best.

Further, there is no mention of the one time I gave the command to "Fix bayonets!" and led the charge into a German position where we cut them up. I killed one with my trench knife and took out two with my bare hands. That is one memory that is still with me, unfortunately.

In short, what I have created is, hopefully, easy reading. There are numerous maps, photos, and original copies of orders. Consult them, for they will shed some light on my life in the Army of World War II.

Respectfully,
Captain (Retired) William Frodsham, Jr.

1994
PROLOGUE

Under cover of darkness, we had crossed the Vire River deep inside occupied France and were now behind enemy lines. It was very early on D-Day plus 7, and I was the lieutenant in charge of Third Platoon, G Company, 175th Infantry Regiment, part of the 29th Infantry Division.

The day before, on 12 June, our Company had made an aborted attempt to cross this key river in boats. But the Germans had turned us back with harsh counter fire. Now we were in a sort of frustrating stalemate, with the Jerrys holding one bank of the river and our Company holding the other.

We were dug in and waiting for orders. After fighting our way a dozen miles into Normandy, my men were worn out and tired. Our bodies were dirty, our minds numb. My men were hungry, their bellies empty. But they weren't complaining.

I was proud of my men. They had fought well. We had already been through a lot together. Our unit had been on the move, with only one day's rest, since just after sunrise on 7 June, when we landed on the coast at DOG GREEN BEACH in the second wave.

Soon new orders arrived from our Company commander. We were to move further south along the river to a point where intelligence had determined the river to be only two feet deep. We were to traverse the river at that shallow point, move cross-country, then seize and hold the several bridges where an important road crossed the Vire-et-Taute

Canal. This was the only route Allied armor could use to push further inland. But, in crossing the river at that shallow spot, we would end up several miles behind known German lines.

The Company was beefed up with the addition of a section of heavy machine guns from H Company. In total, our force now numbered more than two hundred men, including our Regimental Commander.

Moving out now in a column of platoons, by 2300 hours we arrived at the point where we needed to cross. It was dark, very dark. No moon. No light whatsoever.

An hour later, at 0003 hours 13 June, I was in the black water leading my men across the river. The information was correct, at least in one respect. The water at that spot was only about two-and-a-half feet deep.

But, beneath the water, there was more than a foot of gooey mud. This made for a rather messy crossing. To keep our weapons dry, we held them over our heads as we quietly slogged and slopped our way through the water and muck to the other side.

Half-covered with mud now, we fanned out on the opposite bank and positioned ourselves to move quietly cross-country. My platoon was on the left, Second Platoon on the right and First and Fourth Platoons in the rear behind Second. Fourth was our Heavy Weapons Platoon.

We edged forward. All of this was done with extreme quiet. We were behind enemy lines. No conversation. As little sound as possible.

We passed by a tiny, no-name hamlet, my platoon still on the left as we advanced. The rest of the Company passed through the center of the village. Less than a mile further on we ran into trouble.

Reading maps and plotting our position had become a practical impossibility in the black of night. We relied instead on our compasses and our intuition, a near-perfect recipe for making a mistake.

Moments later all hell broke loose. My Third Platoon had stumbled onto a German patrol bivouacked for the night. Most of the enemy was asleep. No matter. A short but vicious firefight ensued. It didn't last long. Conditions favored my men and we killed a lot of sleeping Germans without any losses to our own forces.

Success in hand, I rapidly disengaged my men and we continued toward the bridges. At least I hoped we were headed in the right direction, as we were still traveling somewhat blind in the dark.

In the minutes ahead, the sky began to lighten as dawn approached. I broke out my flashlight and buried myself under my raincoat. Hidden this way, with a little natural light, I was finally able to check our position on my map.

What I discovered made my heart skip a beat. We were south and east of la Roy. That meant our connecting file was gone. This was dangerous. *We were advancing without contact with the rest of the Company.*

I needed a moment to think and decided this would be a good place for us to stop for a short rest. We had been on the move for nearly twelve hours now.

By 0700 we were up again and moving. I was determined to push my men until we reached our objective, the bridges.

We continued to observe complete and total silence. I controlled my men's movements with hand signals. Going was slow, though not as slow as it had been during the night.

Each hedgerow represented a new danger, every hidden spot a possible German position. Each field — as well as the hedgerow beyond — had to be thoroughly scanned before risking an attempt to move out into the open and cross it.

Caution, caution, caution. These were our watchwords.

In the dark we had moved in a tight group, fairly well bunched up. Each man followed the man in front of him so as to not get lost.

But, as the sky lightened, our tactic had to change. I decided to employ a skirmish line: two squads up front, the third holding back.

With the platoon dispersed this way, enemy resistance would not have a concentration of men to fire upon.

My men understood my motives. It was simple economics. Spread out this way, an exploding mortar round would take down fewer of us, leaving more of us alive to carry on the fight. We moved forward slowly and carefully.

About 0800 we came upon a small farmhouse with what appeared to be an upstairs loft. Two of my men spoke fluent French, so I kept them at my side as I entered the house. An older French man and woman — probably husband and wife — stood inside the door. They held on to one another, obviously frightened. I couldn't blame them.

Who among us wouldn't be terrified if a contingent of foreign soldiers brandishing automatic weapons entered their home, drenched in mud, sweat, and blood?

And, even if these people did recognize us as being American, even if they did recognize us as being allies in common cause to expel their Nazi occupiers, we were still fierce-some looking men — and we were still present in their home without so much as an invitation. That would scare me too.

I could see the fear in the old man's eyes. He and his wife were at once frightened and excited. We were liberators, yes. But we were also destroyers. Our armies were about to tear up their fields and their homes and their towns as we drove relentlessly toward the heart of Germany. And, in our wake, we would leave behind stinking corpses and dead bodies for them to clean up after, as well as mountains of rubble and debris.

I turned to one of my translators. "Ask these people if there are any Germans in the area?"

He did and they quietly whispered "Non." But they pointed nervously toward the ceiling over their heads. We got their meaning and immediately proceeded to fire a clip apiece into the ceiling.

Plaster fell everywhere. At the sound of gunfire, the old woman began to scream. Her husband clamped his hand over her mouth to keep her quiet. I could imagine my own wife Connie in the same situation. She would have fainted, I was sure.

At the corner of the room was a ladder-style stairway to the loft overhead. I poked my head up through the opening and spied two German soldiers lying on the floor badly wounded and moaning. Our wild firing had hit them.

Holding tight to my weapon, I climbed up through the opening in the floor. Several of my men followed. On a table in the corner of the loft we discovered a field phone. Now everything was clear. *This was an outpost. These men had probably seen us approach, maybe warned others in the vicinity.*

I instructed my men to pull up the phones and cut the wires outside. I had my aid man shoot up the Germans with morphine and bandage their wounds. Then we were out the door and again on our way. *But I was troubled.*

Despite our every effort, silence had now most definitely been broken. There was a small chance that the sound of our guns being fired had been muffled because we were inside the house.

But that was a big maybe. Plus, those Germans had probably alerted their unit of our approach. But, maybe, if we moved fast, we would be okay. Resuming total silence, we crossed the next three fields nearly at a run.

Once I felt we were out of immediate danger, I stopped my platoon in the shadow of the closest hedgerow to check my map and verify our position. We were almost to the road that crossed the Vire-et-Taute Canal.

I didn't want to remain out in the open long, so I decided to stay off the road and confine our movements to the fields that ran parallel to it. The bridges were close. Probably only a couple hundred yards off. We couldn't see them yet. Maybe another field or two.

Because the road was as important to the Germans as it was to us, I knew we had to be extra careful now.

Scrutinizing every inch of the field ahead of us and the hedgerow beyond it, we saw no sign of the enemy. I signaled my men to climb over the hedgerow and start across the field.

But we only got about ten feet into the field when the Germans opened up on us with rifle and machine-gun fire. They had been well hidden behind that next hedgerow. Probably alerted to our presence by their comrades when we knocked out the outpost in that farmhouse loft.

I urgently shouted "Back!" to my men, and we beat a hasty retreat back over the hedgerow we had just crossed.

I was not at all happy with what had just taken place. I looked anxiously about, did a quick headcount. The men in my command seemed none the worse for the wear. But it was a close call. Somehow, none of us had been wounded or knocked down by enemy fire.

Now we responded in kind. We started firing back. I ran along the line of bushes shouting to my men, "Shoot only at what you can see!"

Soon we were in a full-blown fight. Within minutes, a couple of my men caught bullets. Doc, our aid man, sprang into action, quickly bandaged the two men, after which they again took up positions beside the hedgerow.

But we had a problem. The vegetative growth atop the hedgerows blurred our sightlines. We were shooting blind. Fortunately, the overgrowth across the way was quite sparse indeed.

Our tactical position was simple enough. We were pinned down. We were pinned down in a smaller field, with larger and wider fields on each side of us. A flanking attack would certainly meet with stiff resistance. For the moment, the enemy was firing in great volume at us with machine guns and rifles. Thus far, there had been no mortars flung our way. I thanked God for that one.

To hold them off, I moved B.A.R.'s to each flank, keeping one gun in the middle. These were Browning Automatic Rifles, and they were very effective guns. The Browning had a high muzzle velocity and was accurate out to about six hundred yards with sight adjustments. Our Brownings were the newer models, the ones with a skid-footed bipod fitted to the muzzle end of the barrel, as well as a redesigned magazine guide. My B.A.R. men were crack shots. Not to brag, but so was I.

The enemy continued to fire, and we continued to return fire. With the B.A.R.'s in place, we were being more effective knocking them down. Even so, several more of my men got hit, one badly.

The opening into the field in front of us was at the middle of a long hedgerow across the way. Suddenly, four Germans swung open the gate and set up a machine gun right there in the opening. I was amazed. It was as if they were going through a parade ground exercise rather than lethal battle.

Right about then, my B.A.R. man in the center of our line got hit in the left upper arm. I saw him go down and grabbed for his gun. I had no problem taking out the four enemy machine-gunners busy setting up their gun at the opposite gate.

In the minutes ahead, we kept picking away at the enemy. The moment we spotted someone stick his head out or saw a weapon protruding over the hedgerow, we would shoot.

About ten minutes later, another set of four Germans began to set up a second machine gun at the same spot, right smack in the middle of that opening.

I couldn't believe my eyes. I was still at the B.A.R. where I promptly dropped the four of them. I thought they must be nuts. *Why didn't they set up the gun over top of the hedgerow?* I couldn't figure it out. They had now lost eight men in a stupid move.

It was at about this time that I decided we needed reinforcements. I'm not sure what made me come to that decision. Maybe I reasoned that any force that could withstand the loss of eight men in rapid succession without withdrawing had to be much larger than my own.

I called over my Staff Sergeant. He was a good man, and I trusted him implicitly. Like me, his first name was Bill. I told Bill to work his way back and to the right to find the rest of the Company and to tell the Colonel of our plight. "Ask him for support," I said.

Bill left as ordered. But I never saw the man again. We didn't know it at the time, but the rest of our Company was fighting a losing battle some six hundred yards up the road to our right.

No sooner had Bill taken off, than there seemed to be a sudden, large increase in volume of fire from across the field. Jerry had brought two 40 mm anti-aircraft guns into position. The explosive rounds were now hitting the hedgerow, spraying us with small but deadly shrapnel.

I was still manning the Browning when suddenly I noticed that my men on the right flank had started to increase their rate of fire. Jerry was trying to sneak along the hedgerow, trying to outflank us on that side.

So far, our rifle and B.A.R. fire had them pinned down. To drive the enemy back, we tossed in a couple fragmentation grenades. That tore them up badly, knocking down perhaps eight of them at one time. The rest beat a hasty retreat.

My bazooka men had but two rounds remaining. I knew we had to use them judiciously. I gave the men orders to aim for the location where the 40 mm rounds seemed to be coming from, then crossed my fingers.

My men fired one round. It hit the hedgerow near the top. A miss. *Damn!*

My men moved a little to keep the Germans off-balance, then fired again. This time they aimed just a bit higher so the round would clear the bushes. *Bingo!* The second round — our last round — exploded just beyond the hedgerow. That AA gun fell silent.

Now, yet a third enemy team set up a machine gun in that opening. *These guys must be absolutely crazy*, I thought, as I dropped them with my trusty B.A.R. They had now lost twelve men trying to set up that gun.

My original B.A.R. man was now bandaged and back in the line of fire. I gave him back his piece. I don't remember the man's name.

The volume of fire from across the field seemed to lessen, if only for a moment. Then, another machine gun started up, this time from over top the hedgerow. *They had finally gotten smart*, I thought.

Again the fire from my men on the right flank got heavier. The Germans were trying yet another sneak move along that hedgerow. This time they didn't get far at all. My third B.A.R. man had moved to where he could fire his Browning from the opening across the entire field. Three of my riflemen were there alongside him. The opening was only about twenty feet from the corner of the hedgerow.

I figured the Germans had only recently moved to their current position. They were probably called back from defense of the bridges and were therefore not well dug in at all. *This might work to our advantage*, I thought. Plus, the absence of mortar fire indicated they were likely a rifle company not a full infantry company. That meant they were armed with lots of machine guns and Schmeisser MP 40 automatic guns but no cannons. I had seen at least four machine guns so far. A typical German infantry squad had at most two.

But then the situation changed drastically. We were suddenly under sustained fire from heavy cannon, my worst fear.

Based on what I could see through the bushes, the Jerrys had moved in two 88's, probably self-propelled. The big guns were positioned just behind the hedgerow. The 88 mm gun was a German anti-aircraft gun. It was used widely throughout the war and could be found on just about every battlefield, where it was often used as an anti-tank weapon. This particular pair of guns was about two hundred yards away and firing instantaneous detonator shells, very bad stuff.

With this new weapon now in place, a murderous barrage began to descend upon us. It ran the length of the hedgerow as their fire systematically traversed it from one end to the other. *The results were devastating.*

With nearly every explosion, now, my men were getting hit. One of my two men who were fluent in French went down with a big hole in his leg. I went over, cut open his pants, tore open a packet of sulfa powder and sprinkled it over the man's wound. I bandaged him best I could, shot him full with morphine using the syrette in his bandage pack. Then I laid him back against the hedgerow.

I moved to the right and found my B.A.R. man dead. His assistant now manned his gun. Everyone else was hunkered down. One of my Sergeants was dead. Another had half his right arm gone, plus a big, gaping wound in his abdomen. He, too, was dead.

There was a brief pause in the cannon fire. I glanced along the hedgerow counting heads. Some of the wounded were moaning in pain.

It looked as though I still had ten, perhaps as many as twelve men in position and still firing spasmodically.

But the firing was sporadic and accomplished little. The men fired only at what they could see, which wasn't much. Ammunition was low. So low, we were almost out of it. Whenever a man went down, we would take his ammunition, refill the B.A.R. magazines and distribute the rest. We had already fought for hours, stretching out what little remained.

From where I was, near the center of our position, I started left to check on my men on that side. I was in a crouch, running. After about two steps, there was an explosion on top of the hedgerow beside me. Something that felt like a rod of hot steel rammed into my left leg just above my knee. I knew I had been hit. But the sensation was short-lived. Within moments I passed out as I was lifted violently into the air.

I don't know how much time passed before I came to, perhaps minutes, maybe only seconds. But through a fog, I heard one of my men yell, "The Lieutenant's dead!"

Me, I was dazed, not dead. I raised myself half-up on my arms and answered his frenzied call.

"In a pig's fuckin' whistle, he is!"

But my bravado didn't match my condition. I was splayed out on the ground about ten or twelve feet from the base of the hedgerow, lying in a pool of blood — my own. The explosion must have flipped me through the air.

Rolling, now, onto my side, I pulled myself back in the direction of the hedgerow using my arms and hands. I cut open my pants leg where it hurt, and sprinkled the last of my sulfa powder into the wound. It cooled the fire of pain down a bit. But the damn thing still hurt like hell.

I had no bandages left, nor any morphine. I had used the last of it minutes ago on another man. I thought to call our aid man for help. But from where I lay, I could see that he too was dead. There would be no relief for my pain, nor any bandage for my wound.

My B.A.R. man was dead. He had been in the center of our line near where I lay. So I rolled over, picked up his piece and propped myself against the hedgerow. I was hurting badly. But I wasn't defeated. I selected a few targets, managed to squeeze off a couple bursts. Our fire had dwindled to almost nothing. We were badly beaten down. It was over.

At about this moment, thirty or more Germans came pouring through the opening in the hedgerow to my right.

I yelled, "Cease fire!" to my men and threw down the Browning in defeat. I raised my hands best I could and said, "Kamerad!" I was surrendering my command, what little was left of it.

The German closest to me looked as mean as I looked scared. He raised his gun, pointed it at my head.

I judged my alternatives. Only two things could happen to me in the seconds ahead:

Either I was about to be shot dead or I was about to become a prisoner of war to the Third Reich.

At that moment in time, I wasn't sure which fate was worse.

7 DECEMBER 1941

Ah, what a glorious December day! Sunny and pleasant. Not your usual winter's day in upstate New Jersey.

At about two o'clock p.m. on that wonderful day, I picked up my girl and together we set out on a short afternoon drive. Connie huddled close to me in the car as we headed up through the Palisades Interstate Park. I loved being behind the wheel, and I loved being with her.

Car radios in those days were not very good. The one in my Plymouth coupe was out of order that day and refused to emit anything but a few squawks and a lot of static. So we turned it off and simply enjoyed each other's company. Before long, we found ourselves nearing the U.S. Military Academy at West Point.

When I was younger, my folks had often taken my sister and me up there on Saturdays. My father had great respect for the military — had served himself in World War I. Something about the place drew him back time after time. Together, we would watch the weekly parade of cadets across the grounds. I must have inherited that great love of his, for the sight of that long gray line of soldiers marching in perfect alignment — and with flawless precision — never failed to quicken my heartbeat or stir my soul.

Unfortunately, on that Sunday, there was no parade. But I had some familiarity with the campus, having visited it so many times before. This was Connie's first time, and I was proud to show off my knowledge of the place.

We explored, walking along the old battlements. Some dated back to the days of the Revolutionary War, when West Point was the site of a fort on the bluffs commanding the Hudson River fifty miles north of New York City. The place was like an outdoor museum, with countless muzzle-loading cannons of the old style, still displayed in position, seemingly ready to be fire upon British warships moving up the river. At various other places around the grounds, we saw mementos such as tanks and artillery pieces from previous wars.

Soon we found ourselves at the Academy's magnificent chapel. From there we drove over to the stadium. Not even the "Plain" — the cadets' name for the parade ground — escaped our scrutiny. The Academy had an aura of beauty and strength. Just being there filled us both with pride. We were proud of our country, proud to be Americans.

But December days are short, and this one was rapidly coming to a close. Soon darkness would be upon us. We headed home taking a different route. Shortly, we were in Paramus driving south on Route 17 toward Hackensack, where I lived.

We hadn't eaten all day and by now were feeling a bit hungry. I knew that Gorman's Silver Glen lay just ahead. So I decided to stop. The place was owned by the parents of Frank and Dick Gorman, two of our close friends from school.

The Silver Glen had become a favorite watering hole for our circle of friends, what a later generation might call a hangout. Dick Gorman was working the bar, his usual Sunday chore.

The atmosphere in the bar was unusually somber, even though the place was relatively crowded for a Sunday afternoon. The jukebox was silent, not even lit up, like it had been unplugged. I found that puzzling.

The buzz of conversation around the bar was noticeable. Patriotic music came from a small radio behind the counter. Dick came over to take our order.

"Hi, Connie, Bill. What'll you have?"

"Hi. Why are things so quiet in here? Is the jukebox broken?"

"Haven't you heard?" he answered. "The Japs bombed Pearl Harbor!"

"What?!?"

Connie and I were both shocked. My mind raced.

"You're kidding," I said.

"Where's Pearl Harbor?" Connie asked.

2

"I mean it. Pearl Harbor's a Navy base somewhere in Hawaii. It's been all over the news. We get reports on the radio every ten minutes or so. How could you have missed them?" Dick asked.

"We were out riding. The car radio's broken."

We ordered hamburgers and drinks, which came quickly. While we ate we listened to the radio. Bulletins came every few minutes. It was true, what Dick said. Little Japan had pulled a sneak attack on our Naval base. According to what sketchy information came across, there was a lot of damage and many people dead. *Those Japanese people must be crazy*, I thought.

America had kept out of the war in Europe. Now, most certainly, we would be in one. I could feel it in my bones.

Connie and I ate, then left quickly. Mildly confused and gripped by a growing rage, I dropped Connie off at her house and headed home.

Just who the hell did these little people think they were? Did this mean all-out war? If so, I would be part of it. There was no other way. It was in my blood.

When I walked into the house, my mother was sitting there, listening to the radio. She barely looked up, didn't say hello.

"Well, where is your uniform?"

Mom was just being herself. The woman was so patriotic, a timid fellow like Nathan Hale would look like a draft dodger by comparison. My own father had gone to war in 1916, and she was proud of him. Very proud.

The next morning I left the house early and went directly to the Army recruiting office. I would make her proud of me too.

8 DECEMBER 1941

There were no recruiting offices in Hackensack, New Jersey, where I lived. The closest recruiting offices to my home that I knew of were in Paterson, seven miles to the west. The recruiting offices were located in the same building that housed that town's main post office.

I arrived on the doorsteps of the post office shortly after eight o'clock in the morning, went directly to the door marked Marine Corps. I wasn't the first to arrive. Ten or twelve men were already in line ahead of me. Together we waited as the Marine Sergeant opened the place for business. He talked to us in turn and, before I knew it, I was sitting at his desk.

For more than a year already, America had had a military draft. However, the Marine Corps did not draw from that pool. Their physical standards were still very high, and my glasses immediately disqualified me.

Undeterred, I went next door to the Navy office. The Chief Petty Officer in charge gave me the same story. My eyeglasses disqualified me.

His recommendation was the same as the Marine Sergeant's had been — try the Army recruiter down the hall. I went home.

A week later, accompanied by my father, I returned to Paterson, this time to visit the Army recruiter. Because of my age, parental consent was required. I was still twenty at the time. Dad was willing to sign the necessary paperwork. But, as I discovered later, that wasn't his only reason for being there.

Dad's underlying purpose for accompanying me to the Army recruiting office was to enlist himself. Because of Dad's prior service, the Warrant Officer in charge advised my father to make inquiry directly to the War Department in Washington, D.C. His civilian position as Assistant Chief of the Hackensack Fire Department would probably qualify him for a direct commission as an officer.

Dad later negotiated a deal with the Department of the Navy that would grant him the rank of Commander with responsibility for firefighting instruction at the Bainbridge, Maryland Naval Training Center. Our mayor and city council refused to release him for active duty because he was slated to be the next Fire Chief. Dad later became head of Civil Defense for Hackensack as well as the surrounding communities.

Now, with my father's consent, the recruiter signed me into the Regular Army. I would report for duty two months' hence, on February 24, just four days after my twenty-first birthday. That suited me fine, as that would give me time to tie up loose ends, as well as having a chance to celebrate becoming twenty-one with my folks at home. I never registered for the draft.

The time to February 24 passed quickly. The first thing I needed to do was make peace with my employer. I had a full-time job at the Hackensack Post Office, where I was well liked. The Postmaster and his Assistant were sorry to see me go but understood perfectly. They gave me their blessings and assured me that my job would be waiting for me when I returned. Nobody said, "IF you come back." People didn't think like that.

Those sixty days were a busy and exhilarating time. I quickly put my few affairs in order. With it being the holidays and all, there were several farewell parties, each filled with plenty of emotion and more than passing wistfulness. My friends gave me the impression that I would be missed. Certainly a grand sendoff for a young man who had enlisted!

On the morning of February 24, I said goodbye to Mom and to my sister Margaret at home. There were tears on both sides of the aisle. I had said goodbye to my girl Connie the night before.

Dad drove me to the recruiting office in Paterson, where I was sworn into the service along with thirty other men. We had time only for a quick handshake and goodbye before all us recruits were directed to board a waiting bus for the trip to Newark. There we would undergo a physical examination, complete with vaccination and shots.

The bus took us south, directly to the National Guard Armory in Newark. It was a cool and drafty place. For hours, three hundred of us wound our way from table to table in the roomy drill hall. It wouldn't have been so bad except for one thing. Aside from for our shoes, every last one of us were naked and carrying our clothing rolled into a ball. *Talk about your goose bumps!* Remember, it was February, never a warm month in my home state.

Thinking back upon it now, I must laugh. What a sight we must have been. Three hundred naked men. A virtual cross-section of the human male anatomy. All sizes. All shapes. All inching their way slowly around the giant hall, moving from station to station as we were processed. And we weren't alone. With us were twenty or thirty Army nurses doing what nurses do. But they looked as if they couldn't have cared less.

The examination took nearly five hours, the first of many lines I would stand in as a soldier. Finally, they organized us into busloads for a trip to who knows where.

Our next destination proved to be Fort Dix, also in New Jersey, but further south still. The installation was enormous, much bigger than I expected. We were deposited outside a mess hall, probably one of several on base.

By now, of course, we were all tired and hungry. Most of us had been up since early that morning and had hardly eaten since. The Sergeant in charge of the bus called roll, after which we went in and ate. Army grub served up cafeteria style. *Yuck!* After years of enjoying my mom's fine home cooking, this was no bargain.

By the time we exited the mess hall, the buses had departed, probably to pick up more recruits. Men were pouring in daily. Our Sergeant called roll again, then turned us over to a Corporal. He marched us along a gravel road to a barracks area, where we were each assigned a bunk. As we walked, I thought again of those splendid marching soldiers I had seen with my folks now and again at West Point. Our line was not nearly so well organized, nor so pretty.

At the barracks we received our first instruction. The Corporal demonstrated how a bunk was to be made up, Army-style. No sooner were we done with that, than we formed up outside and roll was called again. It seemed there was going to be a lot of that. As we marched off, it dawned on me that it would be some time before any of us had a chance to sack out. *Those freshly made-up beds would have to wait a while longer.*

Next stop, the Quartermaster warehouse. This was a big operation, very important. The Quartermaster issued us uniforms, what they called OD's, for olive drab. As it was February, we were issued olive-drab wool uniforms, fatigues, field jacket, wool overcoat, raincoat, fatigue hat, olive-drab hat, socks, underwear, toilet articles, two pair of carefully-fitted boots that came above the ankle, as well as a canvas, barracks bag to carry it all in. Actually, the issue was complete, even down to a pair of olive-drab colored handkerchiefs, toothbrush, and set of towels.

We formed up outside the QM, gear in hand. Roll was called yet again. Wearily, we marched back the way we had come, full barracks bags slung over our shoulders.

Each barrack was identical. On the ground floor were two private rooms, a latrine, and a large squadroom. Upstairs was a second squadroom plus three private rooms.

Now, finally, we hit the sack. It was late. Everyone was asleep within minutes. Soon the place was filled with every type of snore. High, low, stuttering, whistling, even booming sounds arose from the sleeping troops. Surprisingly, the noise did not seem to bother anyone. We were so tired, our ears went to sleep along with our brains.

Thus ended my first day in this man's Army.

25 FEBRUARY 1942

Suddenly, we were awakened by someone yelling.

"Rise and shine! *Mess Call* in fifteen! Put on your OD's! Form up outside in the Company street! We'll march as a unit to the mess hall!"

At the sound, I sat straight up in my bed, tried to remember where I was. Then I looked outside. It was still dark. My wristwatch said it all. Five forty-five a.m. We had had about three hours' sleep.

Confusion reigned. Seventy to eighty men had to get out of bed, make a stop at the latrine, wash up, and get dressed. We had sacked out last night without a thought given to how our barracks bags were packed or to even where we set them down. Now clothes flew everywhere. Somehow we managed to make it in fifteen minutes, though I don't quite know how.

I could almost seeing it coming before we got out the door. The first thing the Corporal did was call roll. Then off we marched, this time to a different mess hall, one closer to our barracks than the one we ate in last night.

I have to admit, the food was a little better. But then, breakfast food is a little more difficult to muck up than supper.

After eating, we formed up outside and — you guessed it — roll was called again. We were instructed to return to our barracks where we would have free time until eight o'clock. Nearly everyone used every minute of that "free time" to make their beds and organize their uniforms. This time, clothing was folded neatly and barracks bags were repacked in a more sensible fashion.

At eight o'clock, we formed up in the street and, after the roll was called again, got our first instruction of the day. We learned how to stand at attention and how to salute. We were lectured on military courtesy then spent the rest of the morning at close-order drill, learning how to march.

Our Corporal was good. He knew how to get results. After the midday meal, we spent another two hours marching in formation, becoming progressively better at it each time we practiced.

Finally, about three o'clock that afternoon, we were given the rest of the day off, although we were warned to remain in the area. Most guys sacked out almost immediately, lying on top of their made-up bunks. We had been warned earlier that once a bed was made-up in the morning, it must remain that way all day until lights-out at night.

Just before five o'clock that afternoon, the Corporal came in, blew his whistle, and yelled, "Form up outside for *Retreat*!"

Most men did not know what *Retreat* was. On a military installation, bugle calls are used to indicate changes in the daily routine. They are usually centered around *Mess Call* or the raising or lowering of the flag. At the start of each day, before breakfast, *Reveille* is sounded and the flag is raised. At the end of the day, before supper, the flag is lowered and *Retreat* is sounded.

We stood, now, in formation outside our barracks. Once again, roll was called. We could hear a distant bugle sounding *Call To Retreat* followed by *Retreat*.

A bugle call is a beautiful thing. It consists only of notes from a single overtone series. This is a requirement, for the call must be played on a trumpet or bugle without moving any valves.

Once the flag was down, we then had a short time to clean up before supper. Following supper, we were off for the rest of the day. The Corporal told us that *Tattoo* (Army talk for lights-out) was at nine-thirty p.m. and that *Taps* would be played thirty minutes later. Everyone was to be in bed by then. Twice again that night we heard the sounds of a distant bugle instructing us what to do.

As an interesting aside, let me mention this. As a soldier with all of two days' service, I had no idea what "Tattoo" really stood for. It sounded like such a strange term for such an important moment in the day. Later, I learned. The term Tattoo dates from the seventeenth

9

century when the British Army was fighting in the Low Countries of Belgium and The Netherlands. Drummers from the garrison were sent out into the surrounding towns at 2130 hours (nine-thirty p.m.) each evening to inform the soldiers that it was time to return to barracks. The process was known as *doe den tap toe* (Dutch for "turn off the tap"), an instruction to innkeepers to stop serving beer to the soldiers and to send them home for the night. The drummers continued to play until the curfew at 2200 hours (ten p.m.).

Funny what we learn as we go through life.

.
.

The next morning, we were again awakened by our Corporal at 0545 hours. We formed up in the street. Roll was called. We stood *Reveille*.

After breakfast, we had to completely clean the barracks, leaving out no detail. Mop the floors. Do the windows. Clean the latrine. Make beds. Lash barracks bags to the foot of each bunk. Then form up to begin two days of testing in the Reception Station area.

There were two tests to be taken. The first was the Army General Classification Test — what amounted to an IQ test. The second, a day later, the Mechanical Aptitude Test. I found out later that my score (164) on the IQ test was the highest ever recorded by a recruit since the inception of the Station more than a year ago. My score on the Mechanical Aptitude Test (154) was also high.

But don't get the idea that I was some sort of prodigy. Only a week later, my record IQ score was beaten by another recruit, a former truck driver.

Not that anyone of us were particularly homesick. But our lives had now changed in every possible way from the lives we once knew. Just getting up from the couch and going to the refrigerator for something cold to drink was a thing of the past. Not only was there no refrigerator in the barracks, but from the moment we woke up at 0545 hours until the moment we lined up for *Retreat* at 1700 hours, our lives were under complete control of someone else. True, we did have our evenings free. But, without exception, we all found ourselves restricted to Post.

2 MARCH 1942

Three days after completing our testing, assignments began to trickle in. All day long, for the next few days, groups of men were called up and shipped out.

This was when I first became aware of how the Regular Army took care of its own. Three months ago, back in December, when I first enlisted, I had selected Ordnance as my preferred branch and asked for assignment to the Army base at Charleston, South Carolina, where I hoped to be trained as a welder. It seemed I was to remain here, at Fort Dix, until a spot opened up for me there in Charleston.

Now, as other men were shipped out and new recruits were arriving, I was temporarily assigned to another barracks in a different area of camp. Here, my barracks mates were a mixed lot, some regular Army enlistees like myself, some re-ups (trained men who had re-enlisted), and a number of former General Prisoners who had served time in the Army stockade after being convicted of felonies. This last group of men were a special lot. They had been given the opportunity to earn an honorable discharge in exchange for a period of clean and honorable service.

Being exposed to these previous-service soldiers at this point in my career made me very self-conscious of my shortcomings as a raw recruit. Above all else, I didn't want to look the part of the newbie or the "green" tenderfoot. This fear of rejection, perhaps ridicule, prompted me to engage in a bit of subterfuge. I quickly learned how to take advantage of some of the many services and items for sale at the Post Exchange, the PX.

The first step in my metamorphosis from tenderfoot to "experienced" soldier was to have my uniform altered so it would fit me to a tee. I bought Second Service Command patches, as well as brass indicators of the artillery branch for my newly tailored uniform.

To further enhance my transformation, I purchased a different model overseas cap from the one I had been given. This one had red piping on it, for artillery. A pair of low-cut quarter shoes made of tanned leather completed my makeover from raw recruit to what appeared to be a soldier with some service under his belt. The Second Service Command patches on my shirts and blouse made me appear to be what in the service was referred to as "Permanent Party," an established soldier with experience.

The final touch would have been to apply a glistening shine to my wonderful new leather shoes, something I couldn't easily do in my quarters. It occurred to me that a good shoeshine could be had in town. Only, I lacked a Class A pass which would allow me to get off Post. Permanent Party soldiers could leave the Post any time they weren't on duty. The pass covered travel off Post as far away as fifty miles.

I considered my options, looked at the identification card that came with my Army wallet. If a fellow didn't look close, the identification card resembled a Class A pass. Properly filled out with my name, rank, and Service Serial Number, I forged the signature of an officer. I was confident it could easily pass the MP's rapid inspection at the gate.

In those days anyway, it was easy to get in and out of Fort Dix by taxi. All it meant was stopping at the gate and presenting your pass. Actually, if a man exited the main gate at a peak period, which I always did, all he need do was flash his pass and the MP's would wave him on through. To improve my odds, I dirtied the celluloid window in my wallet to make the details on the pass a little more difficult for those fellows to read.

Now, with my revised appearance and phony Class A pass in hand, my life changed immeasurably. Now I was off Post nearly every night. A couple times I even took a bus and headed home for the weekend. Home wasn't far away.

Amazingly, my subterfuge actually worked. By using the same gate every time I came and went, my face became a familiar fixture to the MP's on duty, and they always let me through. After a while they wouldn't even look at my pass. They would see my face in the taxi and wave the cabbie on through.

During the days I would draw all kinds of work details. When a man is on Post and not assigned to a specific unit, the Army made certain each soldier was productive in some way. At first, because I could type, I found myself working in the Reception Station every waking hour.

This quickly became tiresome and boring, so I applied for, and received, assignment as permanent Latrine Orderly. This wasn't as bad as it sounds. Each day at 0800 hours I would lock up the latrine and clean it until the darn thing shined. At 0900 the barrack was inspected by an officer along with the First Sergeant. After that I was free for the rest of the day. I spent most of my free time at the Post Exchange or playing pool in the dayroom.

But after a time, even that became tiresome. There's only so much polishing and mopping a man can do. So I applied for the job of night fireman. Another snap job. Each night, before *Tattoo*, I would bank the furnace. In the morning, I would build the fire back up and clean the furnace room, all in preparation for the inspection at 0900 hours. Again, nothing to do all day. Someone else drew fireman duty on weekends.

I moved into one of the private rooms upstairs in the barracks with a fellow who had been a General Prisoner and who had taken the advantage of an opportunity to earn an honorable discharge. I'll call him Hanrahan.

In my new digs, I set myself up comfortably. Trips to town became less frequent but only because money was running short. On the other hand, movies cost nothing and there were several Service Clubs on Post. Plus, let's not overlook the Post library. Life as a "fat cat" was okay.

Comfortable as my room was, and with such light duty, I did have one thing that provided the occasional blip. Hanrahan was a nice, almost pretty young, blond guy. But he did have one hang-up, the same one that put him in the stockade originally. The man was a complete and total alcoholic. Hanrahan was so bad, a single beer from the PX would leave him drunk.

When Hanrahan got drunk, he became wild and pugnacious. More often than I can remember, I would be sitting there, relaxing on my bunk, when somebody would dash in and tell me that Hanrahan was under the influence and picking fights in the PX.

I had no choice but to interrupt my free time, dash off to the PX at a run and try and extricate the man from whatever jackpot he put himself in before the MP's arrived and slapped him in shackles. Then it was back up to the barracks, where I tossed him into a cold shower and tried to sober him up. Somehow I had become something I didn't want to be, the man's keeper. After about four weeks of this, Hanrahan was shipped out and I breathed a long sigh of relief.

You might recall I told you earlier that when I initially enlisted my first choice of assignments was to be posted to the Army base at Charleston, South Carolina, where I hoped to be trained as a welder. But, by early April, I was tired of waiting for the Army base at Charleston to place a requisition for recruits. I had decided by then that I wanted to get out of Fort Dix and on with my war.

One of the senior officers in the Reception Station was a Major who had served with my father in the First World War. I requested a meeting with the Major, explained my situation, and indicated that I would accept any assignment, thereby changing my original request for assignment to Ordnance.

Thankfully, the Major was a man of action. In a matter of days, my orders came through. I was to be assigned to Fort McClellan, Alabama, for basic training effective 19 April 1942.

19 APRIL 1942

I was part of a contingent of men that left Fort Dix by train the night of 17 April 1942.

Now you have to understand one thing about me. As a young man, I was comparatively well traveled. My parents believed deeply in the family car vacation long before such things became fashionable.

By age seventeen we had motored at vacation time across the country, in one instance all the way to California where my father was born and where my grandmother still lived. By then I had traveled with my parents through twenty-five of our forty-eight states as well as three of Canada's provinces. One trip included the Century of Progress World's Fair in Chicago in 1933.

But I didn't know the South well, and I hadn't traveled by train this far from home. I certainly had never taken a train trip that lasted nearly two days. I'm guessing we crossed parts of only four or five Eastern states. But at the time, it felt like twenty.

Much of the terrain we crossed was hilly and mountainous. Almost all of it was wooded. All night long and into the next day, we seemed to bounce from one train line to the next, first slowing, then speeding up again, constantly moving through switchyards and little towns.

Finally, late in the morning of 19 April, we arrived at the Fort. *But what a ride it had been!* I swear our train car had square wheels!

The train had followed a circuitous route through the mountains, and sleep had been hard to come by. We were traveling in coaches, after all, not sleeper cars, and we had ordinary seats, which were highly uncomfortable and certainly not designed for long-term travel.

During the long trip which, like I said, seemed to follow every branch line ever built, we made but one stop. It was late in the afternoon, when the train slowly ground to a halt somewhere in the middle of nowhere.

During that brief stop, we were allowed to get out of the cars to stretch our legs. I looked around, got my bearings. We were surrounded on three sides by heavily wooded hills. A small gravel road ran parallel to the tracks. Just a short way down the road I could see a house of sorts, as well as some people milling about.

From appearances, I decided we must be somewhere in what is now known as Appalachia. That means we were in Kentucky or West Virginia or Tennessee or North Carolina, maybe South Carolina or Georgia, perhaps Alabama or Mississippi. Take your pick. I did not know where we were, and no one told us. So making a clear identification of our location was next to impossible. Maybe it was supposed to be that way. It was wartime, and we were soldiers.

During our stop, we were made to stay close to the train and ordered not to speak to the folks we saw. All we could do was wave, which we did. The people waved back but did not approach.

I watched the goings-on with interest. The train took on water and then we were quickly on our way again. This outpost in the boonies couldn't have amounted to much, as the branch line we were on had but a single pair of rails. It was about halfway along in our journey south or perhaps southwest.

Fort McClellan is situated some six miles outside of the small town of Anniston, Alabama. The Fort was what the Army called a Branch Replacement Training Center, or BIRTC in Army-speak.

McClellan was a decent post. The cantonment area was spread across a slightly rolling plain. There was only one hill — Trench Hill — at the north end. The training Regiments were made up of four Battalions each, set in squares around a large parade ground. I emphasize the word "large," for the parade grounds were surely the largest I had ever seen. The arrangement of Battalions loosely resembled the organization of an active-duty outfit, with each Battalion consisting of four Companies.

Post Exchanges were scattered throughout the area. These establishments stocked practically anything a soldier might wish to buy, the Army's version of a modern convenience store.

There also were a number of enclosed theatres on base, at least two of which were "tent" theatres, which is to say, under canvas. Another theatre was open-air. During the day, the theatres were used mostly for lectures. At night, movies were shown.

There was a hospital, a Post QM, an athletic field and an artillery range. Also, a number of chapels. The Army saw to it that no soldier was ever far away from a chapel. Plus, two large Service Clubs.

I was assigned to Company B, 15th Battalion, 3rd Training Regiment. The 15th was bivouacked at the foot of Trench Hill, location of Regimental Headquarters. I found out later that, in a strange quirk of fate, I was in almost the same location as my father had been while in training with the 29th Division prior to going overseas during World War One.

The physical layout of each Training Company was exactly the same. There were four, one-story buildings in each camp. They were the mess hall, the Day Room, the latrine, and the supply room. All four buildings looked precisely alike from the outside and were situated at opposite ends of the Company street, with each pair facing the other down that "street."

Unlike my setup in Fort Dix, we no longer slept in barracks, but in large winterized pyramidal-shaped tents. The tents were mounted on a firm wooden base with walls about three-and-a-half feet high. Above the walls was a four-piece wooden framework over which the canvas was hung.

Each tent was furnished with a small heating apparatus known as a Sibley wood-burning stove. The Sibley stove dated back to late in the previous century and was hardly up to the task. It was made of iron and had a conical shape. It was fueled with a small amount of wood and regarded by some as quite efficient. Smoke was carried out via a stovepipe that passed up through the center of the tent. This was an obvious fire hazard, and it occasionally resulted in tents catching ablaze. The Sibley stove's heat output was very limited, and it was the subject of frequent jokes and ridicule. Enlisted men slept on canvas cots, though spring bed frames were eventually provided.

The mess hall was both our kitchen and our dining room. The latrine was our bathroom, complete with sinks and toilets. An adjoining room had showerheads placed all around the exterior walls. Privacy was now a thing of the past. There were eight of us bunking in each tent and many times that number sharing an "open" latrine arrangement.

We each slept on a small bed with a mattress and pillow. Each soldier was issued two OD wool blankets, two sheets, and a pillowcase. As before, our barracks bags were lashed to the head of the bed and our shoes, laced up, were placed under the bed. There were no cabinets or closets to hang clothing, so we had to become proficient with folding our uniforms carefully to keep them from becoming wrinkled.

20 APRIL 1942

Beginning with *Reveille* on the morning of 20 April, we found ourselves immersed in basic training.

Reveille was at 0545 hours. It came in the form of a bugle call from atop nearby Trench Hill.

We got up. Then, a few minutes later, we formed up at the command of another bugle call sounding *Assembly*. *Assembly* was sounded by our own Company bugler in our own Company area. Similar soundings could be heard from neighboring Companies all up and down the line.

Next, we fell out in Company street and formed up into our new platoon assignments. Then came the reports of each platoon Sergeant — "First Platoon, all present or accounted for, Sir!" — and so on with each of five platoons. Then we were dismissed to wash up, shave, and dress, something that wasn't as easy as it sounds, as two hundred men were all trying to do the same thing at once, and in the same place — the latrine.

The next call sounded by our bugler was *Mess Call*. We ate quickly. Then we hurried back to camp to clean up our tents, make our beds, and police the area around the tents. We did all of this each morning, as well as wash and scrub the wooden floors of our tents and scrub down the latrine. All these duties had to be done before *First Call* at 0800 hours, also referred to as *Call To Duty*.

As you can see, we lived by the bugle. This was still the old Army. Little had changed in this regard since probably before the Spanish-

American War. The Army was expanding rapidly in numbers, now, especially since the United States entered the war after Pearl Harbor.

But the bugle still told us what to do — and when. During the day you might hear *Sick Call* or *Pay Call*, among other calls. On Sundays, *Church Call*.

About noon each day we would hear the call for the noon meal. After lunch it would be *Assembly* to fall out for an afternoon of training.

At the completion of our duty day, we would return to our Company area to wash up and dress in Class A uniforms for *Retreat*.

First the bugler would sound *Assembly*. We would form up in the Company street. At precisely one minute before the scheduled lowering of the Post Flag, the bugler would sound *Call To Colors*. Then the bugler would sound *To The Colors*, during which time we would stand at attention and hold a salute until the *Call* ended. As I said, we lived our lives according to the bugle.

During the week, our tents were inspected each and every day by the First Sergeant. On Saturday mornings, we stood a formal inspection by a team of inspectors — the Company Commander, his most senior Captain, the First Sergeant, and our own platoon leader, a 1st Lieutenant. This inspection took place beginning at 0900 hours and lasted about one sixty minutes. Each soldier stood at attention at the foot of his bunk while the inspection party was inside, and remained inside until the entire Company had been covered. These inspections were tough. Everything had to be perfect and in order. Pity the soldier who cut corners or erred. Extra duty was a sure penalty. Often, whole tents would be gigged.

After Saturday inspection, we were free for the rest of the day. But, as we were still in training, we were restricted to Post.

Honestly, this was really not as bad as it sounds. On Post, there were many things for us to do. In addition to getting caught up with the cleaning and maintenance of our uniforms and equipment, we could take in a movie, visit the Service Club, hang around the Post Exchange or the Company area, engage in any number of athletic activities, read, write letters home, or just plain sack out.

Every Saturday night, at both Service Clubs on Post, there was dancing to a live big band (soldier musicians), as well as ample refreshments. Women were brought in from many of the surrounding towns, some from as far away as even Birmingham, Alabama, sixty miles to our west. Our civilian neighbors really went all-out for us. Each group of visiting women was accompanied by a chaperone from their hometown. The rules were simple. They were permitted to tell us only their first names, nothing more. Of course, rules are meant to be broken, and more than one short-term relationship was hastily formed.

To those of us who enjoyed dancing — and count me among them — Saturday nights were great. Not only was there the dancing. But the chance to make new acquaintances and to spend time with a woman was a real break from the strict routine we lived under the rest of the week.

I have to thank my mother for my love of dance and my love of music. She helped me to develop an appreciation for what was then, modern American music. She taught me that such music was very danceable and, at age fourteen, she taught me *how* to dance to it. That confidence on the dance floor later helped me pick up lots of girls.

As long as I'm on the subject of my mother, let me tell you something else about her. Mom was ahead of her time. She was one of the first women in town to get a driver's license. Imagine that!

Plus, let me tell you one more story about her before going back to my own. Before the war, back in the days of Prohibition, my parents would vacation up near the Canadian border. The four of us — me, Mom, Sis and Dad — would stay in a farmhouse just this side of the U.S. border. Each day we would make a trip into Montreal. So far as I could tell, there was only one purpose for these trips, to enable Mom to smuggle a pint bottle of booze back home each night inside her girdle. HA! And to think she later dared to call me a rascal!

Okay, back to Fort McClellan. Sundays were completely ours. There was no *Duty Call*. Essentially every minute of the day was our time to spend as we liked, so long as we stayed on Post of course. Naturally there were church services at each chapel. All denominations were represented by the Army Chaplains. A soldier had only to select the service that most-closely suited his religious calling. In our Company even Sunday meals were different. Each Company had its own cooks. Very often they would whip up a special baked food that was available to us at breakfast. Sunday dinner was probably the best meal of the week.

Our Day Room was a favorite spot for me. This or that women's club in Anniston had seen to it that the Day Room was furnished with writing desks, easy chairs, even a fine pool table that got plenty of use. Plus, we had a small radio set up on a table in one corner. To my memory, it was never turned off. It always seemed to be on, playing round the clock.

24 APRIL 1942

Among the very first things they taught us in basic training were the correct way to stand and the correct way to march. Close on their heels came lessons on military courtesy, proper hygiene, care and cleaning of ourselves as well as our uniforms. In short, how to look and act like soldiers.

Close-order drill consumed an hour out of each day, physical conditioning another hour. Although most of us came into the Army believing ourselves to be in good shape, we were not. For the first few days of conditioning, it seemed as if every muscle constantly ached. But soon we were getting hard, and the stiffness disappeared.

For me anyway, close-order drill did not pose much of a challenge. I found it easy, thanks to prior training I received as a member of the drill team while active in the Order of DeMolay. This was a youth organization sponsored by the Masonic Lodge in my hometown.

Even if close-order drill was a snap for me, this was not true for the majority of recruits. For most of my buddies, the whole idea of military discipline was a new experience. The idea of moving in concert with thirty-five to forty other men at the discretion of some noncom was unnerving. You would be amazed how many of my fellow recruits had trouble distinguishing their right foot from their left.

But, with practice came achievement. Soon we were moving correctly, and with precision. On account of my previous experience and admitted proficiency at this simple task, I was made squad leader.

With the new position came an elevation in rank, purely ceremonial, I assure you. As the unit's new "Adhesive Sergeant," I now wore stripes made from strips of adhesive tape on the shoulder of my uniform.

Aside from close-order drill and physical conditioning, the other six hours of our duty day were consumed by lectures and instruction. These covered a variety of skills and knowledge we each, as soldiers, needed to acquire.

The instruction went on for days. We wondered whether we would EVER be issued an actual rifle. It became almost an obsession with us. *How could we call ourselves soldiers if we didn't have a weapon to call our own?*

Meanwhile, I continued as an Adhesive Sergeant and soon became Platoon Guide. This position is normally granted to the second in command behind the Platoon Sergeant. Our Platoon Sergeant was a Buck Sergeant named George Huffmann. George was a Regular Army man with about ten year's service. He was a Georgia farm boy who had originally gone into the Army because jobs were so difficult to find. Our platoon leader was 1st Lieutenant Baker, another Southerner.

It goes without saying that whenever we moved between training areas during the day, we always marched. But that wasn't the end of it. In addition to our daily hour of physical training, we conducted a ten-mile march at least once a week. Plus, we were physically active in our off-time, regularly playing volleyball, for example, in the Company street. We had a number of teams, and the one I organized was the best in the unit, rarely losing a game.

One of the more interesting physical challenges we faced was the base Obstacle Course at the opposite end of the camp near the Drill Field. The course was difficult, about eight hundred yards of pure physical pain. Naturally, we competed against one another.

Each man strived for proficiency and speed, and each Company had its own champion team. Regimental meets were held to determine an overall Regimental champion. I had three special buddies on my team with me: Millard, a student at Florida State University; Alonzo, a postal clerk from Kingsport, Tennessee; and Stanley, a New York City policeman. We four were good and fast, and we made it our business to win the Regimental championship.

That was one of the things I liked best about the Army, the constant physical activity. Even as a young man, I was always athletic and always physically competitive. As a boy, I ran Track & Field. High jump. Broad jump. Discus and javelin. Ran the 440.

As a teenager, living near Riverside Park in Hackensack, me and about a dozen other neighborhood boys organized a club, The River Rats. In summer, we fielded a baseball team, a football team, built a boxing ring behind a neighbor's garage.

In winter, we skated on the inlets of the river. In high school, I did not try out for my school's baseball team — but with good reason. By age fourteen I was playing on an *adult* men's semi-pro ball team, the Bergenfield Blue Sox. One season I batted .682 over twenty-two games. This was against MEN, mind you. I was just a boy. That season I hit twenty homeruns, twelve triples, and countless doubles.

So, when I tell you the four of us made it our business to win the Regimental championship, you can be sure I did my part to make that happen.

10 MAY 1942

After what seemed like an eternity — though it actually amounted to only a couple weeks — we were finally issued rifles. You would think these guns were made of gold, the way we cradled them in our arms.

But the truth was: these rifles were outdated weapons that bordered on being relics. They were the 1917 Model Enfield Rifle with bolt-action. They had been taken out of storage, where they had remained since the closing days of the First World War. The clips held all of five rounds of ammunition. *But they didn't give us any bullets!*

For the first five days after we were issued these weapons, what we did learn was the Manual of Arms. The idea of a Manual of Arms dated to before the American Revolution. Such manuals were especially important in the matchlock and flintlock eras, when loading and firing a gun was a complex and lengthy process usually carried out in rapid-fire fashion. Our Manual was of course updated. It taught us the proper functioning of the weapon, how to disassemble the rifle, then how to put it back together again.

One of our early challenges was to learn how to break down the Enfield Rifle then quickly reassemble it with competence. Doesn't sound like much of a challenge unless you consider that we had to do it blindfolded and in a space of under two minutes.

We learned how to properly clean the piece, how to keep it that way at all times. When it came to cleaning, this meant the entire weapon, not just the firing chamber — all metal parts, the entire wooden stock, plus the leather and brass on the sling.

For five long days, four hours a day, we did these things over and over again. The monotony was beginning to get under our skins. *Goodness! When would they actually permit us to shoot one of these damn things?*

When the first morning of the next week arrived, every last one of us was convinced that this would be the day, the day they would hand us bullets and ask us to begin target practice.

But it wasn't to be. The entire second week was spent on "dry fire." We had to learn the prescribed positions for firing. We had to practice developing a good trigger squeeze. We had to learn a proper sight picture, without which we would not be able to hit the side of a barn. We had to practice loading and reloading the weapon smoothly, all with dummy ammunition. *Boy, were we disappointed!*

But these were valuable lessons. We studied the characteristics of different ammunition. This is a bit of a science, and it has become ever more so in the modern era. Muzzle velocity. Throw-weight. Flight path of the projectile. Line-of-sight versus actual trajectory. Range limitations. Kinetic energy. Striking power or energy retention upon impact.

We studied these characteristics not only for bullets, but also for armor piercing rounds, as well as tracers.

Throughout these many training sessions we never fired a single round nor even saw a round being fired. Up to this point, no live demonstrations whatsoever, just instruction and films. Remember, we weren't out on the base Firing Range at the time, but inside camp in the cantonment area. *But things were about to get more interesting.*

On Monday of the following week, we moved out to the rifle range. Now began our demonstrations, followed by familiarization firing, and finally, firing for record. *I simply loved it.*

But you would be surprised by how many men closed their eyes when they pulled the trigger, how many flinched when firing. For the great majority of men in the Company, handling and firing a gun was a brand new experience.

The cadre of officers and enlisted men who trained us worked hard every day. But they clearly enjoyed seeing us evolve from newbies to competent shooters. I have only good things to say about these men. They were good instructors. Under their tutelage, ninety-six percent of our Company became qualified on the range. I just missed Expert by one point.

For me, the worst part of this segment of our training was learning how to properly clean the rifle after it had been fired. The work was quite tedious. But, within a week, we had all become very good at cleaning and oiling the firing mechanism and barrel to prevent pitting from the salts and residue of the powder. A dirty weapon could lead to a misfire and death.

Once we were qualified on the Firing Range, our life changed. For one thing, our quarantine ended. Now we were able to obtain one-day passes to get off base on Saturdays or Sundays. The nearby town of Anniston became our immediate objective.

Scuttlebutt around camp had it that if you attended church in town, an invitation to Sunday dinner would almost certainly be extended by one of the local families. So, naturally, with my very first Sunday pass in hand, I attended services at the Presbyterian Church in town. The scuttlebutt proved right.

During the Sunday morning service, in the portion of the service devoted to special announcements and community events, the Minister asked all servicemen in attendance to stand and to give their names, as well as their hometowns. The congregation immediately broke out in applause.

Sure enough, no sooner had the service ended, than I was approached by a nice family of three who invited me for Sunday dinner. I accepted immediately.

My new friends were the Nelson family, father, mother, and lovely daughter Joan. As luck would have it, Mr. Nelson was a Postal Clerk in the Anniston Post Office. *Talk about a small world!* We immediately had something in common, something to break the ice, something to talk about.

I had my camera with me that day, and sometime that afternoon I snapped a picture of Joan, a picture which I was fortunate to have and cherished often.

I stayed with the Nelsons at their house that day all the way up to five o'clock p.m., when I returned to the Post. That small act of kindness, that simple gesture of inviting a stranger into one's home to break bread, remained with me the rest of my days. I couldn't have had a better Sunday if I had tried.

A week or two later, on another Sunday pass, I made a tentative exploration of the town. That day I had a more specific goal in mind. Some of the guys had told me of a small sweet shop in Anniston, where an equally sweet girl worked as a waitress. Reports were she had a sparkling personality. So I came prepared. I took that girl's picture as well.

I can't entirely explain why, but recently, that beautiful girl has popped up in my mind time and time again. I hardly remember a girl with a more ready smile, or one who bubbled over with more effervescence and friendliness. Far from home, in a highly regulated environment, occasionally lonely, such things meant a lot to a fellow.

It was apparent, now, that basic training was drawing to a close. None of us knew for certain how long basic training would last. But something about the tenor of our trainers told us we were nearing the end. Hopefully, by now, we had learned all the many things which, with practice and application, would classify each of us as a "Basic Infantryman."

Looking back, now, upon my training, I realize that I became most proficient where it counted most for an infantryman — the deadly use of force. I was proficient with every weapon in our arsenal. — Rifle. Bayonet. Light machine gun. 60 mm mortar.

I was equally proficient with the lethal use of my hands as weapons, both in knife fighting and unarmed combat. I had learned how to kill with what the Good Lord gave me. Of equal importance, I had become proficient in map reading and aerial photo reading.

Because I had excelled in each of these vital areas, that led to me being placed in a position of leadership as Acting Sergeant for our next and final phase.

For the lion's share of our early training, emphasis had been placed on building the skills of each individual soldier — but as an individual, not as part of a team. Now things changed.

Now we embarked on squad tactics, working together as a unit. This phase of training — what I will call our combat exercises — required the use of large tracts of land. We now found ourselves out in the maneuver areas of the camp for long hours each day, all daylong.

One of the earliest skills we mastered was a carefully orchestrated set of hand signals. Actual combat is noisy and chaotic. Speech, if not impossible, is subject to misinterpretation. Sometimes a unit had to operate in total silence, to avoid giving away their position.

But there were other skills that had to be mastered. The ability to read maps and interpret aerial photographs became a valuable commodity. In our war games, we had to learn how to make map overlays, how to report "enemy" activity, both orally and in writing. We had to master proper use of a radio in our communications, a tool new to every single one of us. As Acting Sergeant, I was put in a position of leadership for these simulated combat exercises.

The grand finale of our segment in group-tactics consisted of a five-day, four-night bivouac in the maneuver area. We established a base camp composed of pup tents, set up a field kitchen, dug a latrine and fire hole, spent each day doing our thing.

I have to tell you, the exercise wasn't entirely realistic. Sure, we spent one entire night practicing night maneuvers and learning the finer points of moving as a unit through a black forest. But each night, after supper, we formed a large circle around a huge bonfire and sang songs, told stories, and generally horsed around. Oh yes, the Post Exchange had a truck out there as well. There was more than enough beer to go around, as well as ice cream, soda, and the like. A fine time was had by all, despite the many hours of hard work.

But soon the bivouac was over, and so was basic training. We marched back to our Regimental camp at the foot of Trench Hill confident of the skills we had acquired.

We unpacked our gear, cleaned up our equipment and ourselves, and began to decompress. The following Monday they ordered us to turn in our gear, keeping only our personal issue. *Training was over!*

By Wednesday, men started to ship out. Every few hours, our First Sergeant would form us up in the Company street and read out a new list of names. Those on the list would return to their sleeping quarters, shoulder their barracks bags and be marched across camp to the Post Headquarters, soon to be shipped out. By Friday, our Company had been reduced to all of four men: me, plus my three special buddies — Millard, Stanley, and Alonzo — the same team that had been champions of the obstacle course. *Had we done something wrong?* I wondered.

We were about to find out.

20 JUNE 1942

It was now late June, 1942. Me and my three buddies had not been held back because we were in trouble. We had been held back on account of our proficiency and enthusiasm. Not to put too fine a point on it, but we had been elevated to the status of Cadre Men. This meant we were now part of the training staff. Our war would have to wait.

Almost as soon as the four of us graduated from basic training, we began to receive men for the start of the next training cycle. These men were largely from three states — Kentucky, Tennessee, and West Virginia — and they had a lot to overcome. Many were children of extreme poverty, the kind of poverty that is unknown in America today, but was common in the hills of Appalachia at that time. For some of these "mountain people," becoming a soldier meant wearing their first pair of real shoes. Just getting some of these men to stand straight at attention was a problem because they had a built-in slouch to overcome. Further, many of them could not write, and almost none of them could read.

But don't misunderstand my criticism. These men were not dummies. They simply lacked adequate schooling. As Cadre Men, our work was cut out for us.

But there were some rewards. On 8 July 1942, I was promoted to Corporal, the first of my buddies to receive an elevation in rank. The others made Corporal a week later. I outranked them by date of promotion, but was certainly well down the list from the older regulars who had been in rank for years.

About a week later, my father surprised me when he arrived unannounced for a visit. He had traveled by Greyhound Bus all the way down from New Jersey and didn't even know of my promotion when he arrived. Talk about a proud father. Wow!

Dad took a hotel room in Anniston and came out to McClellan every day to see me in action and to rekindle some old memories. Of course I was busy with my duties, so Dad became fast friends with my First Sergeant and our Captain. He even came out early a couple days and ate breakfast with the Company. Every lunch and dinner as well, always sitting at the Cadre table. A former Army man himself — and a Sergeant, no less — Dad got along just beautifully with the rest of the Cadre. There was just something about my Dad. The man had a natural commanding aura, I could see that now. At home he was the Assistant Chief of the Fire Department. The man conveyed an attitude of one accustomed to being in charge, a man used to issuing commands. It's funny how your parents always seem to get smarter and grow in stature as you yourself get older and become a man.

The fact that my Company turned out to be physically located in close proximity to the area where he himself had trained before going overseas in World War I added a lot to his obvious enjoyment of the visit. Even now, I can almost hear my dad reporting it all in detail to Mom on his return home to Hackensack.

It was fortuitous, but we were at that point in the training cycle where I was able to spend most of my day in the Company area. So I saw a lot of my father over those few days. He was accepted into our life almost as if he were one of the gang.

After eight days, Dad had to leave. At dinner the night before his departure, the Company baker treated my father with a cake he made to honor Dad's last meal with us. After dinner, just before he left to begin the long trip home, the First Sergeant took Dad and me aside. Somewhat secretively, he directed us to the Orderly Room, where he broke out a bottle of bourbon. This was a pretty big deal, as hard liquor was absolutely not permitted on Post.

Rules or not, the First Sergeant poured us each a measure. Then, we clinked glasses and made a toast to our continued good health. *What a splendid farewell drink!*

The Sergeant made sure I accompanied my father back to his hotel in Anniston, where we said our goodbyes. I have no doubt my father's visit to Fort McClellan lived in his memories until the day he died.

.

.

The training of our group of "mountain men" continued apace. This was a funny lot. They didn't take orders well. Nor were they easy to shape up as soldiers. But, they were crack shots with a gun.

Many of these fellows had been hunters from the time they could walk, often hunting small game like squirrels, rabbits and such. They were very much at home with a gun. All us trainers agreed: Never before or since had we seen so many sharpshooters in one small, tight-knit group.

A record number of these men qualified on the range. They proved to be absolute naturals when it came to the handling of arms of any sort. Plus, they excelled at being able to move quietly about from cover to cover, again probably on account of their background as hunters ranging over the hills of Appalachia. I guarantee you, whatever outfits these men were eventually assigned to, got some really good, scrappy soldiers.

The next batch of men we received for training consisted mainly of men from the steel mill areas of western Pennsylvania, West Virginia, and Ohio. Again, the vast majority of them lacked adequate schooling. On the other hand, they were formidable men, very well built and physically strong.

As this second group of men was arriving on Post, we were busy converting the last of the winterized tents — like I had been housed in as a trainee — to somewhat more substantial huts. These huts were more like barracks, rigid buildings that had been erected on top of the old wooden tent bases. Each of these huts was designed to hold more men than the tents they replaced.

One night, several weeks into this new group's training cycle, I pulled the assignment of Charge of Quarters. This meant I was the ranking person in the Company from *Taps* to *Reveille*. Everyone else in authority was off duty.

No sooner had the "lights-out" command been given, than a fight broke out in one of the huts. I ran there immediately.

Upon entering the barracks in question, I saw two men, both heavily muscled, hurling foot lockers at one another across the room and yelling epithets in Lithuanian. I didn't understand a word. But here were two men, each of sufficient stature to be able to pick me up with one hand and toss me aside, and they were in the midst of a horrendous fight.

I yelled at the men to stop fighting, and lo and behold, they did!

Don't ask me why, but for some reason, when these two giants saw it was a Corporal yelling at them, they stopped fighting. They even stood at attention.

I was encouraged by their respect for authority. So, I lowered my voice and began to talk with them quietly. It seemed one of the men had insulted the reputation or looks of the other's sister. Apparently, the trouble began at the Post Exchange, where they had imbibed a few beers.

But now, tempers cooled. The two men were actually the best of friends, having come from the same hometown and having been co-workers in the same steel mill. The little guy (about five feet nine and two hundred pounds) apologized to the big guy (about six feet two and two hundred fifty pounds) and then all was well.

I had them straighten up the place. But I did not put them on report. There seemed no point to it.

LATE AUGUST 1942

By now, I and my three Cadre buddies had settled into somewhat of a routine. Not all our off-time was spent in the Company area. Stan had met a nice girl, Mary Crawford, who was a student at Jacksonville State Teachers College in the small town of Jacksonville, Alabama, just eight or nine miles up the road, though in the direction opposite from Anniston.

Stan started to see Mary whenever he could. To get to where she lived, he had to take a bus from the Main Gate. In no time at all, Stan had talked me into going to Jacksonville with him.

While he was busy with Mary, I would spend my time in the town's huge recreation building. I judged it to have been built with government money, perhaps a program dating from the Great Depression.

But now, with my regular trips to Jacksonville, I had a chance to renew my acquaintance with Alice Clark. This girl was a beauty. On a previous occasion, I had taken her to a movie one night in Anniston and then danced with her at one of the Service Clubs on Post. It was at that same time that I also met a girl named Vera, who was the best dancer I ever knew.

Vera lived a few doors down from Alice, which meant nothing to me until I found them both in the Recreation Center one night, squared off and arguing over me, of all things.

It was a downright fierce argument, and *all I had ever done was dance with the silly girls!*

That put an end to my trips to Jacksonville. The last thing I wanted was trouble with the locals. So, instead, I started going to Birmingham for fun.

One Sunday I traveled to the small town of Pell City, well west of Anniston, halfway to Birmingham. We had heard that one of the churches in town was putting on an "All Day Sing With Dinner On The Ground." A girl I met at a Service Club dance invited me to go with her. For a fellow who was basically a city boy, this was my first exposure to an old American tradition. It was great fun.

•

•

With summer now drawing to a close, the nights grew a bit longer and the days a bit cooler. This was nothing like a New Jersey fall, not the kind I was used to anyway. But it clearly approximated some sort of autumn.

In late September, my unit Captain called me into his office. On three previous occasions, he had tried to convince me to apply to Officer's Candidate School. But I wasn't having any of it.

What I didn't know was that in the meantime he had written to my father. The two had met back in July when my father made his unexpected visit. They had become fast friends. The subject of the Captain's letter to my father was to see if my father could shed any light on my continuous refusal to apply for OCS.

Dad wrote back and told the Captain how I had written my father and told him that some of the officers I had met, who were products of this or that Army school and who were assigned to us for further seasoning, left a lot to be desired in terms of their ability.

Well, now, with my father's letter in hand, the Captain read me out for about fifteen minutes. Then, he threw the green DD Form 150 across his desk at me and ordered me to sign it.

Too scared to argue, I signed the form and indicated my first choices of duty as either Tank Destroyer or Air Corps Administrative.

•

•

On 26 October I was ordered to report to another part of the Post for an intensive, highly competitive Preparatory Course of Instruction.

There were one hundred and eighty-eight of us present and accounted for. Some, like me, were noncommissioned officers. Quite a few were just Buck Privates.

The school was conducted by teaching officers sent down to us from West Point. Discipline was very strict. Spit and polish was the order of the day, even to the point of having our fatigue uniforms starched and pressed. I resorted to carrying a spare handkerchief in my pocket solely for the purpose of combating dust on my shoes, as well as a toothbrush to use many times a day on my weapon. Each night a lot of time was spent preparing ourselves and our uniforms for the following day.

Instruction was fast and furious, information and specifics presented only once. You either absorbed it or you didn't. No halfway measures here. The object was simple. We were being prepared to attend OCS, where we would hopefully earn a commission.

In all the time I had been a soldier — nearly eight months already — I had never once even seen a state-of-the-art M1 (Garand) rifle. The country's entire production of Garand rifles was being rushed to active units, outfits on the line in North Africa or elsewhere.

We spent a whole day (eight solid hours) on the M1. Instruction covered nomenclature, function, assembly and disassembly. *All in one day.* Compared to the more than one week we spent on the much simpler, bolt-action Enfield, this instruction was tough and rapid fire. You either got it or you didn't.

In a matter of days, we covered every facet of basic soldier instruction, each subject presented in the same rapid-fire style. At the completion of each segment we had to sit for a written test. These tests were not easy. Our attention and concentration had to be intense and complete. No late nights in town for us now.

By the end of the first week of instruction about twenty men had been washed out. We would be sitting in class, and all of a sudden a name or two would be called out. Those named would leave class and report to the school office. When we returned to quarters at the end of the day, we would see their stuff gone and their beds rolled up. By the end of the third week, the original class of one hundred and eighty-eight had shrunk in number to less than a hundred. By the end of the course on 21 November, only sixty-seven men remained.

Then came the interviews. Each of us appeared before a panel of five officers. They quizzed us closely on our specific branch preferences, as well as what assignments were available to be filled. They grilled me on the specifics of my first and second choices for assignment — Tank Destroyer or Air Corps Administrative.

But I was turned down on both counts. They turned me down for Tank Destroyer on account of insufficient mathematics in my schooling. Air Corps Administrative was scratched because they currently had no requisitions for bodies.

So, at their urging, I chose Infantry. I was, after all, already an Infantryman. I was assigned to attend the Army's Infantry School in nearby Fort Benning, Georgia.

Orders were cut. I packed my gear and shipped out 30 November 1942, thereby missing payday by just one day.

I had a grand total of two dollars and twenty-six cents cash money in my pocket.

1 DECEMBER 1942

My arrival at Fort Benning was inauspicious. The group I was attached to was temporarily quartered in one of several antiquated World War I hutments located in a fairly remote part of the Post. That's saying quite a lot, because Fort Benning itself is in a rather remote location. The Fort Benning Military Reservation is located approximately halfway between Montgomery, Alabama, and Macon, Georgia near the Alabama/Georgia border. In other words, right smack in the middle of nowhere.

The hutment buildings we stayed in were so old and in such disrepair, the siding boards that ran up and down the exterior, had dried up and shrunk. Dilapidated as they were, the boards no longer kept out the weather. Wind whistled regularly through the cracks. It was December, remember? The only heat we had was supplied by a wood burning Sibley stove, much like what we had back in Fort McClellan, and just as inefficient.

In short, we were roughing it. On a positive note, mess was good. That took some of the edge off the whole experience.

Once I arrived onsite in Fort Benning, I discovered that I had been assigned to a class that didn't begin work until 7 December. I don't know why that date stuck in my memory. But it was probably because this was a year to the day after the Japanese attack on Pearl Harbor. That left me a few days to kill before moving into more modern barracks for my formal training.

With nothing to do, and a mere $2.26 in my pocket, it seemed life would be quiet and boring for the next six days.

But I was a resourceful fellow and I quickly devised a plan. Before that first afternoon was out, I tracked down a nickel and dime crap game, where I won a couple bucks.

Now, with just over four dollars in hand, I set out for the nearest town. This proved to be Columbus, just over the Alabama border.

Buses left the Post each hour, though the use of the word "bus" to describe this form of transportation might be a bit of a stretch. These conveyances were actually open-air tractor-trailer arrangements that carried up to seventy men.

But, they were free. And they were relatively fast. Even after making several stops inside the Post along the way, we were generally in town within about thirty minutes. The bus stop in Columbus was in front of a big USO Club. Return trips back to Post began at that same spot as well.

I went into the Club, got a haircut (free), shave (also, free), including razor, shave cream and towel, all supplied gratis by the USO. My uniform was wrinkled, so I stopped across the street at a tailor shop where, for a quarter, I had it sponged clean and pressed while I waited. *Now, I was ready to see Columbus!*

I walked two blocks over from the USO Club, turned right and, within two more blocks, found myself in the busy part of town. I stepped into the first restaurant, where I literally absorbed a large steak. The darn thing was delicious, one of the best I had ever tasted. It cost only one dollar, and that included a baked potato and a cup of coffee. Only later did I discover what I had eaten — horsemeat!

Turns out, Georgia and my home state of New Jersey were the only two states in the Union where horsemeat could be legally sold as food.

Well, it couldn't be helped. Dessert was a walk around town, getting to know the lay of the land, as they say. I took the next transport back to the Post.

•
•

For the next several days, all I did was hang around the Post engaged in "sack time" or writing letters or playing cards. One diversion was the almost-constant crap game. I kept winning a couple bucks each day and even made a good friend out of the deal, Sergeant Bill G. Sergeant Bill was the reigning Regular Army middleweight boxing champion. He and I went into Columbus several times together.

One night, while in town, the two of us decided to go on the prowl for some fun. Fort Benning was home to not only the Infantry School, but also to the Parachute Infantry Battalion. Airborne soldiers were assigned to the parachute training base.

Scuttlebutt had it, Airborne soldiers liked to amuse themselves by getting officer candidates like Bill and me into trouble. The idea was to get some of us thrown out of OCS. We were easy marks to identify.

Each officer candidate had been issued a distinctive shoulder patch for his uniform. Plus, we each had distinctive patches affixed to our overseas caps. On our cap, in the same spot where officers usually wore their insignia of rank, we had applied small, round blue patches with a gold bar. An OCS candidate could be seen a mile away.

Bill and I were passing the entrance to an alleyway when four Airborne soldiers jumped us. Their intent was clear. They meant to work the two of us over. They would mess us up, mess up our uniforms. We would get into trouble when we checked back in at our billets and be thrown out of OCS.

But these clowns picked the wrong two guys to beat up on. Like I said, Sergeant Bill was the Army's current middleweight boxing champ. The man wasn't about to back down from a fight, even outnumbered. — Nor was I.

The Sergeant and I dropped the four Airborne toughs in no time at all. We knocked them down, then they jumped up and ran.

Bill and I pursued them into the alley. But the fight was soon forgotten. We hadn't realized it at first, but the alley doubled as an emergency exitway from the adjoining movie theatre. One of the exit doors was slightly ajar.

I looked at Bill, and he looked at me. We pried open the door and slipped inside, quickly finding a seat in the darkened theatre. I don't remember what movie was playing, but I do know I enjoyed it immensely. Airborne soldiers were supposed to be the elite of the Army. We had not only beaten them at their own game, we also got a free movie out of the deal.

•

•

On 5 December, we moved out of our antediluvian hutments and into new Company quarters. These were first-rate. Now, with one day to go still, before training began, I used my free time to explore this area of camp. I located the nearest Post Exchange, the chapel, and the Post movie theatre. Then I went to look up my friend Stanley.

Stan had gone into the Preparatory Instruction Course at McClellan one week ahead of me. Like me, he was one of the relatively few in his class to graduate. Now his Company was sited just across the road from mine. His class number was 215. Mine was 220.

With the two of us now living in such close proximity, we once again had a chance to spend some free time together. He and Millard had gone through the Preparatory Course of Instruction together. But Millard had been sent to Fort Sill, Oklahoma to train as an officer at Artillery School. After I said goodbye to Millard at Fort McClellan, I never saw or heard from the man again.

My other good buddy, Alonzo — Lonny, to his friends — had not gone through the Preparatory Course. Though Lonny was asked several times — as I had been — he steadfastly refused to accept a chance to earn a commission. When we parted paths back in McClellan, he too became part of my past.

7 DECEMBER 1942

Now our formal training began in earnest. After the stiff program I had survived at Fort McClellan, this program was a snap. The subjects were identical, almost laughably so.

But I didn't laugh them off, I simply became more proficient.

At the outset, Stan and I saw a lot of each other, even on occasion going into Columbus together. Later, as the training became more intense, we found that our free time dwindled.

With Christmas just around the corner, our trips into town took on new meaning. Each time we stepped off that bus in front of the USO in town, it would be to the sounds of Bing Crosby or others performing traditional songs of the season. Their voices blared out of a big sound system. Like the men around me, my thoughts turned to home and hearth. But of course home was far away.

Soon, though, an alternative presented itself. Stan's steady girlfriend, Mary Crawford, was to spend her holiday break from college at home with her mother in LaGrange, Georgia. She invited Stan and me to come spend Christmas Day at Mary's home with her and her mother. It promised to include an old-fashioned Christmas dinner.

LaGrange is a small town about forty-five miles north of Fort Benning. We checked the bus schedule from nearby Columbus. Several buses ran each day in both directions. If we had passes, we could easily get to Mary's house and back without problem. *But we didn't have passes!*

I'm not entirely sure what was running through my head at this particular point in time. Maybe I was homesick. Maybe I had a bit of an

43

ornery streak in me. Certainly, I enjoyed taking chances. Maybe getting away with a little skullduggery was too hard to resist.

In any case, Stan and I opted not to even try and request passes but to simply go AWOL instead. A risky move, to be sure. If we were caught "Absent Without Leave" we would be tossed out of OCS, perhaps even the Army. I suppose being thrown in the brig was among the possibilities.

It was a calculated risk. Even on an active Army base, the day before Christmas — 24 December — was likely to be a short day. But we would have to be smart about it.

Stan and I packed the least we could think of. A change of shirt, underwear, and socks, plus a few toilet articles. We stuffed them into our musette bags. For those of you who don't know what a musette bag is, it is a haversack, standard issue for an infantryman. This sort of bag is essentially a sheet of rugged khaki-colored canvas that folds around its contents. It is held together by flaps and adjustable buckle-straps. No one on Post would think twice about us carrying our musette bags under our arms.

Our plan was simple. We would walk as nonchalantly as we could across the Post to the bus terminal. We would board the earliest transport that included LaGrange on its route. In about an hour and a half we would be there!

As we saw it, the only "iffy" part of the whole caper would be at the bus station. There would likely be Military Police checking passes at the gate. Neither of us had one. Our only hope was that maybe the MP's would be merely spot-checking passes.

Surprise of surprises . . . Not a single MP was in sight when we purchased our tickets and boarded a waiting bus. *Maybe they were using the restroom or having a cup of coffee.*

This was 1942 and the Greyhound buses of the time were long affairs with the motor sticking out in front of the driver. Except for a bus-wide backseat and the area around the driver, a narrow aisle ran down the full length of the interior of the bus. There were two seats on either side of the aisle. Above the seats, on both sides, was an open luggage rack which also ran the length of the inside of the bus.

The bus was heated, but only to a degree. No heating unit of the day was capable of keeping the entire bus warm in the middle of winter.

Such conveniences wouldn't be perfected for a decade or more yet. It was December, and the early morning air was cold.

But now, after sweating out the possibility we might be stopped by MP's checking passes, we breathed a sigh of relief as the driver started up the motor. *We were on our way!*

The bus wasn't even close to being full. In our pockets was a bus schedule we had picked up at the ticket counter. We had memorized the departure times from LaGrange for our trip back. There were several buses late into the night and into the wee hours of the morning.

Our bus made a pit stop of five minutes at some small town along the route. But that was the only stop. We arrived on schedule in LaGrange at 1000 hours.

As we came into town, I noticed a firehouse a block or two back. That gave me an idea. As soon as we got off the bus, Stan and I returned to the firehouse on foot. I was confident the firemen could give us accurate directions to the Crawford residence.

This was a trick my father had taught me. The men in a firehouse know the streets of their city even better than the police. They have to. Fighting a fire is time-critical in a way that solving a crime never is.

On foot now, with accurate directions, we arrived at the door of Mary Crawford's house in under twenty minutes.

We were warmly welcomed. Mary gave Stan a hug and a kiss by way of greeting. Mrs. Crawford was a great looking woman who possessed an incredible knack for conversation. I, on the other hand, had always treated simple conversation as largely a waste of time. It was one of my big failings.

But Mrs. Crawford was something else. She had me talking as I never had before — and on a broad variety of subjects. This worked out to be a very good arrangement, as Stan and Mary only had eyes and ears for each other. They ignored us totally and, soon enough, the two left to take a long walk together. The cold start to the day had morphed into something beautiful with warm sunshine.

Naturally, with the two of them gone for the balance of the morning, I helped Mrs. Crawford finish getting dinner ready and onto the table. The woman was a great cook, and before long the four of us enjoyed a fine meal. I couldn't help but be drawn to Mary's mother and must admit to having enjoyed every minute of our time together.

We four ate leisurely, then the lot of us pitched in and did the dishes. Before long, it was time for Stan and I to catch our bus back to the Post.

After saying our goodbyes and thanking Mrs. Crawford for her hospitality, Stan and I walked back across town to the bus station. A bus was just leaving as we approached. But it was crowded. We could not get on. This worried us a little. But we knew three more buses were scheduled in the next two and a half hours. We would just have to be patient.

The next bus arrived, and it too was crammed full. No seats, not even standing room.

Then — you guessed it — the third bus arrived, and once again, not a space was to be had.

Now we were really beginning to sweat. If we didn't get on that last bus of the night, we would not get back into camp in time to report for *Reveille* in the morning. Then our goose would surely be cooked! We would be busted as well as being charged with AWOL.

We asked at the ticket counter why the buses were running so full. Apparently, every soldier in camp had gone to Atlanta for the holiday, which meant every single one of these buses was already full from their starting point.

Finally, about 0200 hours, the last bus of the day arrived. Like the ones that had come before, it was full to the brim.

But, by now, Stan and I were done being polite. We pushed and shoved our way onboard. Being just a bit larger than most men, we managed to force our way into the throng.

There were no seats to be had. But that didn't stop us. I don't suppose you'll guess where we ended up. Stan and I found space in the luggage rack above the seats. No sooner had the driver closed the door than we were fast asleep.

Someplace between 0300 and 0400 hours that morning the bus pulled into Columbus. We walked over to the USO with only one thought in mind. Would transports to the Post still be running at this hour of the morning?

Hooray! A truck-bus was ready to leave. The tractor-trailer made its usual fast trip back to Post, and we snuck into our Company area hoping to reach our barracks without being found out. No one checked passes for returning soldiers, only for ones leaving.

I slipped into my barracks, turned down my bunk, and fell in, still fully dressed. The time now was shortly before 0500 hours in the a.m.

Reveille was at 0600, so I got perhaps fifty minutes of sleep. But, it was enough. I was up and at 'em with a bit of a grin to spare.

We had made it clean! And what a splendid twenty-four hours it had been!

Thus ended my first Christmas away from home.

9 JANUARY 1943

Near the center of our Company area was a Duty Board. Each day they posted the following day's schedule. Today it showed a light schedule with formal training only in the morning. Our printed schedule showed a night exercise.

Such schedules were always light on details. Today's had no indication what type of night training was in store. But the required equipment was simply stated as "Light Pack." That gave some indication of what was involved.

Late in the afternoon, we were instructed to load onto waiting trucks. They would take us out of the Company area and up into the maneuver area. You have to remember that Fort Benning is a vast area, much of it nearly wilderness, with wild hills, thick forests, and churning streams.

The trucks took us up a gravel road, around a few bends. We stopped near the summit of one of Benning's many hills, where we were told the upcoming exercise would be a night patrol.

The instructors organized us into four-man patrols. Every so often, a truck would stop and drop off one of these four-man groups beside a white stake that had been driven into the ground beside the road.

I was designated patrol leader of my particular group. That's when the scope of the exercise became clear. We were given no flashlight, nor any maps, just a compass and an eight-inch by ten-inch aerial photograph. I noted that the white stakes had been planted every twenty feet or so along the road. *That's when I figured it out — this was a competition.*

Our first order of business was to identify exactly where we were on that aerial photograph. This took a bit of doing.

I looked first at the white stake beside us. It bore the number 23. Certainly that was of some importance, though I didn't yet know what.

Reading an aerial photograph is part art, part skill. In full daylight, with the sun beating down on the glossy surface of the photograph, interpreting such a photograph is sometimes difficult.

But this was a night exercise and the sun was already low in the sky. It made all the difference in trying to "read" the terrain off the photo.

Once I had determined with some precision our current position, I had to map out a plan how we might get cross-country to our objective. It was marked on the photograph with a small white X.

Fortunately, sundown was still some thirty minutes away, so we had a flicker of natural light to work with.

But I knew darkness would come quickly. It was January, after all, and days were short.

One other piece of good fortune: the skies were only partly cloudy, with a big moon overhead. You would be surprised how much moonlight can reflect off a bank of patchy clouds at night.

After about fifteen or twenty minutes of planning, I had plotted out a route in my mind. We took off from our starting point on the rise.

The route I chose for us to follow looked fairly easy in the photograph. Unlike the satellite images of today, identifying poorly-defined rises and drops from an aerial photograph circa 1943 is not easily done.

But we set off nonetheless. We went down, then up, then through some wooded areas, then down and up again, across two small streams, and a narrow field. We did all this in the dark. No map. No flashlight. Only instinct and a sketchy aerial photograph.

After working our way cross-country for about four hours, we finally came upon a road. It too was on a rise and clearly showed on the aerial photograph. By now we were tired, our feet were wet, and the January cold was starting to penetrate. To a man, we hungered for the exercise to be at an end.

When we climbed up that final slope to the road, we came out about four feet from a white stake. I had one of my men go over and check the number on it. Sure enough, the number was 23, just as I guessed it would be.

My chest swelled with pride. We had worked our way across three-plus miles of rugged, unmarked territory, done it at night with only a medium-quality aerial photo to guide us, and had hit our objective almost precisely on the head!

Probably the best part was the canteen cup of HOT coffee that was waiting for us when we arrived. Of all the four-man patrols in our Training Company, my patrol had come in closest to its objective. Others did well but missed by larger margins, some all the way up to three hundred yards. More than a few never found their objective. They might be wandering around still, if not for the Instructors. They were still onsite until well after dawn, picking up stragglers.

14 JANUARY 1943

The next phase of our OCS training centered on the proper use of weaponry. As in everything we did, our training followed the pattern of basic training, only with much greater detail and from a slightly different perspective. Officers had to be competent teachers as well as competent commanders. We had to learn how to teach others what we learned, as well as learn it ourselves.

There is perhaps no more violent way to kill a man than with a bayonet. It is up close and personal in a way that shooting a man with a gun can never be. Spilling blood at arm's length is an unspeakably violent act.

I was exceptionally skilled with the use of a bayonet. My training at McClellan certainly helped in that regard.

But it may have been something more than that. Give a man a basketball, order him to shoot lay-ups all day, and eventually he will learn to sink a shot. That still doesn't mean the man will hit anything but the backboard in the heat of a real game. Some had a knack, others did not. I had a knack for the bayonet.

On the other hand, the 60 mm and 80 mm mortars were strangers to me. I had been through a short course on the 60 mm back in basic. But the 80 mm was entirely new to me.

In each mortar squad, the squad leader is the Forward Observer, the man who is usually in an elevated position where he can visually observe see the target. That man directs the fire.

As we trained, we rotated through each position in the squad so that we could each learn just how it was done. We began with the 60 mm mortar.

When my turn came to be squad leader, I was given a target. It was a fifty-five-gallon drum — what us Army types call a "GI can." It was set out in a field about six hundred yards away.

I made my estimate of azimuth and range and called my instructions back to the gunner by radio. The gunner, who can usually *not* see the target, adjusts the gun sights as directed and sets its position. My estimate of range and elevation were okayed by the Instructor before I was permitted to radio them back to the gunner.

At the other end, beside the gun, another Instructor checked the settings I had radioed in before giving his okay to the gunner to fire his weapon when ready. Because we were working now with live ammunition, the instructors closely monitored our every move.

Firing a mortar is mainly a question of ballistics along a high-arc trajectory. The further a projectile must fly, the larger amount of kinetic energy is required to propel it on target. Thus, the size of the powder charge will vary with the intended range. To match the range called in by the squad leader, the gunner must remove from the projectile the requisite number of powder segments.

Once everything checked out, he got the final okay to fire. The assistant gunner dropped the charge into the tube, and yelled, "On the way!"

A mortar shell is not like a bullet. A bullet moves swiftly and — for the most part — in a horizontal flight path. Mortar shells do not move rapidly. Plus, they move along a highly elliptical arc. Their flight path is impacted by a crosswind to a degree most bullets are not.

From my vantage point out front, where I had a clear view of the target, I watched my first shot go. It flew over my head and in the direction of the "can."

To my great satisfaction, the shell came down squarely and actually went *into* the barrel. The fifty-five-gallon drum blew apart with a loud bang. *On my first try I had done something very, very rare.*

The Instructors were suitably impressed. They gave me a new target a little farther out and to the right. I called my corrections back to the gunner and, within moments, the second round was on its way.

With fingers crossed, now, I watched as the second shell landed about ten feet from the barrel and exploded. It made a large crater in the ground. A good shot but not the cigar.

They gave me a third target, far to the left and just a little closer. Again, a miss of about ten feet. Pretty darn good even if it didn't hit the target square.

My shooting was the talk of the barracks that night. In spite of the variables created by the wind, in spite of the fact that a projectile like a mortar moves relatively slowly and cannot "fight" the wind as well as a bullet, we had squarely hit the target. Busting out that barrel was a rare feat for an officer candidate.

.

.

A day or two later, we took up the 80 mm mortar. As the shell was much larger, it had a much longer range. Now most of our targets were out beyond one thousand yards, nearly double that for the smaller weapon.

With a larger, more lethal weapon came more difficult challenges. Sometimes, the firing was directed using maps to locate the target because the target itself could not be seen directly.

In battlefield applications, this larger weapon filled in the gap between the 60 mm mortar an infantryman usually carried and the 105 mm towed howitzer. It was a bit more complicated to fire and often involved filling a draw in the terrain with highly explosive rounds.

The projectiles were big, more than twice the size of a 60 mm round. But they operated in much the same fashion, adjusting distance by the removal of powder increments.

As might be expected with a larger round, when these big shells detonated, the explosion shook the air with a truly awesome, loud shock. The destruction they caused was far greater. *Here was a weapon with some real punch.*

Here again, we rotated through the various positions of responsibility in the squad. When it was my turn to be squad leader on the range, the day was cold and rainy. That added to the difficulty.

The first target I was given was an old truck out some eleven hundred yards from our position. I made my calculations, radioed in my instructions. Right off the bat, our first projectile came down right beside the truck. The point of detonation was close enough to overturn the vehicle in a big splash of mud and smoke. I was feeling good about that one.

My second target was a spot about a thousand yards out and to the left of the now overturned truck. It was a small area marked in outline with white lines, a parallelogram actually. It ran obliquely to the left and was maybe one hundred feet across in size.

The rectangle represented a draw, which is to say, a small valley or depression in the landscape. The assumption was that an enemy gunner sat in this draw. We knew the enemy gunner was there but we couldn't see him directly, so we had to hit the same general area multiple times to be sure the enemy threat had been wiped out.

The object here was to put three rounds into that rectangle. This called for quick adjustments to our fire to cover the differences necessary to keep within the target before it could "move."

My first shot was in the box on the side closest to me. My second shot was also in the box but near the line. My third shot was again inside the box, almost in the center.

Bingo! Three for three! I was good at this, very good. The instructors were almost ecstatic.

22 JANUARY 1943

Weapons instruction moved in phases through every weapon in an infantryman's arsenal. We were instructed in, and fired familiarization courses on each — the .50 calibre machine gun, the Bazooka (which was, at the time, a new anti-tank weapon), as well as the .45 calibre semi-automatic pistol.

Other weapons were fired for record. The .30 calibre Heavy Machine Gun. The .30 calibre Light Machine Gun. The .30 calibre Browning Automatic Rifle (my personal favorite). The .30 calibre M1 Carbine. The .30 calibre M1 (Garand) Rifle.

We received advanced instruction in the details and finer points of close-in fighting, both with a knife and with bayonet. We ran exercises time and time again. I was already an expert with both, as well as in killing a man with only what God me, my bare hands.

As I said, we fired many of our weapons for record. The day we were on the range and fired the B.A.R. for record was picture perfect. Warm, with an overcast sky, but excellent visibility. When I fired the weapon, I set a student record for high score.

Not every January day was so fine. Georgia can get cold in winter, cold and wet. On just such a day I found myself on the range firing the M1 for record. Visibility was poor. At three hundred yards I could just barely make out the targets.

In spite of the adverse conditions that day, I fired well enough to qualify as a Sharpshooter, the second highest rating on the Army's skill scale.

•

•

After weapons training, our next subject was Tactics. As a reader, it is important you distinguish between Strategy and Tactics.

In the military, Strategy deals with the planning and directing of projects involving the deployment, movement, and application of large forces. Tactics deals with actual processes, the handling of the many smaller units that make up these larger forces. Our assignment was to learn small-unit tactics.

We began this segment of our training with the smallest infantry unit, the squad. From there we progressed to the platoon, then to combinations of platoons, and finally, to an entire Company of platoons. For each level of organization, in addition to the "skull work," we conducted simulated combat exercises.

When we finally reached the level of a full Company exercise, each man in the Company was given a specific assignment. Some were designated as riflemen or B.A.R. men, others as machine gunners or mortar men. A select few were given positions of command as squad leaders or platoon sergeants. I was given a rather large responsibility as Company Executive Officer. That made me second in command for the entire Company.

I have to admit, I was disappointed with this assignment in one respect. I enjoyed getting my hands dirty, and this was an uncomfortably "clean" assignment. On the other hand, it said something about the level of respect I had earned among the Instructor Staff.

The Company-wide exercise was conducted in Benning's maneuver area. The Army had built an entire small town on this location for the sole purpose of making such an exercise as realistic as possible. Our mission was to take the "town," which was currently being held by hostile forces, the "enemy."

This was no casual drill. This was a full-blown deal, complete with a large contingent of "umpires." Their job was multifaceted — Create problems for the combatants to solve. Declare every move successful or failed. Designate men dead or wounded. Grade each man on his ability to perform his designated function.

The position of an Executive Officer is generally at or near the rear. He is to establish the Company's command post. Of course, in a rapidly changing battlefield, especially one where a strong frontal attack is underway and moving forward, the command post must be kept moving forward to stay with the action.

Like I said, I was disappointed to be to the rear of the action. But five minutes into the attack, things changed markedly. The umpires declared the Company Commander dead. *That meant I was now in command!* I immediately moved to exercise my prerogative. I fairly dashed to the front, where I found our attack stalled at the edge of town.

The enemy had strategically positioned two machine-gun nests — firing blanks, of course. But, from this position, they could directly confront us with grazing fire down Main Street. In short, they had engineered a perfect killing zone and my men were bogged down by it. Umpires had already declared eight men dead, including the Company Commander.

I called in my four platoon leaders and gave them orders to establish what we called a "fire base." The fire base was to be composed of one Rifle Platoon as well as the entire Weapons Platoon. I instructed Second Platoon to advance down Main Street while the fire base unleashed a deluge of covering fire. Third Platoon was to be held in reserve.

This was a risky move in at least one respect. I had concentrated all my firepower at my fire base. This force consisted of the machine gun and mortar crews, plus all the riflemen, the Bazooka man, and the B.A.R. gunners from the Rifle Platoon.

On my mark, the platoon leaders began to execute my plan. The men of Second Platoon advanced down Main Street under the covering fire. They worked their way forward, remaining close to the buildings. At each doorway they entered the buildings and methodically cleared them of defenders, one by one.

In almost no time at all, the umpires declared the machine-gun nests destroyed. *We had the first block!*

Suddenly, at the next corner, a force of defenders (trainees from the 29th Infantry Regiment) started to move in along the street on the right. At about the same time, a second force moved in directly ahead of us. Now I had trouble on two fronts.

From what I could ascertain, the force advancing on us from the right was the stronger of the two enemy forces. I threw my Rifle Platoon from the fire base at them, with instructions to the rest of the fire base to concentrate their fire on the advancing troops.

Now I threw Second Platoon at them. Second had hunkered down after clearing the surrounding buildings. Now they took up the fight without advancing further. I still had Third Platoon in reserve. They followed closely behind Second but had not yet engaged.

With the help of the fire base, Second Platoon attacked the enemy on the right and put a stop to their advance. The umpires declared Second Platoon successful and ordered the "enemy" to withdraw.

Now I concentrated all my firepower strictly and mercilessly on the defenders directly ahead of us. I committed my Reserve Platoon and shifted the efforts of the fire base.

I ordered my reserve platoon — Third Platoon — to pass through the position held by what had, up to now, been my attacking platoon — Second Platoon. I placed Second Platoon in reserve.

Now we drove forward. Each step of the way, I advanced Weapons Platoon as needed.

All of a sudden, the umpires declared us to be under heavy artillery fire. We hunkered down to protect ourselves amidst an explosion of noise and smoke. After about fifteen minutes of this "shelling," the umpires declared the barrage ended.

We took advantage of the lull in the fighting to once again advance forward. But we found the "enemy" gone. They had abandoned their forward position after the artillery attack.

This was not necessarily a good sign. The enemy wasn't stupid. It was entirely possible that they might be laying a trap. They might be waiting for us to be suckered into the center of town before attacking once again.

On the one hand, my Company had been successful in taking control of the town. But, in so doing, we had lost contact with the enemy. *The battle wasn't over.*

I called in my platoon leaders and we set up defensive positions at the far edge of town. This entailed setting up platoon areas, designating fields of fire for the automatic weapons, as well as designating target areas for the mortars and Bazookas. The idea was to position the heavy weapons where they were certain to inflict the most punishment.

No sooner had we set up our defensive positions, than the umpires declared the exercise ended. We had been at it, now, for more than six noisy, busy hours. In the morning we would find out how we scored on this most important of simulated combat exercises. A lot more than just pride was riding on the outcome.

18 FEBRUARY 1943

From every indication, I performed well in that final, Company-wide exercise. After the original Company Commander "died" trying to take the town, I was elevated to Company Commander.

Under my leadership, we recovered from the loss of our leader and went on to win the game. That win definitely went on my record. How do I know? Because things kept popping up later in my career, things that almost certainly had their genesis in that key bit of information.

For instance: Upon my graduation from Officer Candidate School, I was one of only two newly minted Lieutenants considered for assignment as General's Aide to the commanding General of the 75th Infantry Division. I probably would have gotten the job too, except for one thing. — I wasn't connected. The guy who got the job was a close relative of a Midwestern banker. That particular banker was one of President Roosevelt's big financial backers. *You don't suppose that had anything to do with it, do you?*

•
•

As the date of our graduation from OCS drew closer, we spent the better part of two days with representatives of the firms that manufactured officer's uniforms. We were measured for size and orders placed. Our uniforms were to be delivered to us on or before 3 March.

In January, the Army had increased the uniform allowance for new officers from one hundred and fifty dollars to three hundred and fifty dollars. The idea was for each graduate to purchase a complete set of uniforms manufactured only to the highest standard.

Not one of us ordered the ultimate dress blues with cape lined in infantry-blue silk. The reason was simple. Unless a man was assigned to the brand new Pentagon Building in Washington, D.C., there would be no call for it. The Pentagon, by the way, had been under construction since ground was broken on 11 September 1941, and had only recently been dedicated, just days ago, on 15 January 1943.

Nor did any of us buy khaki or light cotton shirts in quantity. We opted, instead, for the time-honored tradition of having a swatch cut from the tail flaps of our shirts. Shoulder epaulets were made from these pieces cut from our shirts. Thus the origin of the term "shavetail," to describe a newly minted Lieutenant.

•

•

The tailored uniforms arrived, as promised, on 3 March. In the meantime, many of us had been busy making tentative travel plans to stop by our respective homes enroute to our next Post. Only, as of yet, we really had no clue where our next assignment would take us. Orders were to be issued just one day ahead of our "graduation," now scheduled for 6 March 1943.

You may have noticed that I put the word graduation in quotes. There is a reason for this. When 6 March finally arrived, our graduation was less pomp and more circumstance, heavy on protocol, light on celebration.

In one swift wave of the hand, each of us were summarily discharged in rank from the Army of the United States effective 12 midnight 5 March 1943, then sworn in as 2nd Lieutenants effective 0001 hours 6 March 1943. This swearing-in time was formally our "Date of Rank." On more than one occasion, that date and time would prove crucial in determining seniority.

On the morning of the sixth, we received pay for service through the fifth and were given travel allowances in cash to cover our trip from Fort Benning to our new posting. I was granted a "Delay in Route" amounting to nineteen days. This meant that those nineteen days would not be deducted from my annual leave of thirty days. On the other hand, those days would not accrue for later if I did not use them now. Frankly, I was delighted to be able to go home for a spell.

I don't know where it began, but there has been a longstanding tradition in the military that the first soldier to salute a new Lieutenant was to be given one dollar by that new Lieutenant. My good friend Stan had received his first salute from me. That had been the week before, as his class graduated ahead of mine. I still had that dollar bill in my shirt pocket. Now I paid it out to a young Corporal from the school troops. He was the first man to salute me.

My orders assigned me to the 75th Infantry Division at Fort Leonard Wood, Missouri. All I knew so far about Fort Leonard Wood was that it was located somewhere in central Missouri, and that I had until 24 March to get there.

Along with another man from my class, a man named John from Paterson, New Jersey, I made tentative reservations to fly on Eastern Airlines from the airport in Atlanta to the airport outside Newark. I had never been on an airplane before, but my friend John had. He reassured me that it was safe to fly. Besides, there really was no other way to get home. Our flight was to depart about 2100 hours that same night.

By noon on that day, John and I left Columbus onboard a bus headed towards Atlanta. We arrived there about four that afternoon. Our flight didn't leave for several more hours. So we walked about for a while then decided to have a first-class dinner in one of the nearby hotels.

As luck would have it, four Army nurses — lieutenants all — sat eating dinner at the table next to us. Naturally, me and my buddy John struck up a conversation with these girls. Just as naturally, we invited the four for a drink in the bar after dinner. Well, one drink led to another, and before I knew it, the two of us were scotched.

Now time was getting short. John and I said our goodbyes to the nurses, then poured ourselves into a taxi for a quick dash to the airport.

Airport security was lax in those days, certainly nothing like what passengers have had to endure since the terrorist attacks of 11 September 2001. Even so, drunkenness was forbidden. For John and I, that was a bit of a problem. We had had so much to drink with the girls, we likely breathed toxic fumes of alcohol. I was afraid the officials would not allow us to board the airplane. Drunks were flat-out not permitted to fly.

Somehow, though, our luck held. John and I were able to convey the impression of being sober, or at least sober enough to board. We got on. The airplane was a DC 3.

As I said, I had never flown before. I didn't entirely know what to expect. But, Oh, my Lord, what a flight. We must have stopped at every airfield between Atlanta, Georgia, and Newark, New Jersey. No sooner would we get up in the air, than we would be landing again.

Aside from the fact that we were constantly landing and taking off, the worst part is I really had no clue where we were or what the landscape looked like below us. Security precautions demanded the window curtains be drawn closed the entire time, though I'm not entirely sure why.

After what must have been hours, we finally put down in Newark. I said goodbye to John and caught a late-night bus for Hackensack. After a grueling day of travel, I finally arrived home about six in the morning.

My folks were ecstatic. *The son was home.* Mom almost ignited with pride. Dad did not say much. Not that he wasn't happy to see me. But I'm not sure he trusted himself to talk without crying. My sister Margaret was happy for me. But she had her own worries. Fred, the man who would soon be her husband and father to her children, was headed shortly for Alaska with his unit.

•

•

The next day, Mom made her first and only request of me, one I was only too happy to oblige.

"Walk up and down Main Street with me," she said. "I want to show you off."

Well, you know how mothers are. Plus, she had her reasons. My mother had been a poor girl growing up. Over the years she had made many friends, some of whom were much higher on the social scale than she. Now she had something to strut about, something to be proud of, something to show off to her friends.

Our trip up Main Street was one for the record books. Mom must have introduced me to thirty women.

"Hello, Mrs. So-and-So," she would say. "This is my son, Bill. You remember him. Oh, yes, in those days he was a bit of a rascal. Now he's a Lieutenant in the Army."

Naturally, I was wearing my "pinks and greens." This was Army lingo used to describe our Class A uniform. The shirt and tie were beige, with a slightly pink hue. The service tunic had a somewhat greener cast. The trousers had the same pinkish beige hue as the shirt and tie. We servicemen referred to the ensemble as our "pinks and greens."

As soldiers on leave, we were required to exclusively wear our Class A uniforms, when out in public. Mom was proud of me and beamed with joy.

•

•

Almost every evening of my leave was spent with Connie. I had not seen her since last summer, when she came to visit me at Fort McClellan. I don't think I mentioned this visit earlier. It was overshadowed in some ways by my father's visit.

But now we spent every free moment together. We went dancing — alone — or sometimes with whichever of the old crowd was around. There were parties, a few special dinners. I was the center of attention.

Great!!!

22 MARCH 1943

Here I was, in the Army just over a year. I had advanced in rank from Buck Private to 2nd Lieutenant. Quite good.

But I was still in the United States. Not so good. The war was overseas, both east and west, and I was eager to be in the mix. At least I had now been assigned to a "line" outfit. Maybe I would soon get "over there," wherever over there might be.

Officer's Candidate School had been a snap. As a graduate, I reflected, now, upon my original decision not to attend OCS. As an excuse to avoid attending, I had cited to my superiors the poor examples of 2nd Johns that had been assigned to train us back at Fort McClellan.

But now I came to a realization. Those officer-graduates I once detested so much back in basic training had been sent to us, not so much for *our* benefit as for theirs. By trying to train us, it helped put the finishing touches on their own training.

Only by trying to command a Company of unruly soldiers could these recent graduates of OCS hope to become effective commanders. I knew that now. Leadership was a quality — and it improved with experience. In retrospect, I realized that the attitude of us Regular Army noncoms was wrong, and wrong in the worst way. That attitude bordered on arrogance — but an arrogance born of ignorance.

Now my orders called for me to report to 75th Division Headquarters at Fort Leonard Wood, Missouri, not prior to 21 March 1943 nor later than 24 March 1943. My orders stated that I was to be attached to the 7th Service Command.

At this point, I was not yet aware of one very important fact — the 75th Infantry Division had not yet been activated. The 75th was to be a brand new Division, and I had been selected to be part of the Activation Cadre. Me, and others like me, would be taking the new outfit through basic training to the point of combat readiness. Clearly, a long haul lay ahead.

As the time remaining in my "Delay in Route" drew to a close, I made arrangements to travel by train via the Pennsylvania Railroad to Saint Louis. From there, I would change to the Frisco Line and proceed to the small town of Rolla, Missouri, where I would pick up a bus for the final leg to Fort Leonard Wood. The trip would take about two days.

I told my parents goodbye at home. Connie and her mother, Elsie, accompanied me to Penn Station located in the heart of New York City. My train was to leave at five o'clock p.m. (1700 hours in Army time).

Although I would have preferred to have had some final private time alone with my girl, there was a perfectly legitimate reason for her mother to accompany the two of us to New York City. This way, Connie would not be forced to make the long, return trip alone.

All too soon came the conductor's call — "All Aboard!"

Connie and I kissed goodbye, and I climbed onto the train. I was one measure sad and three measures happy.

Sure, I was leaving my girlfriend behind. But wonder of wonders — I was now on my way to my first posting as an officer in the United States Army!

I stuck my head out the window, now, and waved goodbye. The train was already in motion.

Unlike that earlier train trip south when I first enlisted, this time my reservation included a Pullman berth. The conductor checked my reservation, assigned me to a bunk. I went there, stowed my gear.

After everything that had happened, I thought a good, stiff drink might taste good right about then. But the conductor delivered some disappointing news. The train did not have a club car. Only later in the night, when we were nearer Washington, D.C., would we be adding a section that included a club car. *Damn! I sure could have used that drink.*

Somewhat dispirited, I returned to my seat. My only remaining diversion was a pocket book Mom had given me before I left. I pulled it out, now, and began to read.

But then my luck turned. A gorgeous girl of about twenty came over and sat down beside me. Her name was Carol. She had a topnotch figure and a head framed with strawberry blonde hair. My need for a drink was quickly forgotten.

Carol and I struck up a conversation. She was a member of the Radio City Corps de Ballet. That meant four live performances each day at Radio City Music Hall, a place of glamour I had only heard of but never been. It also meant she was physically fit in every imaginable way.

Daily live performances of the Corps de Ballet alternated with the more-famous Rockettes between movie films shown in the Music Hall. As a curious aside, I learned the next day that The Rockettes were founded twenty years earlier in the very town our train was headed to, Saint Louis. In those days, The Rockettes were known as the "Missouri Rockets."

I asked her why such a pretty girl would be traveling west alone and Carol explained. She was on her way to an Air base in Texas, where she was to be married to her boyfriend, an Airman.

(As a point of reference, at this point in time, the Air Force was not yet a strictly separate branch of the military, but still part of the Army, the United States Army Air Forces, or USAAF for short.)

Maybe an hour after our departure from Penn Central Station in New York City, we arrived in the train yards at Harrisburg, Pennsylvania. Here, the so-called "Washington section" of train cars was added. As promised, it included a club car.

The porter came through. He wanted to make up our berths. The seats on the floor converted to lower berths. Upper berths were pulled down from above.

As the porter shooed us all away, we headed for the club car at the rear of the train. Carol and I threaded our way back through four or five crowded cars to reach it in the rear.

The club car was crowded. This brand new 2nd Lieutenant quickly surveyed the landscape. Almost everyone in the car was military. Only problem was, aside from me, every single man in the car was at least a Major.

As in any circle of alpha males, the single best way to draw everyone's attention is to show up on the scene with a knockout babe hanging from your arm. That certainly was the situation here.

No sooner had the two of us stepped into the room, than some officer got up, offered Carol his seat.

I motioned to a waiter to bring drinks. Liquor was flowing freely. It was wartime and everyone onboard seemed plenty intent on having a good time. A baby grand piano stood near one end of the car. Someone of rank was at the keyboard playing. Those who weren't drunk and laughing were singing.

Somewhere north of two a.m. — after having absorbed more than my share of alcohol and after receiving much advice on how to conduct myself in my new assignment (much of it given by half-drunk senior officers) — Carol and I headed for bed and lights out. Abundant singing and raucous conversation had made the time fly.

I think she was the more sober of us two, as I only remember following her as we wound our way back to our berths. By now, of course, the berths were made up. I took the lower, she the upper.

I don't remember saying goodnight, as I was fast asleep within seconds.

23 MARCH 1943

About 0800 hours the next morning, I woke up, raised the window shade, looked outside. The train was at a dead stop. We were standing in some railroad yard.

The porter came through, told us we had arrived in Saint Louis. Those of us who had slept in Pullman berths for the night, now dressed and performed our morning ablutions in the restrooms at the end of the car. Carol exited the restroom looking quite stunning.

Freshly shaved, I was ready to continue my journey. This pretty girl, who was my temporary companion, had until three p.m. before her train departed for Texas. My train was scheduled to leave hours later, around eight o'clock that evening.

With plenty of time to kill, the two of us left the station, which was downtown, and wandered about. I treated her to breakfast. Later in the day, as we roamed around further, I treated her to lunch as well. We did a pretty good job of seeing the sights but didn't wander more than a few blocks from the railroad station.

I saw Carol off on her train but still had five hours to kill. I treated myself to a nice meal — no horsemeat, this time! — then hung around the station until it was time to board.

•
•

The train rolled into Rolla, Missouri, about 0500 hours the next morning. This was the twenty-fourth, the day I was supposed to report for duty.

Rolla was a small town — maybe forty-five hundred people — and finding my way around was easy. I found the bus terminal, booked a seat to Fort Leonard Wood, about forty miles further on. By 0630 hours, I was at the front gate. From there, I took a taxi to the 75th Infantry Division's Provisional Headquarters.

A taxi, you say? Yep. Fort Leonard Wood was so large and so far away from dense civilization, it housed its own civilization population that rivaled a small city in size. Perhaps thirty-five hundred non-military people lived and worked on the Post. Some had their own cars. There was a Civilian Club. The Civilian Club had its own restaurant and bar. Both were off limits to military personnel. Some taxis operated strictly within the confines of the base, others from the gate to places further afield.

As required, I reported to the Garrison Adjutant, turned in a copy of my orders. I was assigned to G Company, 2nd Battalion, 290th Infantry Regiment. At the various levels of the Army, an Adjutant is a staff officer who assists the commanding officer with the details of his duty. There are Adjutants at every level — Regiment, Battalion, and Garrison.

I found my way to Regimental Headquarters, where the Adjutant assigned me quarters. As an unmarried officer, I was assigned to the Bachelor Officer Quarters (BOQ), which I found easily. In a large military installation, everything is well marked. All buildings on base are named and numbered with small signs. That's the Army way.

The building, one of three, housed officers of the 2nd Battalion. From the outside, the three buildings of the BOQ looked no different than conventional barracks.

Inside, though, everything was different — and better. The inside of each building was subdivided into a number of private rooms, one officer per room. Each room was decorated roughly the same. The exterior wall was finished with wallboard. Two, if not three of the other walls were unfinished. No wallboard. Exposed studs, wiring, and plumbing. These were the order of the day.

Furnishings were sparse. A cot with mattress. A pillow. Straight-back chair. Small, wooden table.

A clothes rack was built beneath a shelf along one of the "raw" walls. The floor was bare wood.

Order of arrival into camp favored the early-comers. Because I was only the second officer to have been assigned to the Company, I had a wide choice of rooms when I arrived. I picked a room on the upper floor on the side away from the parking lot and near the center of the building.

Now, after two days of nonstop travel, I felt overdue for a shower and a shave. I stripped down to my skivvies and headed for the latrine on the ground floor.

As I entered, I heard a powerful, baritone voice belting out a song from a nearby shower stall. He must have heard me come in, because suddenly, the shower stopped, along with the singing, and out stepped a big, hairy, strongly built soldier measuring over six feet tall.

Towel in hand, the big guy dried himself off, shook my hand and introduced himself. He was Captain Costello, the newly assigned Commander of the Anti-Tank Company.

Costello had been on base no more than an hour longer than I had. But in that short time he had already made a date with two nurses for this very evening. If I wanted to come along, one of those nurses could be for me.

That's the kind of offer a guy finds hard to turn down. But, I did. Captain Costello was an outgoing guy of French-Canadian stock. Obviously, he was a fast worker in the picking-up-women department. He was already charged up for this evening's dates and pressed me to change my answer.

I reluctantly declined. Maybe I felt a little guilty about spending so much quality time with women other than Connie. Besides, I had already decided I would spend the rest of the day getting my things in order and settling in. Costello shook it off as the good-natured fellow he obviously was.

I showered, put my room in order, then set off to explore this corner of the base. I quickly located the Regimental Officer's Mess and the accompanying Day Room, sometimes referred to as the "Club."

The mess hall looked like any Company's mess hall but with one big exception. Inside it had tables for six spread across the dining area.

71

The Club also looked just like a Company mess hall from the outside. But, inside, it had certain amenities, the most prominent of which was a small barroom. The lounge area housed a large pool table as well as a bunch of living room type furniture and a juke box. There was an area, slightly raised and devoid of furniture, suitable for dancing.

The small barroom had a single, large mural that wrapped around the four walls from left to right. It portrayed an idyllic scene.

Some artist, perhaps a civilian, had painted the mural to convey a series of erotic images. When a man sat with drink in hand at the bar, he felt as if he were floating in the center of a small, woodland pool. Bare maidens were painted all around. They were cavorting in various attitudes of play and bathing. Whoever had painted those vivid images had clearly been talented.

Aside from the mural — which had almost certainly been approved by the previous Division — all the furnishings inside the Officer's Club had been donated by this or that local women's club or church group for the comfort of our soldiers.

I continued my tour of the grounds. I was already familiar with Battalion Headquarters, as that's where I had first checked in. Next I found the G Company area. The Company Commander was not in. But I did meet the First Sergeant and his clerk. They informed me that no soldiers had yet been assigned to the Company, so there would be no *Reveille* in the morning. *Duty Call* would be at 0800 hours.

As that first day wore on, there was a continuing influx of officers into the Company area. By the time evening mess came around, the officer's quarters were nearly full. I went to the officer's mess hoping operations would be up and running and that they would be serving dinner. About thirty officers showed up, all with the same idea. Story swapping began in earnest as we ate. Each man had a different tale to tell as to how he found his way to Fort Leonard Wood.

After dinner, just about everybody repaired to the Club. This is where I met the Battalion Commander and his Executive Officer, as well as the Commander of 1st Battalion, every last one of them a Colonel or Lieutenant Colonel.

Both the Battalion Commander and the Commander of 1st Battalion had come to Fort Leonard Wood from the 88th Division at Camp Atterbury in Indiana. Both were heavy drinkers, maybe too heavy for their own good.

Even before I arrived on the scene, the bar was already in action. Apparently, some men had skipped dinner and gone straight to the drinking.

Protocol here was simple. Each officer had his own private bottle of his own favorite poison. These bottles were kept beneath the bar in separate niches, each labeled with the name of whichever officer it belonged to.

To make this place work, each of us paid a small monthly membership "fee" into a kitty. This pool of money covered all Club expenses, as well as payment to the bartenders. These were enlisted men who worked on their own time.

The merrymaking swung into full gear. But by 2100 hours, I was tired and went to bed.

Tomorrow would arrive soon enough.

25 MARCH 1943

Morning came. This was my first duty day, 25 March 1943.

But, this day was unusual. There was to be no morning formation. Instead, I went directly to the mess hall for breakfast. By now, the BOQ had filled up. Officers had continued to arrive well into the night, even past midnight. When I arrived, the mess hall was going full blast.

I ate quickly, then went to G Company Headquarters to report in. Our Company Commander was a big blonde Captain named Parker. He talked with me a short while, sized me up, then put me in charge of Third Platoon. Next, he called in the man who would be my Platoon Sergeant, a Regular Army man, Tech Sergeant Coulter.

Coulter was an interesting fellow. He had been in the horse cavalry for more than fifteen years. But his looks were deceiving. Coulter was a slightly built man. Without his uniform, he could have easily been mistaken for a librarian, if you get my drift.

Formalities out of the way, Tech Sergeant Coulter and I spent the balance of the morning getting to know one another better. We exchanged frank views on the best ways to handle men in our command. The longer we talked, the more I came to realize that here, standing before me, was one really good noncommissioned officer. If the man lived up to indications, together we would have one very sharp platoon.

The Activation Cadre filled out the day. Everyone had arrived. In G Company we had six officers — the Company Commander, his Executive Officer, plus four platoon leaders. Supporting these officers were twelve enlisted men — the First Sergeant, his Clerk, the Messenger, the Supply Sergeant and his Clerk, the Mess Sergeant, First Cook, Cook/Baker, and four Platoon Sergeants.

Now the real work began. Together, we made certain the barracks were completely operational, all beds in place, the supply room fully stocked with all equipment received, functioning and properly in place, kitchen and mess hall ready and stocked, latrine properly functioning. Above all else, everything had to be spotlessly clean.

.

.

Over the course of the next few days, enlisted men — so-called fillers — started to drift into the Company area. First to arrive were several groups of men with prior service under their belt. Any number of them had already completed as many as two tours of duty.

I latched onto several of these experienced men for my platoon. One of these men had already served two tours of duty. He made Corporal before leaving the service. Now he came to us from a demanding job, that of Greyhound Bus driver.

It seemed intuitive to me that such a man was surely familiar with the demands of responsibility. Sergeant Coulter and I considered ourselves lucky to have grabbed onto the man so quickly. A competent man with previous service could be a valuable asset. Such a man could assist us in countless ways to train and develop a good unit.

On the other hand, some of these older, more experienced men came with baggage. Some had psychological problems. Some were what we in the military called "eight balls." It is a slang term. It roughly translates to misfit or sad sack. A screw-up. More than a few of these men had drinking problems. Only time would tell which were which.

A few days later, the bulk of our fillers arrived. These were not men who had volunteered, but mainly seventeen-year olds who had been drafted. Just kids.

The majority of our fillers hailed from Massachusetts and other New England states. The balance came from various spots across the country. It took just four days before we had a full complement of soldiers, actually one hundred and ten percent of our total need. Long experience had taught that about one in ten would washout in early training.

Even though our Division was not yet activated, we began to train our men as if it were. Four hours of each day was spent on things like military courtesy, military bearing, and close-order drill. The balance of each day we used the men to improve our Company area, bring it up to snuff. Work details were organized to do everything from painting walls to scrubbing floors to repairing broken fixtures. Much had to be done to get the place shipshape.

Thus far, Battalion had not issued us any weapons. So that eliminated instruction on their proper use or their care and cleaning. Instead, we concentrated on close-order drill. Although somewhat repetitious at times, such exercises are a superb vehicle for instilling in a bunch of undisciplined men an appreciation for order and discipline.

By the end of the fourth day, the Company was beginning to come together. Now, men could be moved from place to place without looking like fools. Now, when they marched, they marched with purpose and distinction. I began to think of them as "my" men, and I was beginning to be proud of them.

Most of the men in my platoon were from the Boston area. Nearly all were of Italian descent, usually first generation. I loved these men. They were exuberant and lively, and they seemed to take their responsibilities quite seriously. Nearly every day, their question was the same — "When are we going to get our guns?" They would ask me, then later in the day they would ask the same of Sergeant Coulter. "When are we going to get our guns?"

Activation Day approached rapidly. On that day, the 75th Infantry Division was born. The 75th was the first Division in the entire history of the United States Army to be activated at full strength on day one.

Normally, a Division would be activated with a skeleton crew, the Cadre plus a handful of fillers. Only later, after Activation, would the entire roster of Division personnel be fleshed out with additional fillers.

But we were a first. On that special day, we had a Division parade. The men passed in review assembled in Battalion masses.

When you consider that each Battalion numbered in excess of a thousand men, you can appreciate how cumbersome such a procession might possibly be.

But this is where all that time spent on close-order drill truly paid off. Each of the Battalion masses moved smoothly past the reviewing stand, just as if the soldiers were experienced old-timers. The commanding General and his staff were very pleased. They beamed with satisfaction; everyone could see that.

10 APRIL 1943

We started our men through a course of basic training the morning after Division was activated. Here was an instance where my prior experience as a Cadre member at Fort McClellan qualified me as top dog. Captain Parker placed me more or less in charge of training.

This gave me a terrific amount of latitude. Of course, the actual scheduling of subjects, or phases, was out of my hands. These were prescribed by Division G3 Plans and Training Section. In combat, the G3 was the Operations Officer for the Division. That is where Division tactics were determined.

With basic training now under way, duty days began to take on a certain routine. Though I was officially in charge, the reality was that Sergeant Coulter controlled the lives of every single one of these young men in my command. I was lucky to have him. The men responded well to his quiet authority. There were only a few occasions when trouble erupted in the barracks.

The simple truth is this. When you place forty men together in a room, forty men who are complete strangers, forty men who have not had sufficient time to establish a pecking order among themselves — when you force these forty men to live together in close quarters, some feathers are bound to become ruffled.

After all, each man has little more than his own tiny bunk area to call his own. We are talking here about a physical space of no more than five by eight square feet. Everything the man owns — and I mean everything — must fit in that one tiny space.

Not only that, everything the man owns must be arranged per regulation, right down to how he folds and arranges the contents of his footlocker. A uniform on a hanger had to be hung a certain way, facing the door, with all buttons secured. Any shoe not currently on a soldier's foot had to be lined up a certain way. It had to be shined and laced up. Lace ends had to be tucked in. The regs went on and on in this manner.

Plus, the men had absolutely no personal freedom. For the first week of training, the men were restricted to the Company area. For the next two weeks, they were restricted to the somewhat larger Battalion area. Then, for the subsequent three weeks, they were restricted to the Regimental area. A total of six weeks would elapse from the start of their formal training before they would be allowed license to freely roam the Post.

But even at this juncture, not a single travel pass to exit the Post had been issued. If the men wanted to buy personal items such as toothpaste or razor blades or shave cream, they had to do it at the Post Exchange in the Battalion area. Among other things, the PX had a soda fountain. In these early days, it was constantly busy.

On the other hand, officers had plenty of freedom. When they were off duty, they could leave the Post anytime they pleased. Because Captain Costello had his own automobile, we often went out together in the evenings. This was usually in the company of two or more off-duty nurses. He, especially, was a strident appreciator of women.

Together, we explored the many delights of the region. Missouri is pretty country, hilly and wooded. But it is also sparsely populated.

About six miles west of the Main Gate was the tiny town of Waynesville, permanent population six hundred and fifty. Wow. Some town. Barely qualified as a village where I came from. The main street had perhaps two dozen fledgling businesses. Most of them were military stores. But there were also a handful of drugstores, small eateries, and bars. The largest and newest building in town was the Public Health Center.

A little further on was Rolla, Missouri, about forty miles east of the Main Gate. Compared to Waynesville, this was an immense metro area, with a population of a staggering forty-five hundred.

Other than Rolla, the only other nearby town of consequence was Lebanon, about thirty-five miles beyond Waynesville and approximately equal in size to Rolla.

The Big Piney River courses from north to south through the eastern edge of the Post. There were four large Service Clubs on base. If a man was so inclined, and if he had time off, he could draw a boat and fishing gear from the Club and go fishing or whatever.

But the Big Piney was more than just a fishing hole. There were many spots along the river where a man might pitch a tent and camp overnight. Camping gear could be drawn from any of the Service Clubs.

Other diversions included the base movie houses. There were six in all on Post. They were air-cooled and pleasant. During the day they were used as lecture halls. But at night they came alive with many good films, and some not-so-good.

Women are universal objects of pursuit for all soldiers, even married ones. In Waynesville there were several dancehalls, each with a bar. One of these dancehalls was quite large and was even written up in an issue of Life magazine.

I cannot say from firsthand experience. But not every lady who frequented these dancehalls was a lady. At least a few of these "ladies" were on hand to do more than just dance and converse with the soldiers.

Even on Post, women presented a bit of a problem. Most of the civilian employees that lived and worked on the Post were women. The great majority were unmarried. They presented a temptation of the highest order to some men.

Officers generally avoided the dancehalls, and with good reason. Instead, they frequented a number of nightclubs scattered in and around Waynesville.

The nightclubs were a bit more expensive than the dancehalls, and a lot nicer. Plus, there was always the issue of officers fraternizing with enlisted men. This practice was strictly prohibited by Army regulations. By going to different places on our nights off, this problem could be mitigated.

The nicest of the nightclubs in the area was a place called "The Cave." This part of Missouri was filled with countless natural caves, some of which were quite large. The owners of this particular cave had converted it into a quiet and attractive meeting place, a nightclub with subdued lighting amidst a completely secluded location. A small band played nightly. Dancing was enthusiastically encouraged.

Like so many natural caves, this one had a large natural pool fed by a small underground stream. The stream percolated into the cave from somewhere deep in the neighboring hills. It flowed over a tiny waterfall then down into the collection pool. Thus, there was always the sound of running water in the background.

And, as a bonus, the temperature inside that wonderful place was always a comfortable sixty-five degrees. No matter how hot things became out on that dance floor, nature's air-conditioner never stopped running.

Costello and I went to The Cave several times with dates. Believe me when I tell you. Even though I lived to a ripe old age, The Cave was one of the finest nightclubs I ever had the pleasure of patronizing.

I suppose by now, with all my talk of dating this girl and dancing with that one, you may picture me as some cavalier Romeo that jumped from bed to bed. Nothing could be further from the truth. Sure, I enjoyed female companionship as much as the next man. And sure, nothing strokes a man's ego stronger than having a knockout babe on his arm. But I was devoted to Connie, and we had been serious for a long time.

One of the nurses I met on Post was a cute little Lieutenant named Baba. We went out together three times. But once I told her that I would be getting married shortly, that was the end of that. I wanted a dance partner, she wanted a husband.

In point of fact, Connie and I had decided that if the 75th Infantry looked like a reasonably long assignment for me — at least six months — that we would get married and that she would join me on base.

As long as we're on the subject of women, let me tell you another story. While I was part of the Training Cadre at Fort McClellan, the Army decided to staff the new WAC Officer Candidate School at Des Moines, Iowa, with men who were already experienced trainers. Some of the Cadre was to be furnished by Fort McClellan. I was one of only three under consideration for this juicy position by my Battalion. *Who wouldn't want to work with legions of young women?*

I didn't get the job. But the man who did was a Sergeant with sixteen more years' seniority than I had. Good choice? I think not. This man had the foulest mouth of any individual I have ever known before or since. Every third word the man uttered was a dirty expletive. Those ladies must have learned some new expressions.

As a consequence, the first WAC I ever met was here, at Fort Leonard Wood. On this particular occasion, I needed a jeep to carry out some minor official duty. I was on my way to the motor pool to draw one.

As I walked across the vehicle parking area of the motor pool, I noticed the legs and butt of a soldier sticking out from under the raised hood of a 2 1/2 ton GMC. Obviously, a mechanic hard at work.

"Hey, soldier," I shouted. "Where can I find the motor pool Sergeant?"

Much to my surprise, a cute little lady soldier emerged from under the hood. She pushed her cap a notch further back on her head, touched her hair with a greasy finger.

"Sergeant ought to be in the repair building, Sir."

I think my jaw dropped. My very first WAC — and an exceptionally cute mechanic at that.

Actually, those of us in the Infantry almost never crossed paths with women in uniform. In those days, such women were still a rare commodity. The Army had only recently established the Women's Army Corps. Similar programs were initiated at about the same time by the Navy, the Marines, and the Coast Guard.

As a modern reader you cannot view these programs as some egalitarian, pro-feministic drive on the part of the military. It surely was not. Public opinion — at least at the start of the war — was generally opposed to the use of women in uniform.

No, the intent of these programs was much more real world, a hardnosed way to deal with a shortage of able-bodied young men for line duty. By the end of the war, more than a million women were in uniform. For the most part, they served with honor and distinction.

22 APRIL 1943

As the ranking member of the Training Cadre, one of my responsibilities was to lead our daily, one-hour-long calisthenics session. One day, late in April, as we were doing jumping jacks, I noticed that I was developing a rash.

At first, this didn't worry me. Even though it was not yet summer, daytime high temperatures were already running into the mid-80s.

A simple case of heat rash, I thought. As soon as I cooled down, the bumps and redness would disappear. At least this had been my experience back at Fort McClellan.

But this time, it was different. This time, when I cooled down after exercise, the rash did not disappear. In fact, it got worse and spread. *This was not good!*

Concerned, I headed for the infirmary. The doctor on duty took one look at me and told me to stay put, he would be right back.

He came back with a clipboard and a nurse. "You have German Measles," he said, writing something on the clipboard. "The nurse will escort you to the base hospital."

I was stunned by the doctor's diagnosis. He hadn't performed a single test or even taken my temperature.

But there would be no arguing with the man. Days of confinement lay ahead. German Measles was serious stuff in 1943. The Army wouldn't be taking any chances with a widespread outbreak.

•
•

I spent the next twelve days in isolation in the hospital. Talk about boring. I was normally what you would nowadays call a hyperactive guy. Above all else, I hated to sit still. Confinement was a special kind of torture.

And, to add insult to injury, *the spots disappeared inside of twelve hours.* I never even ran a temperature!

The only consolation was that the base hospital was big. In fact, it was a series of large, single-story, wood-frame buildings that covered an immense area. Each building housed four isolation rooms, as well as a single, large ward room with forty or more beds. A series of enclosed corridors connected one building to the next.

In my building, there was only one other officer, also in isolation and also not sick, plus two or three enlisted men in the ward. To amuse ourselves, that other officer and I would prop up chairs in our doorways and tease each other mercilessly. Passing nurses received the same treatment.

About the only good thing I can say about these twelve days of confinement were the daily massages administered by the nurses. *Boy, did they feel good.*

Visitors were few. The Captain. That nurse I told you about — Baba. Sergeant Coulter.

Finally, I was released and allowed to return to active duty. I can assure you: Never again would I go to the infirmary of my own free will. I was a bit angered by the whole experience. It was as if the medicos had to validate their existence by declaring healthy people ill, thus filling empty beds with warm bodies.

•

•

During my period of confinement I completed arrangements for Connie to come out from Hackensack so we could be married. But there was still housing arrangements to be worked out, as well as the small matter of organizing a wedding party.

In my short time at Fort Leonard Wood, I had become real friendly with 1st Lieutenant George Carpenter. George was the platoon leader of G Company's First Platoon. Even before Connie arrived, I asked him to be my Best Man.

Another fellow, Johnny Riordan, a 1st Lieutenant from Battalion Headquarters, had rented a small house in Lebanon for himself, his wife, and their four-month-old son. It had two bedrooms. Although Lebanon was not close — forty miles off Post — Johnny owned an automobile, which made this whole caper possible.

Johnny and I made a deal. Connie and I would move in with him and his wife and we would split the rent and expenses down the middle. He seemed okay with that, so when Connie arrived, she settled in with Johnny and family until our big day.

In due course, Connie and I met with the Post Chaplain and a date was set for our wedding. It was to be very simple. George was to be my Best Man and Johnny's wife was to be Connie's Matron of Honor. No muss, no fuss.

But then things spun out of control. The house Johnny had rented was one of more than a hundred similar houses that had been built by some enterprising sorts as part of a new housing development. (In those days, they weren't called subdivisions.) Each house in the development was completely furnished. They were rented exclusively to Army officers and their families. Our Battalion Commander, a Lieutenant Colonel, lived with his wife just three doors up the street from where we lived.

As you can well imagine, in a small, tightly-knit community, a community made up of men who work closely together and who are married to wives that have nothing to do all day but talk and tend to their children, nothing stays quiet or private long. *And certainly not a wedding!*

Before I knew it, the Battalion Commander had swung into action and taken charge of matters. Mine would be the first wedding of an officer in the Division. He took it upon himself to organize everything. Ten officers were designated as Honor Guard. A reception in our honor was set up in the Regimental Club. What had begun as a small, intimate wedding suddenly became a full military wedding with all the trappings.

A few days later, on 22 May 1943, Connie and I were married in the Regimental chapel. Almost every officer in the Battalion, some with wives and girlfriends, attended the ceremony. This was, after all, a social event as well as a wedding. Connie and I passed between the Honor Guard as we left the chapel.

Immediately afterwards, everybody repaired to the Regimental Club, where the reception was to be held. You might remember this place. The mural with its bawdy images raised a few eyebrows among the ladies. But it couldn't be helped.

The cooks and baker from my Company baked a huge wedding cake and decorated it beautifully. Men from my Company were the waiters.

Everyone present had a brilliant evening of partying, dancing, and, of course, drinking. It was a great reception, everyone agreed. The officers in my Battalion covered all the expenses. I was surprised by their generosity and felt proud to be counted as one of their number.

Our honeymoon was mute by comparison. Connie and I had all of two whole days to ourselves. We spent every minute of it in our new "home."

But, bright and early Monday morning, it was back to regular duty for me.

25 MAY 1943

The early stages of basic training were now drawing to a close. The next phase would be weapons training.

Rifles and bayonets were issued to the men, and the hard study began. I was excited, for this was a phase of the men's training that employed my greatest area of expertise.

The Captain gave me the lead here, and I ran with it. As soon as we got into bayonet fighting, I fired up those young soldiers but good.

Being young, my men learned rapidly. The same went for rifle training. They sopped up the information like a sponge.

But, like my own self at this point in basic training, the men wanted to know when they would actually be able to fire these things, not just look at them and learn part names. First came the usual "dry firing" period. Then it was out to the range for them.

In the meantime, natural leaders were beginning to emerge from the pool of men we were training. The man who had come to me as a former Greyhound Bus driver, the man with prior military service, I promoted to Buck Sergeant and made him Platoon Guide. This placed him second in command behind Tech Sergeant Coulter, who was my Platoon Sergeant. I promoted each of my squad leaders to Corporal.

My next task was to assist the platoon leader of Fourth Platoon (Weapons Platoon) in their instruction of light machine guns and use of the 60 mm mortar. Bazooka and .50 calibre heavy machine-gun training would come later.

Each day saw progress in my men's skills. But then, out of left field, I was hit with a new and unexpected assignment. Someone higher up the food-chain designated me Regimental Range Officer. That meant Sergeant Coulter would have to take the platoon through its firing for record without me. I was disappointed.

As Regimental Range Officer, I was now faced with a more difficult task. My new job was to coordinate with the staff of the permanent Post Range Detail and take the entire Regiment through its range season.

Don't underestimate the size of this responsibility. We are talking thirty-five hundred soldiers here. Each soldier had to be closely supervised as we put him through his paces. Thirty-five hundred men firing an assortment of weapons that ranged in size from a .45 calibre pistol up to an 81 mm mortar.

Plus, the amount of real estate I had to cover was immense. In all, there were eighty-four different firing ranges spread willy-nilly across the Post. Thirty-five hundred soldiers, eighty-four ranges, three weeks to complete the exercise. Quite a challenge for a lowly Lieutenant.

•

•

For the next three weeks, I had to be on the go constantly. Each Battalion had only one week on the various ranges. I utilized two jeeps to move about and to keep up with them. One jeep was for me, the other for a Master Sergeant from the permanent range staff. We kept on the move constantly.

One of our jobs was to provide liaison with each Unit Commander. We needed to keep these men informed, yes. But we also needed to keep them happy.

Neither the Master Sergeant nor I was a babe in the woods when it came to dealing with the brass. So I devised a solution.

He and I each commandeered a pair of .30 calibre ammunition boxes, empty, of course. These boxes were made of dense wood, one inch thick, solid and well insulated. There were four wing nuts, one on each corner of the box. If you unscrewed these wing nuts, the top panel could be lifted off and removed.

Like I said, these ammo boxes were empty. But, back in the day when they still held live ammo, the ammunition was encased in a shell of sheet copper. This shell made the box waterproof. *Can you think of a more perfect receptacle for keeping cans of Coca Cola icy cold?* I dare say not.

When a Unit Commander would stop by the range and want to know how things were going, we would quietly offer the man an ice-cold drink. It is amazing how often that cold soda helped solve a problem before it spun out of control.

•

•

With range season at an end, I was returned to my Company to resume my regular duties. We moved next into small-unit training, also one of my specialties.

The 75th Infantry Division was part of the 3rd Army. It was commanded by a Lieutenant General who was a strict disciplinarian. He had two rules, both of which irritated the Cadre members no end.

The first was a requirement that every officer wear his Class A khakis each and every day while on duty. This meant we had to perform our duties in the field each day with neckties tied.

When you consider that summertime temperatures in Missouri can often reach in excess of 100 degrees with high humidity, and that much of our work included tromping down dusty roads and bivouacking through insect-laden woods, perhaps you can begin to grasp how uncomfortable it could be for a man forced to work all day in a necktie and long-sleeve shirt. The enlisted men wore fatigue uniforms, which were loose fitting and did not include a necktie.

The General's second rule was equally annoying but in a totally different way. No officer or enlisted man was permitted to be off Post overnight more often than twice a week.

Given that some of us were married and others had girlfriends in nearby towns, this was a rule that just begged to be ignored — and we did. But, unlike other men, I had a legitimate reason for breaking it.

As I mentioned, our Battalion Commander, a Lieutenant Colonel, lived with his wife just three doors up the street from where Connie and I lived with the Riordans. The Colonel owned a wonderful 1940 Lincoln, one he hardly ever drove. It was the Colonel's habit to spend almost every night at home.

The strange thing was this. For a man who owned such a wonderful car, he did not enjoy being behind the wheel. So, as the Colonel's neighbor in Lebanon, I became his unofficial chauffer. We would leave the Post after work, and he would be asleep by the time we reached Waynesville. I would drop him at home and park the car in front of our house. In the morning, I would pick him up and back to the Post we would go. The only nights I actually spent on Post were the rare occasions when I had Officer of the Day duty.

As the Colonel's neighbor, I was well familiar with his habits. The man liked to drink. Nearly every day, he would have a drink at our Club before going home. Most days, it was more than just one drink. Sometimes he would get quite drunk. When we arrived at his house afterwards, his wife would come out and the two of us would help get him inside.

This way of life troubled me some, as alcohol held no particular fascination for me. Oh, I liked to drink as much as the next man. But I grew up with it. My grandparents, being European by birth, made wine at home each year. I remember it clearly. They would go into town, buy crates of grapes, load them into the car, drag them home, then crush them into wine. There was a jug of it on our table every night. It was part of life, not exciting at all.

But other men were different, and the Colonel was one of those other men. Sometimes, rather than bringing him home after work, his wife would find her own way on Post and she and the Colonel would go to the Officer's Club for dinner. On those nights I would arrive home quite late.

On several occasions Connie would accompany the Colonel's wife on Post, and she and I would go separately to the much larger Club for dinner. On several other occasions we attended dances held by the Battalion officers in our little Regimental Club. This was nice, as it offered us some measure of social activity several times a week.

20 JUNE 1943

The later phases of small-unit training are very hands-on and intensive. To accomplish what were now very demanding objectives, we had to move further afield, out away from the center of camp into the Post maneuver area.

Being further away from the Company area, transportation became something of an issue. We made generous use of several 2 1/2 ton GMC's to get the men back and forth.

One day, late in June, I took my platoon out to the maneuver area in two trucks. Our route took us through a heavily forested area and up and across several hills.

The trucks didn't move fast. But, as we rounded one particular curve, the lead truck swerved slightly, perhaps to avoid a pothole in the road. Recent rains had washed out sections of road, and even though the Engineers had been out to repair it, the shoulder was too soft to support the big vehicle's weight.

The truck began to tip. This of course put the fear of God into the driver as he frantically tried to right the damn thing.

For a few precious seconds the driver struggled with the steering wheel. He tried desperately to keep the 2 1/2 ton on the surface of the road. But he lost the battle for control, and the truck started to tip over.

My heart in my mouth, I watched helplessly from my jeep. The truck rolled over on its side and careened some forty feet down the slope, turning over and over as it went down. It came to rest at the bottom of the slope, sprawled on its back like a flipped turtle.

I stopped my jeep in a flash, dashed down the slope to aid my men. I feared the worst. Right on my heels down that hill were the soldiers from the second truck.

Miraculously, most of the men in the fallen truck were uninjured. A few were bruised, one badly. One had a broken arm.

We quickly extricated two men who were trapped beneath the rig. We wrapped the injured in blankets to stay the effects of shock.

I was never without my radio when we were in field. I instantly contacted Battalion Headquarters, asked for an ambulance to transport the injured to the base hospital. Once they were on their way, the day's training continued minus those who had been sent to the hospital.

Now came time to assign blame. Because I was the senior officer onsite, the blame would naturally fall onto me. After that day's training was over, I went to the hospital, checked on my men. Everyone was fine, including the man with a broken arm. I repaired to my quarters to write up my formal report of the accident.

The report ran several pages. I repeated the same thing in several places and in slightly different words. But the upshot of my report was this: The road had a soft shoulder. The soft shoulder should have been marked by the Engineers who repaired it. My driver had done nothing wrong. In fact, he had been looking out for his passengers — my men — when he swerved to avoid that pothole.

I exonerated the driver completely, placed the entire blame on the Engineers.

The blame stuck, much to my relief. I had visions of being stuck in the Army forever, paying for that damaged truck. It only followed. I was in charge. Thus, I was responsible for every stitch of equipment under my control.

•

•

Long about the same time, our Battalion Commander, my neighbor, was transferred to Division Headquarters. His replacement, a Major, was much less qualified. He had spent nearly his entire Army career in Quartermaster Branch. I couldn't help myself. I was totally unimpressed with this new man. *What was this guy doing in the Infantry, for Heaven's sake?*

No sooner had the new Major taken over, than he transferred me from G Company to Battalion Headquarters Company, where I was made platoon leader of the Pioneer Platoon. The Pioneer Platoon could best be described as a miniature Combat Engineer Unit. *Did this transfer have anything to do with the recent truck accident?* I wondered.

When the Major moved into our neighborhood, he and his family took the house immediately behind ours. This would not have been a problem, except for one thing. The Major had a teenage daughter. He insisted everyone in the neighborhood with a small child use his daughter for babysitting.

Well, as you may recall, my housemate Johnny Riordan, had a young son. *How does a Lieutenant refuse the friendly suggestion of a superior officer?* He doesn't.

Every time Riordan and his wife had a social obligation to attend, they would hire the Major's daughter to baby-sit their son. The girl was nineteen.

But her age wasn't the problem. She had itchy pants. That was the problem.

Whenever Riordan or I would get home, we would find her at the house dressed in practically nothing. Tight, skimpy top. Short, tight, bun-hugging shorts. Worse, the girl directed all her attention to us men, not to the children she was supposed to be babysitting.

As you can imagine, this didn't sit well with our wives. Riordan's wife tried to get this point across to the Major's wife. But she wasn't having any of it.

This made for a delicate situation. The Major was our Battalion Commander. To defy him or to insult him might cost us our jobs. We had no choice but to put up with Little Miss Hotpants.

But my troubles with the Major didn't end with her.

22 JULY 1943

One very hot and humid night in late July, we were given a Battalion exercise, one that ended with me getting myself in trouble.

My Pioneer Platoon had orders from the Major to build three bridges across several nearby streams. This meant pulling out handsaws and felling more than a dozen good-sized trees. Some were more than a foot in diameter.

Once the trees were down, we had to cut them to length and lash them together in such a way as to construct a bridge capable of supporting the weight of a tank.

In today's world, with gasoline-powered chainsaws and the like, this would not be so onerous a task. But, in 1943, the chainsaw had not yet come into wide use. The early models were heavy, two-person devices with long bars. Certainly not the kind of equipment issued to an Army platoon, even one charged with such tasks as building makeshift bridges.

No, felling these trees and cutting them to length had to be done by hand, with little more than hand axes and handsaws of various size and quality. Brutal, hard, backbreaking work. Every man swung an axe until his muscles were literally screaming out in pain.

But no one complained. My men worked hard and accomplished the assigned task in good time and with good results. When they were done, they felt a sense of accomplishment even if most were bone tired.

Along with his orders that we build these three bridges, the Major had issued orders that, when the job was complete, we were to all march back to the cantonment area.

His orders made no sense. My platoon had four jeeps and two trucks at its disposal. My men were exhausted. *Why make them walk when they could ride?*

So, in contravention of the Major's orders, I loaded all my men into the various vehicles, and we rode back to camp. *You guessed it.* The Major caught us as we unloaded in the Company area after the exercise.

As per protocol, we had to sit down for a critique immediately following any exercise. The idea was to highlight what went good and what went bad, while the details of the exercise were still fresh in our minds. By doing so, it could draw attention to areas that needed improvement, perhaps underscore where corrective action might be taken for the next time.

The Major lit into me. He took extreme exception to my use of the platoon's vehicles for carrying my men back to the Company area after the exercise. His orders had been explicit, and I had disobeyed.

Now I did an almost unthinkable thing. I stood up in front of the men — officers and enlisted men alike — squared my shoulders, and addressed the Major in a stern, but controlled voice.

I told him his idea to have the men march back to camp, when there were perfectly good trucks to transport them, was an idea born of a brain full of shit.

All the officers within earshot fell into complete, unbelieving silence. I knew the majority of them agreed with me. But I also knew they would be too timid to support me outloud. To hear a junior officer dress down a field grade officer stunned them one and all.

The Major grew red in the face. But, to his credit, he controlled himself. He immediately confined me to quarters pending further action.

I spent the evening thinking about what I had done. Somewhere between the Major's dumb rules and his unruly, sexpot daughter, I had lost it.

The next day, I was ordered to report to the Regimental Commander, a full Colonel. The Colonel was a little guy with a large waistline. In spite of his appearance, the man was still quite military.

I stood quietly at attention as the Colonel read me the riot act. (In the ranks, it's referred to as "reaming a new anus.")

The tirade went on for about twenty minutes. It began with, "In all my twenty-seven years in the Army, never have I heard . . . " It ended with, "You will report to the Commanding General."

So I did what I was told and reported to the Commanding General at Division Headquarters.

The Brigadier General was a bald-headed man with a fierce look. He picked up where the Colonel left off and read me out for a good ten minutes while I stood at attention before him. When he was finished, he said, "That will be one hundred dollars, Lieutenant."

I had no choice but to pay the fine. Nor did I dare object. But, when you consider that my entire base pay for a month amounted to only one hundred and fifty dollars, surely you can see the weight of that fine. I promised myself I would keep my mouth shut next time.

•

•

Not three days later, I was attached for temporary duty to Division Headquarters. I was assigned to G3 Section under the same Lieutenant Colonel who had been my neighbor back in Lebanon, the same Lieutenant Colonel who I used to chauffer around in his own car. I wondered if, because of our friendship, he had somehow intervened on my behalf. Either way, the Major I offended had gotten rid of me, at least for the time being.

The first task given me in my new position was to rebuild certain facilities on the shooting range. To help me, I was to use Prisoners of War then being held there at Fort Leonard Wood.

Not knowing what to expect, I proceeded to the Prisoner of War area, spoke to the Sergeant in charge and requisitioned one hundred prisoners to set to work on the detail.

The men he gave me were all soldiers from Germany's Afrika Korps. They were mostly big, blond, well-built specimens of the best Nazi Germany had to offer. They had been captured in North Africa only months before, at the Second Battle of El Alamein in early November 1942. Originally, these men were part of Rommel's elite Panzer Division. Six American MP's were assigned to accompany the detail to prevent the prisoners' escape.

These prisoners were a sight to behold as they route-marched to the range area. A route-march, by the way, is one with a reduced level of discipline. It is a mode of marching in military formation where there is no requirement to keep in step. Talking and singing are allowed.

As they marched, the prisoners moved fluidly along with a great rhythm, singing German songs. Their favorite seemed to be one that had also been adopted by many American soldiers, "Lili Marlene." It was a curious example of a song that had transcended the hatreds of war. As sung by Marlene Dietrich, I remember the words —

"When we are marching in the mud and cold,
And when my pack seems more than I can hold,
My love for you renews my might,
I'm warm again, my pack is light . . . "

These men, these men who were prisoners, were good workers. They completed all repairs in just under four days. Not one tried to escape.

•
•

Once the range repairs were complete and the prisoners returned to the POW camp, I no longer had a specific task to occupy my time in purgatory.

So I set about to design a system the Cadre could use for the training and testing of individual soldiers on the range, something we sorely lacked. This would amount to creating an Individual Combat Range.

I pinpointed an area on Post where such a range might be constructed, paying particular attention to issues of safety. I wrote up my plan, presented it to the Lieutenant Colonel at Division Headquarters. He made only slight modifications to my plan and agreed to take it to his superiors.

The way I had the course worked out, we would be able to test a dozen men at a time, without ever shortchanging safety. Each man would be able to demonstrate his expertise in each weapon (including grenades), as he worked his way through the course.

The Lieutenant Colonel presented my plan to the Commanding General and his Staff, got permission for me to assemble a test course. I felt vindicated by this success.

I set right to work overseeing construction of the test site. But, no sooner had construction been completed, than Division got a requisition to supply forty junior officers as overseas replacements. I was one of the Lieutenants selected. Four guys who had been in my OCS class at Fort Benning were selected as well.

One other person of note was also on that list, 2nd Lieutenant Christopher Kilmer. He was another of the platoon leaders from G Company. I mention Christopher, not only because he was my friend, but also because he was the son of poet Joyce Kilmer, author of "Trees" and a famous soldier who died in the First World War. Like his son, the elder Kilmer had also been attached to a U.S. Infantry Regiment, though as an enlisted man not as an officer.

All forty men on that officer requisition list were to be transferred to the Army Ground Forces Replacement Depot No. 1, Fort Meade, Maryland. The orders, dated 26 August 1943, directed us to proceed to Fort Meade, where we were to report not later than 1 September.

Our orders were clear. We were to procure individual clothing and equipment for temperate climate. That meant wool, olive-drab duty uniforms. It also meant we were likely headed for Europe rather than the Pacific. Specific note was made that dependents were not to accompany us. Nor were we allowed to take along automobiles or other personal property.

I was granted two days' leave. I used that time to get Connie packed and ready to leave Fort Leonard Wood. I had already made up my mind not to fully comply with the order that dependents not accompany us.

Then I out-processed from the 75th Infantry Division. Before I left the Post, I stopped by G Company and said goodbye to my former platoon. Sergeant Coulter had done an effective job and whipped them into good shape. A new platoon leader had been assigned to command the platoon weeks ago, when I was transferred to Battalion Headquarters Company to head up Pioneer Platoon.

Connie and I took trains to Chicago and then on to New York. I left her in Hackensack and proceeded to Fort Meade.

Life was about to change.

1 SEPTEMBER 1943

Fort George Gordon Meade is a large military establishment that sits halfway between Baltimore, Maryland, and Washington, D.C. While, in more recent times, Fort Meade is practically synonymous with the National Security Agency, in those days it was a basic training post as well as Prisoner of War camp.

Upon my arrival at Fort Meade, I found an old Army-type cantonment area. The place was a classic beauty, with paved streets neatly landscaped and maintained. Lining those streets were a series of old style, two-story brick barracks buildings, each with a second-story porch that ran the length of the building.

As soon as I got settled, I began to sniff the air to see how long I might be stationed at this location. Something told me it would be for more than just a few days. So I called Connie and asked her to come down to Baltimore. She arrived a few days later. We rented a room near Johns Hopkins University from an unmarried lady who had her own apartment elsewhere in the city.

Once Connie was settled in, she went downtown and landed a job in the administrative offices of the Lord Baltimore Hotel. For the time being, all us replacement officers were considered "casual." That meant we were currently considered "in transit" and not assigned for duty to a specific unit. It also meant we were free most of the time. I spent almost every night off Post.

Before long, my name began to appear on Alert Lists warning of an impending movement. On 27 September more than fifty of us shipped out and were sent to Camp Miles Standish in Massachusetts. The camp was located adjacent to Taunton, a large town about twenty-five miles due south of Boston. Standish had only been open about a year and housed another of America's many Prisoner of War camps.

The first few days were a bit tedious. We spent each and every minute of our duty time making certain each of us had all the prescribed uniforms and equipment.

But nights were free. A group of us went into Boston every night, splitting the cost of a taxi each way. There were five of us in that group.

The first night, we stayed together. One of our number, a California boy by the name of Antonio D'Amato, told us he had an aunt and uncle who lived in Boston and who owned their own restaurant. They served great Italian food, and we should go there to eat. So we did.

Off we went, now, to the Italian section of Boston. It was located in an area of town known as the South End. We were greeted royally at the restaurant door, especially Tony, and we ate. And we ate. And we ate. We could barely move when we were finished eating.

Tony introduced us to a fine domestic wine, Zinfandel, which at the time was produced only in California. All of this — the meal, the wine, the wonderful desert — entirely gratis. Tony's aunt and uncle made our dinner their treat. *Perfect for a serviceman with practically no money in his pocket!*

After dinner the five of us split up and went our separate ways looking for amusement. I soon found myself in one of the larger downtown hotels. It had an elegant bar, one of the largest I had ever seen, some seventy-five feet long. While I sat there, quietly sipping a brandy and doing a little people watching, a warm female voice interrupted my reverie.

"My, you certainly are stuck-up," she said.

I turned and, sitting there, almost next to me at the bar, was a really good-looking woman of perhaps thirty. She was tastefully dressed in what looked to be expensive clothes. She smelled delicious.

My reply to her provocative remark was along the lines of, "No, not stuck-up, just a little aloof."

That immediately broke the ice and we struck up a friendly conversation. I found her to be a very interesting woman. I bought her a drink. We talked. Soon, she said it was getting late and that she must be getting on home. The next day was a workday.

I offered to see her home, and she accepted. When we arrived at her place, before leaving the taxi, she invited me in for a nightcap. Innocently, I guess, I said okay.

Her apartment was tastefully furnished. Coffee table, comfortable chairs, grand piano in one corner. Something about the place said she came from money.

As we were both scotch drinkers, making a drink was simple. She poured us each a drink then excused herself. *Why was it?* I thought. *Women seem to constantly have to go to the bathroom.*

While she was away, I looked around. The woman seemed to have good taste in art. There were a couple of fine pieces that looked like originals. I also noticed a framed picture of an Army officer on the piano. That got me to thinking.

When she came back into the room, she had changed into what — I think you would say — was something more comfortable. I asked who the fellow in the picture was. She said it was her husband. He was a fighter pilot attached to the Army Air Force, stationed somewhere out in the Pacific.

I was a bit shocked, although I think I did a good job of hiding it. After all, she had picked me up. She had gotten me to her place. I had been interested enough to play along.

But now, I knew for certain what game was afoot. Gracefully, I hope, I excused myself. I said I had to get back to camp, that I had an early start in the morning. Whatever she had in mind, I was not having any part of it. I tried to convince myself that all I had been looking for was a nice evening of good company.

Thinking back upon it now, I realize there must have been countless numbers of women in similar straits who did the exact same thing. Like the song says: One is the loneliest number.

•

•

A night or two later, three of us stumbled onto a nice, cozy bar in the basement level of the Hotel Tourraine. It was a very intimate setting, with a small musical group playing basically standards and leaning heavily on the ballads of the time.

Lo and behold, we found another of our number (one of the five original taxi-sharers) sitting and talking with a knockout blonde. She was expensively dressed and looked very familiar, though at the time we couldn't quite place her.

It would have been unseemly for the three of us to have interfered with the two lovebirds, as they appeared to be quite intimate. Our man looked as if he might even be making some progress with her. Our man, by the way, was a handsome Virginia gentleman. From where I was standing, not far away, he seemed to be laying it on thick.

The two left in short order. But thirty minutes later, our man was back. He was alone and wearing a big smile. Naturally, we wanted to know what happened and who that woman was. We bombarded the poor fellow with a dozen questions.

His smile only grew wider. The woman's name was Carol Bruce. Now lights went on in my head. *Of course! That's why I recognized her.* Miss Bruce was a singer and a big Broadway star. And that wasn't the only reason she was well known. She was engaged to be married to one of the President's sons, Elliott Roosevelt, himself an officer in the USAAF and on his second or third wife. That night she was appearing at the Copley-Plaza, one of downtown Boston's better hotels.

(By the way, Carol Bruce is probably best remembered in America today for her recurring role as the domineering and meddlesome "Mama Carlson," mother of the station manager played by Gordon Jump on the CBS show "WKRP in Cincinnati." So far as I know, she and Elliott Roosevelt were never married.)

Our man told us that Miss Bruce had invited him to be her guest that night to see her show at the Copley-Plaza. At his suggestion, she had extended an invitation to us three as well. *Now things were really starting to look up.*

Eager, now, the four of us practically raced to Copley-Plaza. Miss Bruce had reserved a table just for us four. We had a nice meal, then it was time for the show. She was great, absolutely great!

After the show, she visited with us for quite a while at the table. Soon, the three of us left, leaving our man behind. He was not in the cab with us that night, when we returned to camp.

•

•

I was not stationed at Camp Miles Standish for long. But for the short while that I was, I managed to call Connie nearly every day. She was lonely, and so was I.

Suddenly, on 6 October, we were put on Alert and placed under a communications blackout. That put a stop to our daily telephone calls. Any time now, I would be shipping out.

Like the other men in my circle, I was beginning to feel that danger might be closer at hand. Maybe if I went to church, God would watch out for me at some crucial moment down the road.

The next day, I attended Communion Service at the chapel. Just to be sure and to cover all my bases, I attended Catholic and Hebrew services as well. *Why leave anything to Chance?*

I wasn't a religious man. But I had to hope and pray that God would be listening in one of those places.

7 OCTOBER 1943

On 7 October, a large number of us boarded the SS *Mauritania*. It was the *new* Mauritania, and it had recently replaced the original Cunard Line luxury liner of the same name that had been in continuous transatlantic service for more than thirty years.

This new ship was, at the time, probably the largest passenger ship afloat. It had made only one commercial trip before the war broke out in Europe and had immediately been pressed into service as a troop-transport.

We loaded troops onboard for almost two days nonstop. When we were finally loaded and set sail, there were some eighty-five hundred military personnel onboard. We were not informed of our actual destination, though many of us had already made educated guesses.

What happened next — and why — is not entirely clear to me. But for some reason, of all those eighty-five hundred soldiers, I was named U.S. Army Liaison Officer to the senior British Army officer on ship. He, in turn, dealt directly with the British Navy, who actually ran the ship. On top of that, I was designated ship's Sanitation Officer for the entire contingent of traveling troops. *Oh, my.*

Considering that there were more than eight thousand people onboard, Sanitation Officer was a rather large assignment. I began at the bottom, on F Deck, and worked my way up through every First Sergeant onboard.

With each man, I laid down the rules. I made them understand that their entire future career with the Army would depend solely on the performance of their units, and that cleanliness was no exception.

Amazingly, it worked! The SS *Mauritania* was a clean ship.

On each day of the voyage, I would perform an inspection, always at random times. On my rounds, I would pass through the men's quarters, never making a fuss, but always making sure each Sergeant witnessed me come and go. Upon arriving at our destination, both the ship's Captain as well as the senior British officer commended me by letter, a letter that wound up in my permanent file.

As U.S. Army Liaison Officer, I had numerous small complaints to take up with the British. It was in the conducting of this official business that I began to understand why I — among so many more qualified men — had been chosen for this special duty.

It wasn't that I was being punished, as I first thought. To the contrary. I was one of a comparatively few Casual Officers onboard. I had no official duties, nor was I assigned to a specific unit. Because this job was so important, the brass could not, in good conscience, remove an officer for this duty from any of the active units. Those officers already had plenty to keep them busy. So, such duties fell to me and a few others like me with similar status.

Included among the troops onboard were four General Hospital Units. That meant there were four hundred thirty-six nurses thrown into the mix. To cut down on the inevitable, the nurses were billeted on one deck, which were exclusively staterooms. Two corridors, or gangways, ran through their living area. An MP was posted at each end of both corridors. That deck was women's country, and absolutely no males were permitted entry. No exceptions.

One of the hospital units was composed of nurses who were predominately from Brooklyn. One of them, a redhead Lieutenant, taught me how to play gin rummy. She promptly took me to the tune of seventeen dollars. After that, I learned.

In addition to the four hospital units, we had several other types of Army units onboard. There were Engineers, Anti-Aircraft personnel, as well as Army Air Force Administrative units. This last group was the most trouble.

Because I was one of the Casual Officers, and because I had some status as a Liaison Officer, I had to spend one twenty-four-hour period as Officer of the Day. That automatically placed me as temporary head of the Military Police detail.

As OD, one of my duties was to make the rounds. After dark on the night in question — accompanied by my Sergeant — we came upon a nurse and a Major (Air Force Administrative) copulating in a relatively obscure spot on the uppermost deck. We had no choice but to arrest the two of them immediately and place them both in the ship's brig.

Of course, the Major complained all to hell. It was not only the ignominy of being arrested, which was bad enough. But he had been arrested by a 2nd Lieutenant (me), for God's sake. That bothered the man no end.

•

•

Internally, the ship was divided up as follows. The main promenade deck, and everything below it, was enlisted territory. The upper promenade decade was open to all personnel. Everything above that deck, mostly the navigation deck and the swimming pool area, was strictly officer country. On those upper decks were a number of lounges, or rooms, where a man might play cards, read, or whatever. Officers were quartered in staterooms, normally six to a cabin. Because of my position as Liaison Officer, I was able to wangle a private stateroom, albeit small, solely to myself.

Despite the strict segregation of officer country from enlisted country, I quickly learned of one exception. Onboard was a woman, a beautiful natural blonde. She was a British Navy radio operator, a post normally held by an enlisted soldier. But she was also part of the Royal family.

Her civilian name was Lady Elizabeth Buccleuch. She was a Scottish cousin of the woman who would eventually become Queen Elizabeth II. Because Lady Elizabeth was who she was, her off-duty hours were largely spent on what was known onboard as the sports deck, even though she was only rated as an enlisted person. That's where I met her.

In our short time together, she and I played a lot of deck tennis. It's an informal sport, sort of a hybrid between regular tennis and a lawn game called quoits. Plus, we talked a lot about everything under the sun. She was easy to get to know. The senior British Army officer, who I reported to, introduced me.

Naturally, I was the envy of nearly every young officer onboard. I completely ignored frequent requests for an introduction.

·

·

The second day out brought gale force winds and some very rough seas. October was a questionable time to be out on the open North Atlantic, stormy and unsettled. Waves approached fifty feet in height, sometimes towering high above the ship. The experience was both dangerous and exhilarating.

Just for the thrill of it, several of us disobeyed orders and worked our way all the way forward, into the bow, where we were actually fifty feet in front of the ship, out in front and over the sea. *Wow, what a feeling!* To say that we got wet as the boat pitched into the crashing waves would be an understatement. The seawater broke over the bow in deafening explosions.

Meanwhile, back in the card room, tables and chairs lurched back and forth across the cabin, as the ship pitched and rolled. The small upright piano slid across the deck, the same piano the ship's surgeon played on for several hours, each and every night.

Further down below, in the lower decks, many of the men became seasick. Sanitation became a bit of a problem. But the men did their jobs well and kept things relatively clean. This torment went on for a space of two full days.

Even though the *Mauritania* was a troop-carrying ship pressed into service by the British Navy, it was still a luxury liner. A full complement of Cunard Line waiters worked the Grand Dining Room where the officers ate their meals. Breakfast each day included a British favorite, smoked kippers, along with eggs and toast. Dinner was also very good and varied from night to night, with plenty of choices.

Both meals were served as in the finest restaurants, with fresh, white linen tablecloths on the tables and white cloth napkins in our laps. We felt like royalty, or at least upper-class patrons. Lunch was less formal, usually nothing more than a mug of hot soup served at various locations on the upper decks.

•

•

Our ship was traveling alone. That meant we were not escorted by battleships or traveling as part of a convoy. There were good reasons for this.

The SS *Mauritania* was one of the fastest ships afloat. We would only be held up by a slow-moving convoy, making us an almost certain target for enemy submarines. Instead, we raced across the North Atlantic, cleaving stormy seas, zigzagging regularly to avoid detection.

We made the crossing, without incident, in five days. On the afternoon of the fifth day our ship docked in the harbor at Liverpool, England. Liverpool is a sheltered, easily defended port along the west coast of England, not far from the Isle of Man.

No sooner had the motors stopped and the ropes been tightened, than we began to disembark.

Unfortunately, the Casual Officers were the last to leave the boat. For two long days we were pressed into service, charged with the responsibility of coordinating the unloading of more than eight thousand troops and associated personnel and gear.

When at long last the lot of us stepped off the boat, ladies from the Red Cross greeted us with doughnuts and hot coffee.

I thought: *This is a war?*

15 OCTOBER 1943

Now that we were back on dry land again, our group of Casuals was directed to board a waiting train. It chug-a-lugged slowly out of the station, pushed off in a southeasterly direction, directly into the industrial heartland of England.

Our destination was the 10th Replacement Depot located just outside Birmingham. The Depot was categorized as SOS ETOUSA, which is to say: Services of Supply, European Theater of Operations, United States Army. It provided logistical support to the burgeoning war effort.

Our group was assigned quarters at Pheasey Farms Estates, a residential subdivision made up of a series of row houses. Pheasey Farms was located in a small village a short distance from the main Post, in suburban Birmingham. The subdivision of row houses was just barely completed when the war broke out and was instantly requisitioned by the military to house troops.

We were billeted eight men to a house, which was uncomfortably tight. There were two tiny bedrooms upstairs, plus a parlor that had been converted to sleeping quarters. On the ground floor was a kitchen and a toilet, but no bathtub or shower. It didn't matter. There was no hot running water anyway.

The only furniture in the place was eight crudely constructed bunks. No chairs, no dressers, no tables.

The electricity and water were turned on. But there were no lamps and only a single sink to wash in.

We did have a small fireplace for heat, which was good, as nights could be cold and damp. But of course there was no wood to burn, only soft coal. It smelled when it burned, smothering us in a cloud of rank, yellow smoke.

There was no stove in the kitchen, which meant we had no way of heating water. If ice cubes could come rolling out of a faucet, well, you get the idea how cold that water was. A bath was out of the question.

I looked glumly around, thought again of that hot coffee and doughnuts those Red Cross girls were handing out at the docks only the day before. *Ah, this is indeed a war!* I thought grimly.

We asked around, found a Quonset hut nearby that offered hot water and showers. There was also a mess hall. The food served there was rather sparse. In fact, the portions were miniscule. It was our first brush with the effects of wartime rationing in England.

The eight of us attended a briefing at the main Post. Those in charge informed us that we would be there at the Replacement Depot only a matter of days while our papers were being processed. After that, we would be assigned to a permanent outfit and shipped out forthwith. Meanwhile, there were "certain duties" that had to be performed. It was all so mysterious.

On the *Mauritania*, we had been traveling across the Atlantic under blackout conditions. Just one little light might be enough to give a U-boat a bearing that would get us sunk. Why, we even lit cigarettes under cover. We smoked holding the lit end cupped in our hands.

At Pheasey Farms it was no different, perhaps even worse. There were blackout shutters on every window and a blanket draped over the inside of every front door. The Germans bombed "Jolly Ole England" nearly every night. We didn't need to provide them with targets, so blackout regulations were strict and strictly enforced.

Now we began with those "certain duties." Each night, some of us were directed to visit nearby towns and pubs to spy on the local populace. Our job was to listen in on conversations around us, especially those that involved American soldiers on pass. We were to make written reports each morning based on the previous night's listening.

To accomplish this task, the Post Commander provided each of us with a command car, as well as a driver. These vehicles were the so-called general-purpose vehicle — GP, for short — the original "jeep." You may have seen pictures. They had four cutout doors.

After the first two nights, it was patently clear that this assignment was a big waste of time. There was no resentment on the part of the locals to the presence of American soldiers in their midst, mostly because those Americans were well behaved. It couldn't be any other way, with MP's posted on every street corner.

So I adopted my own "special duty." Rather than waste both our times visiting local pubs and playing spy, I gave my driver the evenings to himself. I also gave him the command car. Our deal was simple. He would drop me off and pick me up wherever I said. The rest of the time, he was on his own.

I had my driver drop me at the train station. I boarded the first outbound train headed into Birmingham. Once there, my first stop was one of several NAAFI clubs for officers.

The Navy, Army, and Air Force Institute (NAAFI) was an organization created by the British government to run recreational facilities needed by the British Armed Forces, as well as to sell goods to servicemen and their families. They were like a combination USO, PX, and Service Club.

Normally, the NAAFI clubs were closed to officers. But there were a few that made an exception. I ate several good meals at this one.

The rest of the time, I just looked around. England was a strange new country to me, and I wanted to learn everything I could about it. My driver had only to pick me up at the train station when the train brought me back from Birmingham. I prepared fictional reports of my pub "visits" in advance.

Now I know this charade may sound like I was shirking my duties. And perhaps I was. But, something put me off about the Post Commander. He was a tyrant, pure and simple. I found out afterwards that he was later brought up on charges before a court martial. The man was found guilty on several counts, including embezzlement and the beating of his men. He went to jail.

Another officer on "special duty," a man who was a Georgia lawyer in civilian life, took a different approach to our assignment. This fellow would sit quietly in a nearby pub, listen to the rabble, smoke his pipe, and sip his beer. He met a nice English woman on one of those visits and moved in with her.

This woman took care of him in every sense of the word, doing his laundry, feeding him meals, and taking care of the other things a woman can take care of. Her husband was away in Burma, fighting with the British Army. He had been gone nearly four years now. Our Georgia lawyer had it made in the shade with this woman.

Another of our group of eight Casuals was a man by the name of Mack. He had been a 2nd Lieutenant for fourteen years, the last eight with the 14th Infantry Regiment in Panama. One night Mack and I left our drivers behind at the railroad station and journeyed into Birmingham for some fun. We found a lively bar at the end of a narrow alley.

The noise from the bar spilled outside. The place was filled with people of all ages. There were more than a few British Army men, plus quite a few British women, some in uniform, some in civvies. The women in uniform were of two flavors, either WAAF (Women's Auxiliary Air Force) or WRNS (Women's Royal Naval Service). Mack and I took a small table near the door and ordered up some beer.

Now, before I go too far, let me teach you a small lesson, one learned at the cost of one or two bar fights:

Should you ever happen to venture into a strange bar, it is always wise to order up something in a bottle, preferably a beer. A bottle of beer doesn't have too much alcohol. But it does make a splendid, if impromptu, weapon.

Of course, most British beer is available only on draft and normally served in either a glass or a mug. But Mack and I knew our way around a bar, so we ordered a specialty beer only available in bottles.

We had barely taken a sip, when two nice-looking WAAF's at the next table invited us to come join them. Thinking nothing of it, we took our chairs and our beers and moved across to their table.

At about the same time, a few of the more intoxicated civilian women stood up and began to sing. For our pleasure, apparently, they began to belt out a drunken parody of a song popular with American soldiers from the First World War — "Over There."

Their words went along the lines of — "Over Here, Over Here . . . The Yanks are coming, The Yanks are coming . . ."

Immediately I could see trouble brewing. At the next table over, a table crowded with six British Army men, the girls' performance was not well received. In fact, they expressed their displeasure with a loud round of hissing and booing.

Seeing our looks, one of the more inebriated soldiers got up from his table, swaggered over, and placed his hand on Mack's shoulder. I didn't hear his exact words, but they were something to the effect that us Yanks were neither needed nor welcome in these parts.

Mack, still sitting, looked up at the soldier, calmly removed the man's hand from his shoulder, and said, "Yeah, the Yanks are coming. In fact, they're already here. — And you should be damn glad of it!"

Then he reached up and cracked the drunken soldier across the chin with his beer bottle. Now all hell broke loose.

The other five Brits rose up as if one, joined by four from another table, and moved in on us, fists raised. We dropped two of them in short order.

All of a sudden, four Canadian soldiers, who had been sitting quietly at a corner table watching, got into the fray. They were as big as trees and decided that us Yanks, being far outnumbered, needed their help. Believe me when I tell you — we were glad for it.

The Canadians waded in, and before we knew it, British soldiers began hitting the floor hard. But not before someone whacked me across the forehead with a chair leg, peeling back some flesh and drawing blood.

Next thing I knew, every light in the place went out. To my immediate left, something big crashed into the large mirror behind the bar. You could hear the sound of breaking glass flying everywhere. *Probably a thrown chair*, I thought, as I hit the floor.

Mack, the two girls we were sitting with, and I all hit the floor at about the same time. Together, we crawled on our hands and knees for the door then hit the alley running.

When the four of us reached the street, we turned left, ran a few more steps, then slowed to a walk. Our hearts were still pounding hard.

I pulled out a handkerchief and pressed it to my wound. The skin is thin on the forehead, and it doesn't take much to make it bleed. But the actual damage was minor.

With the danger now behind us, there was nothing we could do to stop laughing. We roared for upwards of five minutes, good deep belly laughs.

Then we stepped into the next pub, where we all sat back down and shared a quiet beer. Then we bid one another goodnight. For Mack and me, it was back to dull, old Pheasey Farms.

Thus ended my first week in Jolly Ole England.

22 OCTOBER 1943

After that dull first week, things got rather more exciting. I was placed on temporary duty with a Provisional Ranger Battalion. The Provisional Battalion had been organized by the Division Commander but had not yet been officially recognized by the Army. Thus, despite my temporary posting with the Rangers, my official assignment within the Army's Table of Organization remained unchanged, a Casual headquartered at the 10th Replacement Depot.

At the time of my arrival, the Rangers were training with the British Fourth Commando Group. I was outfitted with jump-gear and fell in step with their program. They were just commencing parachute qualification.

It took only a matter of days, but in no time at all I found myself aching from head to toe. Chalk those pains up to the rigors of learning how to fall properly when leaping off a platform perched sixteen feet above the ground. Yes, you tuck and roll. But gravity is still gravity, and knees are still knees. And the thigh bone is still connected to the hip bone.

Inbetween leaps off that platform, we learned how to pack a chute, where to place the folds, how to apply the talc so it didn't stick. *Talk about your high speed instruction!* A man either learned or he was out.

Rangers liked to fight, and my schooling in unarmed combat back at Fort Meade helped keep me in the game. I suppose that skill, plus my infantryman background is what got me sent to Ranger School to begin with.

We made four jumps in six days. The first was from a height of one thousand feet. The other three were from progressively lower altitudes. Six hundred feet. Five hundred and twenty-five feet. Four hundred and fifty feet.

Believe me when I tell you, that's low. Four hundred and fifty feet is low. You hook up to the line, dive out of the fuselage, feel the shock of the chute opening, swing up, and slam into the ground. Rough. Very rough. But, then again, Ranger tactics called for low jumps.

And you can forget about safety. No reserve chutes here. No margin for error. No second chances. Get it right the first time or perish in a box of broken bones.

I might have stayed with the Rangers, might have parachuted into France instead of wading ashore with the infantry, might have dropped behind enemy lines instead of storming the beach. — But it wasn't to be.

Only days after I arrived, the order came through. The brass at the European Theater of Operations had made a decision. The Provisional Ranger Battalion was to be disbanded.

After more than a year of debate, the War Department had refused to sanction the provisional unit. ETO Headquarters directed that the Ranger Battalion be dismembered and all personnel returned to their original units.

As graduates of Jump School, the only effects we were allowed to retain were our jump boots and our Ranger insignia. I was proud of that insignia. It is a patch sewn on the upper shoulder of the left sleeve of a military uniform. The patch — or "tab," as it is called — is in the shape of an arc with the single word RANGER emblazoned upon it. Gold letters on a field of black with a gold outline.

Wearing the tab is permitted for the remainder of a soldier's military career, even if that soldier is not actively assigned to an Army Ranger unit, one of only four such permanent tabs.

29 OCTOBER 1943

Finally, on 29 October, orders were cut and twelve of us were assigned to the 29th Infantry Division. Each officer was supplied with a train ticket to Tavistock, Devon, where Division Headquarters was located. Tavistock is north of Plymouth, in what might be called the "boot" of England, the southwesternmost peninsula on the island.

Our train left within two hours of our orders being cut. The twelve men onboard included four of my closest friends at the time: Mack, my lawyer friend from Georgia, plus two others.

English trains do not move like lightning. Although the distances we covered were not great, it took us quite a while to get there.

Once we arrived at Division Headquarters we learned that the Division was not concentrated all in one location, but rather spread out all over the place in both Devon and Cornwall. I was assigned, along with four others, to the 175th Infantry Regiment, with Headquarters at Bodmin, Cornwall. My friend Mack was sent to the 115th Infantry Regiment. Two others were sent to the 116th.

We departed almost immediately for our new assignments. No time for long goodbyes. The Regiment supplied jeeps and a small truck for the trip. By now, the day was well on.

I arrived in Bodmin in the wee hours of the next morning. I reported in, got some much-needed rest, a warm meal, a shower and a shave. At Regimental Headquarters they assigned me to the 2nd Battalion, with Headquarters in Helston, Cornwall. Helston was southwest of Bodmin and much deeper still into the "boot."

Off I went, this time in a jeep, for a long, cross-country drive. I might have enjoyed the scenery, for it was beautiful. But I was tired. I hadn't had a stable base of operations for weeks now, ever since leaving America behind.

Helston is a small market town located on the Helston River. It straddles the entrance to a tiny peninsula the Brits call Lizard Point.

Lizard Point commands a strategic location on the map. The Point protrudes into the English Channel and is far and away the southernmost spot in England. It was from here that the British made their first sighting of the Spanish Armada as it approached mainland Britain in 1588.

Because the area around Helston is hilly, the majority of the streets are steep. They are also lined with attractive, old stone houses. Back in the Middle Ages, Helston was an important port. However, in the thirteenth century, all that changed. A naturally forming bank of sand and shingle (stones the size of an egg) silted up the harbor mouth.

Nowadays this rocky sandbar is referred to as the Loe Bar. The water behind the Bar is referred to as the Loe Pool or sometimes just The Loe. After the Helston harbor closed, shipping was diverted thirteen miles to the east, to the other side of the peninsula, where it remained open to the sea.

Although Loe Pool sits near the sea, it is actually a large, freshwater lake fed by the Helston River. Plus, the Pool can claim an interesting history. The Loe is reputed to be the lake in which Sir Bedivere cast King Arthur's sword *Excalibur*. But who knows? The whole area is steeped in so much legend, it is often hard to separate fact from fiction.

Upon reporting in to Battalion Headquarters, I was assigned to be an 81 mm Mortar Section Leader in H Company. Evidently, my record on the artillery range at OCS had become part of my permanent file.

The 81 mm Mortar Platoon was composed of three Sections of two guns each. Each Section was headed up by a 2nd Lieutenant just like me. The Platoon Commander was a 1st Lieutenant. We had seven jeeps between us, two for each Section, plus one for the Platoon CO. It was the largest platoon in the Battalion, numbering sixty-four men.

My quarters were in a small house shared with three other lieutenants. But the Officer's Mess was in a large house where the Battalion Commander and his staff lived.

Each day, when we went up to the Commander's house for dinner, a blackjack game occupied our time while we waited for him to show up for his meal. Under no circumstances were we permitted to even enter the dining room until he made his appearance. *Talk about old Army.* And that wait could get expensive. Unless a man had just the right combination of wit and luck, that blackjack game could eat up funds quickly. I became pretty good at it in no time at all.

There were other challenges. For two hours each day we scheduled athletics. My platoon usually played football. This was full blast, hardcore football, only without protective equipment. Which meant it was easy for a man to get hurt. Playing in the line or being tackled could shake up a fellow pretty badly. Bruises were frequent, some of them serious.

The Platoon Sergeant of my Mortar Platoon was a big, rugged Pollock from Lowell, Massachusetts. (I guess "Pollack" isn't politically correct speech nowadays. But in those days we didn't give it a second thought.) Anyway, the big guy set the tone in any game.

Naturally, when my men invited me to participate in their daily football game, they were meaning to test me. And test me, they did. I received quite the workout that day, and they hit me very hard.

But I understood what was going on. They were checking out this new Lieutenant, seeing what he was made of. Trust me when I tell you — I gave as good as I got. The guys respected that, and it strengthened our relationship. But the tests weren't over, not by a long measure.

That very first day, as we were relaxing after my football "baptism," one of my men offered me a chew of tobacco. Everybody shut up and waited to see how their new Lieutenant would reply.

The man offered me his package of tobacco. It was Beechnut brand. I looked the bag over and handed it back to him.

"No, thanks," I said. "That stuff's too sweet for me. I've got my own."

Then I proceeded to pull out my own bag of Mail Pouch Tobacco. I offered him a chaw, then popped some in my mouth. The men were almost flabbergasted. This new Lieutenant was OK.

Now I know what you're thinking. And I understand that times have changed. In today's world, chewing smokeless tobacco is considered a dirty and dangerous habit.

But that wasn't really the case back then. A man with a plug in his cheek wasn't looked down upon. On the battlefield, under blackout conditions, lighting a cigarette could get a man shot. Plus, a cigarette wasn't so easy to light. Try doing it in a thunderstorm. Or in a gale-force wind. And, cigarettes broke. But a chew was different.

I admit. I had a love-hate relationship with tobacco all my life. Sometimes I smoked, sometimes I chewed. Sometimes I did neither. Sometimes I did both. Mom didn't approve of my chewing, so around her I kept my chaw hidden. But around my own men, well, that was a different story.

5 NOVEMBER 1943

In and around Helston, evenings were spent lounging in our favorite pub or else visiting with some local family. Over glasses of warm, headless beer, we would sit in the pubs and listen to the locals relate stories about the war or about the bombing raids, and we would keep on drinking and listening to their stories until closing time at ten o'clock p.m.

Hard liquor was strictly rationed, and early each evening, when the day's allotment had become exhausted, the man behind the bar would announce with finality: "Gentlemen, we have no more spirits tonight." And that would be it.

But that doesn't mean everyone would simply go home. Each evening, as nine o'clock approached, a noticeable tension would begin to grip the pub. This was a critical time. Everybody would settle down and a hush would fall over the patrons. They would sit quietly and listen to the BBC broadcast as the news came down over the pub "wireless." Britain was a country at war, and things weren't always going so well.

Officers were in demand by the women of the town, and they often organized dances in one of the smaller local halls. I loved to dance and soon became proficient dancing the "quickstep," which I suppose is the British equivalent of our foxtrot.

At the same time, I also learned of certain liaisons between some of our officers and some of these local women. An intelligence officer, for instance, was going with the prettiest Red Cross girl in the district. One of my friends, a 1st Lieutenant with the nickname "Ug," was keeping one of the local teachers warm. Those are but two of several examples.

But I wasn't necessarily critical. I understood even if I didn't agree. Ug had become my special friend. He commanded one of the Heavy Machine Gun Platoons.

There were three Red Cross girls stationed in Helston. They attended to the 2nd Battalion. This was a big job, as the Battalion was spread all across the western part of Cornwall.

To get around, the girls had a 2 1/2 ton GMC at their disposal. On it they carried all their donut and coffee-making equipment, as well as all their supplies. Everything they carried was provided by the United States Army. The truck itself was maintained by our Battalion motor pool. Of the three girls, the least physically attractive one was Molly. But Molly had the greatest personality possible. She was the favorite of everyone I spoke to.

The presence of Molly and the other Red Cross girls compensated a bit for other challenges we faced. Currently, H Company was under the command of a 1st Lieutenant. To protect the innocent, let's call him 1st Lieutenant McHenry. He had recently taken over command of the Company when the former Captain was promoted to Battalion S3 (Operations). McHenry was bucking for Captain. The man was a real pain in the ass.

One evening, Ug and I were having a beer in the pub and talking about the next day's training schedule with a couple of our Sergeants. Ug excused himself to go to the Loo (British slang for john), leaving me talking alone at the table with the men. At about the same time, Lieutenant McHenry came in, sat down alone, and ordered a beer.

The next day I received an official letter from McHenry accusing me of fraternizing with an enlisted man. This is serious stuff. When an officer receives such a letter from his commander, he is required to answer by "endorsement."

In short, what this means is this. The original letter is a charge, and the endorsement is the accused's reply. Then, based on that reply, the originator of the charge must make a second endorsement. All written communications are forwarded to the next higher authority. This endorsement requirement extends up through each echelon until it reaches the top, which in my case was the Colonel commanding the Regiment.

My reply, or first endorsement to McHenry's charge of fraternizing with an enlisted man, was one word — "Bullshit!" Nothing more. Just that one word. "Bullshit!" Simple and to the point.

I returned it to my Company Commander for his endorsement and he forwarded the whole thing along to the Battalion Commander.

What McHenry said in his second endorsement is not known to me. Nor is that of the Battalion CO. But one thing I do know with absolute certainty. The Regimental Sergeant was from my hometown. He told me that when the Colonel read the thing, he laughed for five minutes straight, then recommended "No Action."

A note that I had answered by endorsement was entered, with the date, in my file. I am sure it remains there to this day.

10 DECEMBER 1943

We trained hard every day. There were numerous exercises, all designed to sharpen our skills. Some involved Sections, others just platoons, occasionally Company-wide maneuvers. We spent a lot of time moving back and forth across the surrounding countryside.

On 10 December 1943 I was tapped to serve as an umpire for an exercise involving the 116th Infantry Regiment. This exercise was conducted in conjunction with a British unit of similar size. It was designated by command as "Exercise Eros." The orders came from Headquarters 29th Division. My assignment was to act as umpire for D Company.

The exercise was a complex, two-day maneuver structured around the Division's primary mission, which was to defend England against an invasion. I had a runner assigned to me for the duration.

If nothing else, Eros rammed home to me the precarious position England found itself in, as well as the importance of our Division's presence. Lizard Point and the environs was a natural target for an enemy incursion. Should Cornwall fall, likely the whole island would, and thus the war might be lost. Perimeter Defense, as it was called, was the order of the day.

Later that same month, we began "Exercise Duck," which involved a full-scale amphibious assault of a beach in southern England. I'll come back to that shortly.

•

•

On 6 January 1944, I was again picked for special duty. This time I was designated a Class "A" Agent Officer to distribute supplemental payments to personnel of the 175th Infantry Regiment, 2nd Battalion. In the Army, supplemental payday was always the tenth of each month. Those who had missed the regular payday, for whatever reason, were paid on that day, and always in cash.

To fulfill this duty meant I had to leave Helston late in the afternoon of 9 January and work my way cross-country to a set of map coordinates given me in secret. A pair of armed guards escorted me the entire distance for protection. I had selected these two men personally. Both were armed with Thompson submachine guns as well as .45 calibre automatic pistols. Same went for me and my driver. And it didn't end there. We also wore .45s.

Secrecy was important. It was always possible that we would be waylaid and robbed, especially on the return trip.

We didn't arrive at this secret spot until late that night. Then we had to work our way past heavy security before being granted audience with the Regimental Pay Officer. I signed for the supplemental cash payment and then we returned posthaste to Helston.

All the cash I was given — some thirty thousand dollars worth — was denominated in English currency. It included several bags of coin as well as several stacks of banknotes. If you think about it, the men couldn't be paid in dollars, as they would have no way to convert their dollars into British pounds.

But there was another reason for using local currency. If foreign spies would suddenly see a lot of dollars floating around, they might begin to grasp the size of the coming invasion force.

Even so, I had to figure the men's pay in their dollar-equivalent. This made for a lot of mental arithmetic. Thank goodness I was good with numbers!

To make all these payments, my armed crew and I had to travel all over the western tip of Cornwall that very day, the tenth. E Company was bivouacked at Land's End, F Company near Falmouth, G Company was in Marazion, and, of course, H Company and Battalion Headquarters Company were in Helston. Total distance traveled, nearly one hundred and fifty miles.

At the conclusion of what had become a very long and busy day, I found that I still had remaining in my possession nearly two British pounds in coin. Such is the nature of rounding error. Do enough computations, each with a small percentage error, and it's bound to happen. The Army refers to this as "breakage," and the overage had to be promptly returned to the Paymaster.

With all payments now complete, my driver and I returned, minus the guards, to the original map coordinates and checked in, returning the several pounds of breakage. Then it was back to Helston. I got back on the eleventh. It had been an exhausting couple of days, both physically and mentally.

•

•

A short while later, I was designated to participate in advanced training as a Forward Observer for the Artillery. Forward observers work closely with the Infantry and with other units on the front lines. Their function is to define targets for the Artillery to fire upon and to direct said fire.

Of course, because Forward Observers work on the front lines, their mortality rate is high. Thus, the Army needed to train several layers of Infantry officers to fill in should another man be lost. Inasmuch as I was a mortar man, I was a natural for such an assignment. The danger didn't scare me.

The training was to be conducted at the Artillery Range on the Moor outside of Okehampton. I was assigned TDY (temporary duty) with the Regimental Cannon Company. When I had satisfactorily completed the course, I was to be granted one-week's leave of absence.

The Regimental Cannon Company was equipped with a battery of 105 mm howitzers. I joined the Cannon Company at Bodmin, northeast of Helston, and we convoyed to Okehampton, some forty miles further to the north and east.

After nearly two days of skull work, we finally warmed up our weapons and moved out to the firing line. Because the Cannon Company had been appended to the Division Artillery for purposes of this training segment, officers from that unit were obliged to fire first.

I was second or third on the firing line. As Forward Observer, I was given my target. Now, remember how this works. The Forward Observer makes his estimate of range and azimuth, then calls his instructions back to the gunner, usually by radio. The gunner, who often cannot see his target, adjusts the gun as directed and sets its position. The Forward Observer's estimate of range and elevation must be okayed by the Instructor before the instructions are radioed back to the gunner.

Well, as was my way, I quickly sized up the target and how best to hit it. I called for the gunner to move his gun from the previous target. But, my adjustment was so radical, the Instructors refused to okay the full adjustment I had designated.

The officers conducting the exercise said my adjustment would put the fire outside the safety limits of the range. I thought they were full of it and said so as politely as I could. They overruled me, even though I kept insisting my adjustment was on target and that the shell would not fall beyond the safety range.

The Instructors settled for half my estimate. The resulting round fell halfway between the previous target and the one I had been given. I said nothing. But inside, I was smiling.

So they let me have another shot. Again, they rejected my estimate as being too far. Again, they went for half. Again, the round fell halfway between my last shot and the target.

They gave me a third try. I called for the adjustment that would bring my shot where it would have been had they not interfered and agreed to my first estimate. Finally, they relented. The round exploded right on target, as I knew it would.

This "hunt and peck" method of seeking out a target sounds old-fashioned. And it was. But this was in a time before satellites or overhead drones or laser devices which often aid modern targeting. The artillery system of World War II depended on intuition and skill. It called for searching for a target using one gun only. As the "searching" gun alters its direction and range, all the other guns in the battery follow suit. When the "searching" gun finally finds itself on target, the entire battery fires in a saturation pattern.

After the exercise, the Colonel in charge came over to talk to me. He wanted to know how come I was so accurate. I tried to explain to him that there was a distinct difference between how to properly target a mortar and how to properly target a howitzer.

With mortars, we had to learn to pinpoint our targets, whereas howitzers fired area saturations. Since I had first trained on mortars, accuracy was the name of the game, as our targets were much smaller and our projectiles much lighter. With a mortar, we could not afford to miss our target by even so much as three feet. I simply applied the same technique to firing a larger gun.

The Colonel was properly impressed. I found out later that my exercise had been judged the best of all in that phase of the training.

3 FEBRUARY 1944

Well, there I was, only halfway through the week and still stuck on the range. I had completed what training I was to get, and with flying colors. What to do?

I was due to begin one-week's leave at the end of my TDY with Cannon Company. Which placed me in a bit of a predicament.

Why go all the way back to Helston, only to begin my leave from that distant point? Why not see if I couldn't begin my leave from the range?

In Okehampton, at the range, I was already a quarter of the way to Birmingham, my intended destination. Why not? All it would take is a little finagling — and I was good at that. I would need to convince the First Sergeant of Cannon Company to mark me on his Morning Report as having "Returned to Organization."

But that wasn't the extent of it. I would also need to convince the First Sergeant of my resident H Company to record me on his report as having "Returned from TDY." He would subsequently have to enter me as "On Leave" effective that very same day. Illegal all the way around. — But possible.

Oh, it all sounded so good on paper. But there was a catch, maybe two. In the war-torn England of 1944, long-distance telephoning was not an advanced science. I might as well have been calling the moon. Every night, the Germans would launch a bombing raid somewhere across the island. Telephone service was a shambles.

Somehow, though, I got through to H Company in Helston. After much discussion, I convinced the First Sergeant that my plan was the only sensible way to go. With his approval in hand, I then had no difficulty making my case to the First Sergeant of Cannon Company. Both men would make the proper notes in their record on the day my TDY was supposed to end.

Ah, ha! Now I could leave Cannon Company three days early. That would give me an additional three days of (illegal) leave. Moments later, I was on my way.

From Okehampton, I worked my way up to Birmingham by train. Just the thought of getting there brought back memories of my two weeks as a Casual and the bar fight Mack and I found ourselves in that one night. It seemed so long ago. But it really wasn't.

When I arrived in Birmingham, I secured quarters in a domicile run by the NAAFI and designed specifically for British officers on leave. The accommodations were so-so. But the place did have its own mess. And the daily charge was ridiculously low. So I was set.

My first two days in Birmingham, all I did was explore. On one of these outings, I became acquainted with a British Major who was on his way home. He lived just outside Coventry. He had been in India for six years, part of it in Burma, where he was severely wounded. Now he was on recuperation leave and had stopped over in Birmingham for a short stay. He invited me to be his houseguest for a couple days, an offer which I accepted.

Coventry is perhaps twenty miles east of Birmingham. At the time, it was an industrial city, which made it a prime target for German bombers. Earlier in the war, in a devastating series of German bombing raids, the city had suffered terrible destruction — maybe eighty percent.

We were both horror stricken at the extent of the damage, but none worse than the Major. He had been gone so long, he had no idea the extent of the devastation. No matter which way we turned, we faced bombed out buildings, many consumed by fire.

But the Major lived at the edge of town, and here things were all different. To my pleasant surprise, his home was an estate with a large manor house. Wow!

No sooner had we walked through the door and gotten settled in, than he began phoning people he knew. In no time at all, every one of these people had been invited for a party that night. *And what a party it was!*

Besides getting more than a little inebriated, I met a legion of upper crust men and women. The partying lasted well into the night, only breaking up just before dawn. I assure you. Much fun was had by all.

I enjoyed the Major's hospitality for two more days then returned to Birmingham. With three days still remaining on my leave before I was due back at H Company, I decided more exploring was in order.

The first night back I found a large dancehall. It was beautiful, comparable in every way to the Aragon Ballroom in Chicago, an elegantly appointed dancehall of my era that hosted nearly all of the top names of the Big Band era.

But one thing surprised me right off when I stepped in the place. The preponderance of patrons was female. Yet only a handful of men were dancing. *What an opportunity for a guy who liked to dance!*

The place spoke to me. I put a cigarette in my mouth and reached for my lighter. My hand never made it to my pocket.

Three lighters flamed before my face, each with a feminine arm attached. I grabbed one arm, without looking at who or what was at the other end — and lit my cigarette.

Then, ever so cautiously, I turned my eyes to gaze upon the lady who had offered me that light. She was a real doll, with beautiful strawberry blond hair.

"Thanks," I said. "After I finish this smoke, do you want to dance?" I didn't have to wait for her answer, as it couldn't have been more obvious.

Well, dance we did. And what fun. I have had a lifelong affinity for anything musical. Tommy Dorsey. Frank Sinatra. The Big Band sound. Live performances. That kind of thing. Put me in a place where there is music and dancing and I am a happy man.

Somehow I had lucked out with this woman. She was a good dancer, and we stayed at it for a long time. While we danced, she told me her story.

She had been a showgirl in London, when she was conscripted. English women had a choice when they were called up. They could either go into one of the services or they could become a worker in one of the war industries. She chose the latter. Now she worked in a factory that had once manufactured sewing machines but now made machine guns.

The ballroom had a very pleasant tearoom area. No alcohol was served in the building. But she and I did sit down once or twice for tea and biscuits (that's limey talk, for what we call cookies), then danced some more. I couldn't get enough of it, and neither could she.

Afterwards, I saw her home by taxi, then sacked out in my "digs." (More limey talk.) But the next day, after further exploration of the town and a really decent meal, I returned to the ballroom for one final night of kicking up my heels.

It took me a couple of tries. But, after working my way through several girls, I finally found one who was a good dancer. She kept me busy for several hours.

Finally, late that night, after getting my fill of dancing, I went back to the NAAFI — my "digs" — and packed. Tomorrow would be a long day on the train, with several changes along the way, until I got back to Helston and my unit.

But, oh, what fun!

18 FEBRUARY 1944

Mid-February brought an exercise which involved three companies of men: Headquarters Company, H Company with its mortars and machine guns, as well as F Company. Large exercises like this can often be messy. And I'm not talking mud here. I'm talking garbage. Notes are taken, paper is dropped, things fall out of pockets.

At the end of the exercise, as was true at the end of all exercises, we had the men police up the area. The Battalion Commander, a Major, checked the area afterwards for debris. He was not pleased with what he found. He felt the cleanup was handled shoddily, and he blamed us officers.

So, the next day the Commander issued an order. Every officer under the rank of Captain would re-police the area personally. No enlisted men were to assist.

Actually, this turned out to be a great game with plenty of horsing around. We kidded around a lot, bitched even more, and came up with all of four pieces of paper. You have to remember. The exercise covered more than one hundred acres. We had a lot of ground to cover. *But four pieces of paper?* Hardly what I would call shoddy.

Days later, we participated in a joint firing exercise. This involved our Cannon Company and the 110th Field Artillery Battalion. This was a live-fire exercise, where we were to aim at specific targets.

The 116th Infantry Regiment was to advance to within two hundred yards of the strike area and remain standing. They were not to take cover. Two hundred yards, by the way, was considered the minimum safety factor for purposes of a live-fire exercise. The point of the exercise was to familiarize the men with the effects of close-in artillery support.

As the exercise was about to get underway, a staff car pulled up near my position. General Eisenhower, driven by his driver, Kay Summersby, alighted from the vehicle not twenty feet from where I was standing, partially hidden by a hedgerow. Ike's presence brought the entire exercise to a halt while he conducted his inspection. Summersby, by the way, who is often described as his driver (as I just did) was actually a member of the British Mechanized Transport Corps assigned to be his official chauffeur.

After General Eisenhower completed his inspection of the setup, he departed and we commenced firing. Rank after rank of soldiers from the 116th moved to the front position then were replaced by the next rank in line. Meanwhile, all guns kept firing. It was noisy up where we were, with the guns. I can only imagine what it must have been like for those soldiers standing upright downrange.

Suddenly, a frantic command came across our radios: "CEASE FIRE! CEASE FIRE!"

A moment later an explanation began to make its way up the chain of command. Some rounds had fallen short. Men were wounded.

I immediately ordered my men away from their guns. Nothing was to be touched, nothing was to be moved.

We waited. Before long, a team of senior officers fell upon us and practically accused me and my men of being responsible for the short rounds. I knew it wasn't true. I had faith in my men, and in my own aim.

I explained to the senior officers that I had ordered my men away from their guns when the incident occurred, and that the prepared shells still lay on the ground, just as they were.

The officer team was skeptical. But, they fired each of our weapons and verified that they were, in fact, on target. *We were not to blame.*

Satisfied, they moved on to the next adjoining position. This was a pair of 60 mm mortars. Again they fired test rounds. This time they discovered the culprits. These next two guns had been the ones that fired the short rounds.

It was a needless accident. Five men were wounded by the short rounds. Two others in the thirty-five-hundred-man regiment were wounded by flying shrapnel.

Two hundred yards is a long ways for a man to be off on his aim. Those guns should never have been fired.

1 MARCH 1944

Effective the first day of March 1944, I was transferred to G Company as a platoon leader.

At last! I thought. At least now I would be in a position where I might possibly be advanced in rank to 1st Lieutenant. In any event, being made a platoon leader was a promotion of sorts. I was eager for command.

Once again, I was on the move. G Company, a Rifle Company, was headquartered in Marazion, a small community located about ten miles west of my current position in Helston and perhaps three miles east of the more-famous town of Penzance.

Perhaps you've heard of Penzance. It is that small, oceanside community made famous by Gilbert & Sullivan's comic opera, The Pirates of Penzance.

A little background might be in order here. In the Cornish language, Penzance means "holy headland." And it is truly so. The name is a reference to the location of the chapel of St. Anthony which, a thousand years ago, stood on the promontory west of the harbor. For centuries, this history was reflected in the town's peculiar choice for its symbol: the severed holy head of St. John the Baptist.

Being at the far west end of Cornwall, Penzance and the surrounding villages had been sacked many times in the past by foreign fleets. In medieval times and later, Penzance was subject to frequent pirate raids, including raids by the infamous Barbary Corsairs.

Actually, despite its notoriety, until about the seventeenth century Penzance was overshadowed by my newest home, the town of Marazion.

Marazion is recorded in the history books as far back as the Domesday Book of 1086. It is the oldest chartered town in Britain, having been granted this status by King Henry III in 1257. The name — Marazion — translates literally as "Market Jew" or "Jews' Market," though I am highly skeptical whether people of such descent ever settled in this area prior to the onset of the Middle Ages.

The most prominent feature in the town of Marazion is not the town itself but what sits upon a rock, out in its large, sweeping bay — Saint Michael's Mount. It is in so many ways the British equivalent of the more famous tidal island, Mont-Saint-Michel, off the coast of Normandy. Mont-Saint-Michel, by the way, also translates into English as Saint Michael's Mount. Indeed, the two are closely related in history, as well as geography.

The Mount, as the locals call it, rises more than two hundred feet above the surrounding sea and is topped by a castle. Parts of that castle were built in the Middle Ages, the rest in the seventeenth and eighteenth centuries. The original site dated to at least the eleventh century and was at that time a Benedictine Monastery.

In my day, the Mount was owned by Lord Saint Leven, a descendant of the original owners, the St. Aubyn family. Leven and his wife lived there during the war. Their son, a British Army officer, was away fighting somewhere. At the base of the Mount were a number of houses. This is where the servants and staff lived. I visited the Mount on more than one occasion, usually for Sunday tea. The place was magnificent.

When the tide was low, the castle could be reached by way of a narrow causeway. At high tide, a boat was necessary.

Marazion itself was built on a steep slope. The slope opens onto a fairly broad beach which faces out towards Saint Michael's Mount. Above the town rose hills. They were always green, as the climate was temperate and pleasant.

In fact, nearly all of Cornwall was made up of hills. Many had large, hedgerow-lined meadows on each slope. Most roads in the district were narrow. Beyond the city limits, almost every road was also lined by hedgerows. Within the town proper, there were no new buildings, not a one. Nearly every building in Marazion was old. And, like Helston, they were all made of limestone rock.

•

•

The locals we met around town were friendly. But many were also distant, with a cautious wait-and-see attitude toward us "Yanks." There were few men my age. Most were either much older or mere boys. Great Britain had been engaged in this war for four years already, and the war's manpower needs had sapped the population of eligible men.

Everyone in Britain was subject to call-up. That included the women. Ladies in the requisite age-groups faced a number of possibilities when conscripted and ordered to duty. They could go into an auxiliary branch of the military — Army, Navy, or Air Force. Or they could go into farm work as part of the Women's Land Army, or be sent to work in industry producing munitions. They could also be directed into some form of government effort, like the NAAFI service organization that supported regular troops.

Those men or women who were exempt from service kept things going at home. But, you can be sure, every Brit was making some sort of contribution to the war effort. It was total commitment carried forward with typical quiet, unremitting British grit.

•

•

But now, back to the Army. To make sense of what follows, it is necessary for you to first understand the structure of a Rifle Company, circa 1944. A Rifle Company consisted of three rifle platoons plus a weapons platoon. The weapons platoon had three sections of light machine guns, each with two guns, as well as a pair of 60 mm mortar sections, armed with two mortars each.

Each of the three rifle platoons had thirty-nine men, and each was commanded by a Lieutenant. The Company Headquarters section included the CO (a Captain), the Executive officer (a 1st Lieutenant), the First Sergeant, and the kitchen and supply staff.

Rifle platoons were identified by number — one, two, or three. The Weapons Platoon was the Fourth Platoon. Including the support staff, total personnel in a Rifle Company numbered one hundred and eighty-six enlisted men plus six officers. As I said, I was to be a platoon leader for one of those four platoons in Rifle Company G.

When I arrived in Marazion, I reported in to the Commanding Officer, Captain John K. Singleton. There I met 1st Lieutenant James E. "Speedy" Arrow, the Company's Executive Officer, and First Sergeant George Ingersoll. Company Headquarters were housed in a Nissen hut. It had been thrown up next to an old hotel, one of two hotels in which troops were billeted. Officers were quartered elsewhere.

By way of explanation: a Nissen hut is a prefabricated steel structure. It is assembled from a long sheet of corrugated metal which is then bent into a half-cylinder and planted in the ground with its axis horizontal. It is much like its American counterpart, the Quonset hut, and was used extensively during World War II by both the Commonwealth and the U.S. military to build Army camps and Airbases. The name has nothing to do with Nissan, the auto manufacturer, but rather, Nissen, a British Major in the 29th Company Royal Engineers.

The Captain gave me Third Platoon which, by long tradition, was the platoon where the Army parked its misfits. The officer I replaced, Lieutenant James Flanagan, had already departed. "Speedy" took me to our officers' quarters. We were billeted in a row house on Fore Street across the Town Square from the Nissen hut Company Headquarters.

The building we lived in was narrow, only the width of a single room plus a hallway. The first floor of the house had a dining room, parlor, and small kitchen. The second floor had two bedrooms, as well as a bathroom with a very large bathtub. The third floor had two more bedrooms. All six company officers lived there. We were served by our own "cook" and waiter. These two men also cleaned up the place, although we were to make our own beds. This was a bit of a change from Helston, where I had my own striker.

I said "cook" in the previous paragraph rather than cook, because the man actually procured our food from the regular enlisted men's mess, brought it across the Square and served it to us. About the only thing he actually cooked was coffee. Not that the cook was a bad guy, because he certainly was not. Sergeant "Red" McDonald had come to us from H Company, my former Company, where he was Mess Sergeant. But he had gotten into some kind of difficulty over there — I'm not sure what — and had been transferred over to G company even before I was. So I knew the man.

Our waiter was PFC Touchstone, and he knew his way around a table. Touchstone had been a waiter at the Waldorf Astoria in New York City before being drafted. The man was smooth. Both Red and Touchstone were assigned to Company Headquarters, Red as backup Mess Sergeant, Touchstone as a runner.

3 MARCH 1944

The next day I met my men. The Platoon Sergeant was a young Tech Sergeant named Harold Kinkade. Harold was a Midwesterner from Ohio or Indiana. The Platoon Guide was a Staff Sergeant named William "Bill" Kazanza. He was from the Pittsburg, Pennsylvania, area. My other men hailed from all over the United States, although a great many were from just one place: Maryland. This group of men had been with the 29th Division since its inception. These soldiers had come into the service when the Division was called up from National Guard status.

I told my men a little of my history, that my enlisted duty had been with the Regular Army and that I had earned my commission at the Officer Candidate School at Fort Benning, Georgia. I didn't have to draw attention to the RANGER insignia on my shoulder or the jump boots on my feet. They both spoke volumes. That temporary assignment jumping from an airplane earned me some credibility points.

Then I told my men that no changes were planned for the present, and that for the remainder of the first week things would proceed as normal, with me simply "looking them over." That way I could get to know each of them better and see what they were capable of. After that, I would step in.

Meanwhile, Sergeant Kinkade would continue to run things just as they had always been run. In short, I was telling my crew that they were under scrutiny until I said different. The only admonition I inserted into my little talk was to let them know discipline would be strict and by the book. As I said, Third Platoon had a reputation for housing misfits. This little talk was my way of saying party time was over.

Even so, as that first week progressed, one thing quickly became apparent. Their former platoon leader, Lieutenant Flanagan, had been a slacker. He had allowed the men to become lax, most especially in matters of military discipline.

Flanagan, a former boxer, was gifted in certain ways. He had a pleasing personality and his men (now my men) had obviously held him in high regard.

But a large part of that popularity stemmed from the man's unwillingness to impose any sort of military discipline on his men. Thus, a certain sloppiness had set in. *This just would not do.* These men had to be combat-ready. The war was drawing closer by the day!

I moved quickly — and perhaps harshly — to remedy the problem. Prescribed training for that first week, where I mainly observed, involved squad tactics. As I watched Sergeant Kinkade put the men through their paces it became patently clear. These soldiers were either poorly trained or rusty or both.

The problem was simple. Although most of these men had been in uniform well over a year, it had been soft duty, here in England. Flanagan had been popular, but his doctrine was deadly. He had failed to prepare his men for actual combat, failed to sharpen their military skills as individual soldiers.

If I knew nothing else as a lowly 2nd Lieutenant, I knew this. A poorly trained infantryman does not last long under actual enemy fire. *A poorly trained soldier is a dead soldier.*

But knowing what was wrong and doing something about it were two different things. Flanagan had been well-liked by these men. Either Flanagan didn't recognize his failings for what they were, or else he had been too lazy to do anything about them. Replacing a man like that in the hearts and minds of these soldiers would not be easy.

I guess maybe I deserved Third Platoon. I was a bit of a rascal myself. Even so, here was a chance to turn things around, both for them and for me.

So I set to work to remedy the situation. I gave it to the men straight. I sat them down and told them two things. First, that it was obvious they were a fine bunch of men. But — and here I didn't mince words — they were lousy infantrymen.

To soften the message, I allowed that they were a bit rusty but that I would be laying out a program of tough training which would place great emphasis on redeveloping the skills of each individual soldier as a killing machine.

My men took it well, and even before that first week was out, I felt they were already beginning to sharpen up. I could see that they were standing taller and exhibiting more snap in their relationships with one another. Clearly, they were responding to my earlier dictate that military discipline would be strictly adhered to. But we had a long way to go.

At this point, the entire Company was engaged in various exercises to understand and improve squad tactics. From morning until night, almost the entire day was devoted to actions of each squad. Aggressive attack measures, as well as defensive maneuvers were covered in detail. Practice, practice, practice.

As I noted at the outset, the majority of my men performed with a halfhearted attitude and did not exhibit a well-developed level of proficiency. When they were on their bellies crawling forward over the ground, they exposed themselves unnecessarily. When climbing over hedgerows they took too long and, on occasion, even stood on top of them. Again, this would just not do.

So I came up with a plan. First stop, the Supply Sergeant. From him I procured some equipment and from that equipment I fashioned a sturdy slingshot. Then I went down to Marazion Beach and collected a supply of decent-sized round stones. Now I was ready. I told my men, next time we ran the course, any man who let himself become visible would be greeted by a stone slung their way. Then I demonstrated my accuracy with a rock and a slingshot. Dead on.

The first day I used eighteen stones. They must have stung a little, for only three stones were necessary the second day. We ran the exercises over and over again. I was working them very hard. Within two days that slingshot was relegated to my quarters. The men were developing their individual skills.

Meanwhile, one hour of each day was devoted to close-order drill. Old stuff to them — and perhaps a bit boring — and yet, it was one of those things that require constant repetition. Even today, close-order drill is the single best way for an Army to develop and hone proper discipline.

Here, too, I could see improvement. The men were responding to their training, walking tall, exhibiting snap. Soon their drills were executed with real precision. Also, their uniforms looked better, shoes shined almost to brilliance. Their guns and personal equipment were cleaner. In short, they looked more like a soldier ought to look.

Because of the circumstances of our billets — hotels in the center of town rather than barracks behind a fence or a wall in a segregated camp — there was no practical way to limit a man's movements around town after *Retreat*. It occurred to me that this utter freedom of movement might have contributed to the men's lax attitude, perhaps even to Lieutenant Flanagan's inability to maintain proper discipline in the ranks. So we settled on a rule.

After *Retreat*, every man was permitted to leave his billet so long as he remained in town. If a soldier wanted to go farther afield, say out of town for the weekend, a pass would be required. As a reward for all their hard training, up to one-third of the men would be granted passes at any one time. I was to authorize them and Sergeant Kinkade was to dole them out as needed.

This rule accomplished two things. First, it strengthened Sergeant Kinkade's position. It gave him more authority and tied the men closer to him. Also, it kept the men from feeling too confined. When men feel as though they are prisoners, they tend to want to escape. I'm not speaking so much about AWOL here, as I am about escape in the sense of shirking one's duties or losing a sense of commitment.

Actually, most of the men stuck fairly close to town and weekend passes never once reached the prescribed limit of one-third of the platoon. My policy of granting passes up to some specified maximum was a reflection of my personal philosophy — If a man worked hard, he had a right to play hard. He earned it.

Things got better with each day, both commitment and attitudes. I counseled my men when necessary, joined in on their athletic contests when asked. In many ways I became their surrogate mother and father.

Moral was up.

15 MARCH 1944

One day, while we were discussing cover and concealment, a question came up. One of my men wanted to know how effective our steel helmets were in preventing injury.

I answered the best I could. A helmet went only so far, I said. It might protect a man from flying debris. But it almost certainly would not stop a bullet. I reminded them of my lesson with the slingshot and rocks.

Then, just to prove my point, I took off my helmet, removed the helmet liner, and handed the empty helmet to one of my men. I asked him to run across the field we were standing in and to place the helmet down on the ground beside the nearest hedgerow, then to return as fast as he could.

When he got back, I took my carbine and fired a single shot, hitting the helmet square. I instructed the same man to run over and retrieve it. He was aghast, as were all my men. The helmet had two bullet holes in it, one going in, another coming back out. Every man in my platoon examined it for himself. *Message received.*

The Supply Sergeant painted a new helmet for me, replacing the one I had damaged. The old one was circulated throughout the Company, so each man could see for himself what a single bullet might do to a man's head. A lot of eyebrows were raised.

Captain Singleton did not appreciate my ruining a perfectly good helmet. Nor did he appreciate me firing a live round in an area where weapons were not supposed to be discharged. But he had to agree it was an effective lesson.

My new helmet, like everyone else's, had a 29th Division insignia painted on the front. Those with rank had their insignia of rank painted on front as well. Noncoms had a one-inch by six-inch white stripe painted horizontally on the back. Officers had a vertical stripe of the same dimension in the same location.

No officer, no matter how qualified, can run an effective platoon without the wholehearted support of his sergeants. Fortunately, Tech Sergeant Kinkade as well as Staff Sergeant Kazanza had gotten onboard my tough training program. Their performance was great from the outset.

Now we moved into the next phase — platoon maneuvers broken down by squad. Here's where the men learned how to coordinate squad movements to achieve an overall platoon objective. After the first two exercises, the squad leaders and assistant squad leaders admitted that, for the very first time, they understood what was going on and what was expected of them.

To convey my orders to the squads, I made effective and frequent use of runners. This is an area where Flanagan had failed miserably.

In small-unit tactics, communications is key. It is one thing to formulate an attack plan and quite another to implement it. What looks good on paper may not work in the field. Circumstances change rapidly on the battlefield, sometimes in unexpected ways. A man has to be able to react rapidly to these situational changes and communicate effectively with his men when a change in strategy is dictated.

This is where the runners come in — conveying instructions quickly and quietly. But, for my platoon, the use of runners was a new experience. Now, though, they began to function as a cohesive unit.

•

•

Meanwhile, I was getting to know my fellow officers. 1st Lieutenant Tom Lombardo was First Platoon leader. 2nd Lieutenant George Britto had the Second. 1st Lieutenant John Lister was platoon leader of the Fourth, or Weapons Platoon. In addition to crossing their paths many times a day, we lived together in the same row house. Plus, it was pretty much our habit to congregate each evening in the best pub in town for much drink and conversation.

George was not a regular at our confabs, as he was a bit of a recluse and preferred to stay in and write his wife. Nor was John Lister. John was always on the prowl, looking to meet some lovely young thing. It was easy for him. He was a young, single, good-looking guy.

So, mostly, it was just the three of us — Speedy Arrow (the Company XO), Tom Lombardo (leader of First Platoon) and me. We were the regulars on those evenings.

The public house, or pub, we frequented was actually a small inn with a good-sized, if ordinary, barroom downstairs, plus some sleeping rooms above. The main barroom was partitioned into two sections by a low wall, one side being exclusively for customers of the female persuasion. The wall separating the two parts stood maybe three and a half to four feet tall.

Aside from the main barroom, the inn also had another, smaller room, nicely furnished, complete with piano. This room would also accommodate women, which was good, as there were several local ladies who never seemed to get enough of the place. They were there, in that little parlor, each and every night, rain or shine. As you can well imagine, these girls were full of fun.

Hours during which pubs could do business were set by law, and the laws were strict. From ten a.m. to two p.m., and again from five p.m. to ten p.m. There was no wiggle room on those closing times. When the clock struck ten, doors closed tight.

By tacit agreement, the smaller, side room was "Officer Country," no enlisted men allowed. The main barroom, called the "ordinary" — as well as every other pub in town — was where enlisted soldiers could frequent. Officers would stay away from those places. The arrangement worked out fine.

One of the women who was always in our "Club" was a buxom, attractive blonde named Mary. You know how I like music. Mary would sit at those piano keys every night and play almost the entire time.

But among the several things that were amazing about this woman was that she smoked incessantly. A cigarette was always in her mouth. I never once saw her remove one from her lips.

But the amazing part was something else. I never was able to detect even a hint of ash on her person. *How does a woman do that?* Especially one built like her? Smoke incessantly, play piano, and never get an ash on her dress?

We nicknamed this wonderful girl, "Marazion Mary." Mary was witty and jolly and the absolute center of our evenings. We sang and laughed a lot. Tom Lombardo kept her warm every night after closing.

Speedy and I enjoyed every minute we spent together in our Club. But, unlike Tom, we did not have someone to keep us warm after hours. Sure, I liked being around women as much as the next man. But I was married and had no desire for a short-term bedmate. I can't speak for Speedy. He seemed to be still playing the field.

As for the others. John Lister was always on the prowl, like I said. Tom was with Mary almost every night. And Captain Singleton slept elsewhere. The row house was empty and quiet most nights.

Singleton had married a nice English woman back when the Company was still located in Tidworth Barracks before moving to Marazion. He and his wife had quarters with the Lyster family, British Major (Retired) John Lyster and his wife Pamela. They had a home, named The White House, which overlooked Mount's Bay. Captain Singleton and his wife joined us at the Club perhaps once a week.

Me, I did my best not to be lonely.

21 MARCH 1944

Long about this time, I bought a used bicycle. It allowed me some freedom to explore the surrounding countryside on my own, when time permitted. I like to explore; I always have. It gives me great satisfaction. Nowadays, people say "to go on walkabout." In my time, I referred to it as perambulation.

One day, while I was out riding my bike, I came upon a soldier walking beside the road. It was our cook, Sergeant "Red" McDonald. As you may recall, Red had come to us from H Company, my former Company, where he was Mess Sergeant. When I ran into him, he seemed quite sad. I asked him what was wrong.

He told me that a close friend of his from home had just informed him that his wife was sleeping around. Now Red wanted out of his marriage. Could I help him?

I said I'd see what I could do. Red himself hadn't been faithful. But that was beside the point.

First I went to see Captain Singleton. I would need his permission to approach the JAG at Regimental Headquarters. The Captain was reluctant to get the Army involved but gave his permission anyway.

Next, I contacted the Judge Advocate General and requested his department's cooperation in mounting a case on Red's behalf.

A few days later, the Regimental JAG came down from Headquarters for a visit and gathered what little information Red could provide. They would work through the JAG Department in Washington, D.C., where they would assemble the actual evidence proving the continued transgressions of Red's wife. Then they would sue her for divorce on Red's behalf, and he would be free of her.

This was another example of the Army taking care of its own. In the service, the JAG Department is a soldier's legal representative when needed.

Red was really grateful for my help, even though I hadn't actually done that much. All I really did was to put things in motion for the man. But he had every intention of paying me back in full.

At the time, Red was keeping company with a woman who was the widow of the largest wholesale liquor distributor in the district. She had inherited the business when her husband passed away and now ran it. From the moment I agreed to help Red with his problem, he saw to it that I never wanted for liquor again, even if the stuff was in short supply around those parts.

The truth of the matter was this. We officers were already receiving a monthly allotment of free liquor from the British NAAFI. The allotment consisted of one bottle each of scotch and gin, plus two bottles of sherry and/or rum. So, there I was, adequately provided for by NAAFI but also having a bottomless well of booze at my disposal. I used my good fortune sensibly, to trade for other, more important things, like food. It was the first of my many sub rosa dealings.

As long as we're on the subject, let's talk food. Food is a big thing with soldiers. Next to perhaps women, it is easily the most talked about subject among the men. Its poor quality was certainly the biggest source of complaints. A man can live without a shower or even a decent night's sleep. But a lousy breakfast or a crappy dinner? Now that is something else.

U.S. Army rations were built around three meats — Bully Beef (corned beef), Bologna, and Spam. From time to time we would get frozen meats. Freezing meats was a relatively new phenomenon, although we did notice a carton of frozen chicken stamped as having been packed in a Naval installation, April 1938 Remember: it was now 1944. Those chickens were like rocks. But we had to eat them.

As for vegetables, we had lots and lots of Brussels sprouts. About the only thing that bore even a vague resemblance to home cooking was the first-rate bread supplied to us under contract by a local baker.

It was graham bread, as bleached flour to make white bread was simply not available in quantity.

Lunches in the field consisted mostly of a thick slice of spam or corned beef slapped between two slices of bread. Sometimes it was a marmalade sandwich. Either way, they were unappetizing. Most days, we were out in the damp moors performing exercises. No matter what we ate or how the sandwiches looked when the day began, by the time we put them in our mouths to eat them, they always seemed damp and soggy. Coffee in the field was hot, though, and we quickly got used to midday meals such as they were.

Field coffee was strong. The way it was made had a lot to do with the outcome. The cooks took a large, galvanized-steel ash can, filled it to the brim with water and placed it on a portable heating unit. After the water reached a rolling boil, the cooks dumped in a huge scoop of ground coffee. Then they let it boil some more. I'm not sure how long.

After a time, a scoop of ice-cold water was dumped into the mix and the coffee grounds were allowed to settle to the bottom. The result was wonderful, and the men raved. Hot. Strong. Delicious. It made those limp, damp sandwiches go down more easily.

Seeing my love of food and coffee, Captain Singleton made me Mess Officer. This was a duty I had to perform in addition to my regular duties as a Rifle Platoon Leader. Evidently, Flanagan had filled that position, so, as his replacement, I inherited the job as well. Only problem was, he did neither job well. Me, I was serious about both. Plus, I didn't want to suffer the men's complaints.

During my off-hours perambulating, I became quite friendly with an older pub-crawler we knew only as "Doc." I never learned how he earned that moniker, but it turned out that Doc was the local wholesaler of meats and meat products. *What good fortune!* I thought.

With the dreariness of repetitive meals built around the likes of bologna, bully beef, and spam, my ears literally twitched when Doc told me of his occupation. They positively rang when he eagerly accepted a cigar from me. *Time for some horse-trading,* I thought.

Doc loved cigars. But, in wartime England, civilians found cigars hard to come by. Only I wasn't a civilian. Back in my quarters, stacked against one wall, were nearly fifty unopened boxes of cigars. These were thanks to the PX, and some advance planning on my part.

So I started by slipping Doc a few cigars at a time. This way, he would have some to enjoy at home, where no one else was around to see him smoke.

As soldiers, we normally bought our smokes in the Post Exchange. But, in Marazion, we were located so far from a large cantonment area, there was no PX. Instead, the PX sent out a supply truck to visit us once a month. We had no choice but to buy sundries a month at a time.

At that time, the cigar allotment was three per day per soldier, or ninety cigars for a thirty-day month. Cigars came in boxes of fifty. Rather than break a box, the Sergeant who ran the mobile PX gave us two full, unopened boxes for the month. Not everybody in my platoon smoked. So I put up the money and persuaded several of the nonsmokers to buy their allotment of cigars with my money and hand them over to me. My supply rose and rose.

After a time, with me regularly slipping Doc cigars, he was getting used to never being without. The more cigars he smoked, the more he wanted. The time was growing ripe for a trade. So I struck a deal.

If he would covertly supply G Company with enough fresh meat to feed us all several times a month, I would keep him in cigars and make up the difference in money. I shanghaied all the Company officers to share in the money side of the trade.

Aside from us officers, the only other persons who knew how the fresh meat made it onto our tables were First Sergeant George Ingersoll and the Mess Sergeant. As you can well imagine, secrecy was important as this was a forbidden, black market operation.

In the end, Doc got lots of cigars and the Company had more than a few "Roast Pork Nights." I got more than a few kudos and morale was boosted all around. Captain Singleton was happy. He had made me Mess Officer and I had performed admirably. He had no problem looking the other way.

30 MARCH 1944

Marazion was on the southern coast of England facing the outermost tip of France. We had no rifle range close by. The nearest one was some seventy miles away. With fuel and vehicles in short supply, transporting the entire Company that distance was out of the question. Still, we needed to practice.

They say that necessity is the mother of invention. It must be so, as Captain Singleton came up with an interesting solution to our problem. He ordered a large quantity of balloons from the Quartermaster. When the balloons arrived, each man was issued five and ordered to inflate each of them. Then Singleton marched the entire Company out of town to one of the nearby bluffs which rose above the English Channel.

Rotating the men through one at a time, he had them cast their five balloons into the wind and then wait until they fell to the water. Once the balloons had floated some distance from shore, it was target-practice time. We let the men bang away at the balloons until every balloon had either been sunk or else blown away.

Once the enlisted men had completed their exercise, it was time for the officers. Only this became more of a competition than just a simple exercise. We began by blowing up three dozen more target balloons.

Captain Singleton fancied himself a good shot. He borrowed an M1 from one of the men, and I have to admit, he did well. He shot and hit balloons farther and farther out from shore. I did the same using my trusty little carbine.

But here's the thing. In the hands of a knowledgeable user, an M1 can be very accurate out to as much as a thousand yards. A carbine, like I was shooting, is harder to use and less accurate the farther away a target becomes. When we began, we were shooting at distances under three hundred yards. Plus, we were well *above* the balloons, shooting downhill, as it were. Still, these weren't easy shots, as the balloons rose and fell with each successive wave.

Right off, Singleton noticed how I was hitting the bobbing balloons almost every time. He challenged me, and we started to compete. The wager was one English pound per balloon. At the time, the rate of exchange was in excess of four American dollars to each English pound, a hefty sum on my puny salary. Maybe he thought if he made the wager large enough I would back down. I didn't.

Suffice it to say, the Captain was a good shot. But I was better. When we were through, my winnings totaled four pounds. *Ha!* Pub and cigar money for at least a week.

•

•

There was no denying the fact that Captain Singleton's makeshift "balloon" shooting range was a clever idea. But it most certainly would not do as a long-term solution to our target-practice problem. The Battalion Commander could see that. 2nd Battalion was spread all over the westernmost tip of southern England. We needed a permanent, set location to establish a small rifle range.

In short order, a suitable spot was selected on Lizard Point. You might remember what I told you about Lizard Point. It is below Helston on the tip of a tiny but strategic peninsula, England's southernmost neck of land. A small fighter base was already headquartered out on the tip.

The place we selected to construct our rifle range was on a bluff overlooking the English Channel. Being on high ground would allow us to direct our fire out over the water.

But, because of our range's close proximity to the fighter base, some coordination between our two units was necessary. We didn't want to be accidentally shooting at their aircraft, nor did we want them shooting back. On the other hand, we wouldn't be there often enough to disrupt their operations.

G Company was one of the companies charged with the actual construction of the range. I had some practice with such things after my experience building a range back at Fort Leonard Wood. So my experience counted for something.

Those of us involved in the construction picked up stakes and temporarily moved out to Lizard Point. For a week, we lived in pup tents and ate out of our mess kits. But by week's end, the job was done. We had built a firing range with eight firing positions. It was large enough to accommodate an entire Company for a full day of target practice.

While we were out building the range, I conducted my usual "walkabout." I found a poultry farm nearby, one that was operated by an Englishman who had once lived in California for more than fifteen years. This was a point of connection between him and me, as I had visited California eight years earlier and my father was born in San Francisco. My grandmother still lived there.

The Englishman missed the relatively outgoing American style of living. He found me easy to talk to, and, in the week that I was out there on Lizard Point, we talked quite often and became quite friendly. Next thing I knew, I was making arrangements with him to secretly supply us with large quantities of fresh eggs. *Another black market thing.* I was quickly becoming a criminal!

Actually, that's an overstatement. But then again, anyone who has tried to stomach the dehydrated eggs of World War II can appreciate the underlying purpose behind my machinations. Even a talented cook with the best intentions can only prepare powdered eggs for a large group one way — in large pans as "scrambled" eggs. In such a setting, they took on the texture of foam rubber and lacked good flavor. If they smelled at all, it was a smell a man would rather forget, one with just a hint of sulphur mixed in. Maybe if a man doused the resulting goop in enough salt and pepper and drowned it in ketchup . . .

But now here I was, the bearer of *fresh* eggs, courtesy of my newest friend, the poultry farmer. Ah, what a difference on a Sunday morning!

Now the cook could feature fresh eggs for special Sunday breakfasts. Now the meal could consume an entire Sunday morning, as we allowed the men leisurely attendance. They could drift in when they pleased, order up eggs prepared "their" way — poached, boiled, baked, scrambled, whatever. Add a side of fried spam, maybe some potatoes, a slice of delicious local graham bread. M'mm! M'mm! Good! Another morale booster, courtesy of Mess Officer William Frodsham.

4 APRIL 1944

As officers, we were accepted at court (the King's Court, that is), and therefore included among those who occupied the highest rungs in the still-stratified British society. Common citizens paid us deference. More than a few even looked up to us.

But with this position of status came certain social obligations. We had to always behave well in public. No public drunkenness for us. Plus, we had no choice but to accept a monthly invitation to take tea with Lord Saint Leven in the castle on Saint Michael's Mount. Though the monthly tea was obligatory, it was by no means distasteful.

Lord Saint Leven was gracious to a fault. And the man was interesting. He and his wife would always invite us for Sunday afternoon tea, so as to not interfere with our duties. Their son, as I said earlier, was away fighting for Queen and Crown in the Far East. He, too, was an Army officer. So we had some common ground. Not to bore you, but I have nothing but fond memories of those Sunday afternoon teas.

Another social obligation we had revolved around the Lyster family. As you may recall, Captain Singleton and his wife lived with the Lyster family in a wonderful home — The White House — which overlooked Mount's Bay. John Lyster, now retired, had been a Major in the British Army. He and his wife Pamela had three daughters: Felicity, Rosemary, and Verity.

Felicity was the oldest of the three. When I arrived, she was away in London, acting in a repertory company. Rosemary, the middle one, was a Lieutenant in the Women's Royal Naval Service. The youngest, Verity, was away at school. Mrs. Lyster, Pamela, had been a musical comedy star on the London stage during the First World War. She was vivacious and witty. The Major was quiet and reserved, though always friendly.

With the three girls away and Captain Singleton and his wife living in the house with them, we made it our habit to stop off at The White House nearly every day around teatime. The house was situated at the seawall. It had a patio off the main living room that looked out over the bay.

On the patio was an aviary. It housed about thirty parakeets. They were noisy and amused us no end. One of them, named Dicky, I think, was often permitted to fly about the house. He would perch on your shoulder and, as you talked, would snatch little bits of food from between your teeth. The whole thing was amazing because the bird would do it in a flash and then be gone. It all happened so fast, you were hardly even aware he had done it.

Visiting with the Lysters became part of our daily routine. It was curious, though. Pamela, especially, never quite seemed to understand my taking tea without milk and sugar. She and the Major always seemed to think I was being considerate on their account, given the strict rationing in Britain.

I explained that I had grown up drinking my tea plain. My father had taught me to enjoy it that way. He, himself, had grown up in San Francisco, where there was a large Chinese population. The Chinese always drank their tea plain, without milk or sugar added.

In early April, Felicity Lyster came home for an extended stay. Apparently, the repertory company had fallen on evil times and activities had been put on hold. At about the same time, Rosemary came home on leave. Shortly, she was to report for a new assignment at Falmouth, about thirty miles north and east of Helston. Given the close proximity of her new station, Rosemary would be home often. Speedy Arrow, the Company's Executive Officer, fell for her quickly, and she seemed to reciprocate with ample enthusiasm.

Shortly after the two older girls returned home, the officers in our Battalion decided to sponsor a dance in Helston. The Captain and his wife, living as they were in The White House, found themselves elevated to the status of unofficial chaperone to the two Lyster girls. Remember what I told you about officers being acceptable at Court. A certain decorum was required.

Rosemary and Felicity would attend the party, of course. Naturally, Speedy would escort Rosemary. But Felicity had no date. Singleton had no choice but to instruct one of his officers to accompany the girl. He settled on a married officer, figuring her chastity would likely be safest with one of us. Somehow, I got the nod.

My outgoing personality may have entered into his decision. Or perhaps my well-known love for dance. Whatever the reason, he called me into his office one day a week before the dance.

"Lieutenant, you will escort Felicity Lyster to the officer's dance. I have every expectation that because you are married, she will be safe in your hands. Are we clear?"

I nodded. What he was saying amounted to a direct order. I could not ignore it. Nor could I let him down. I was going to the dance whether I liked it or not, and I was going to take Felicity Lyster.

Make no mistake about it. This was hardly a case of Prince Charming stuck dragging the ugly stepsister to the ball. Felicity Lyster was a beautiful woman. Twenty-five years old. Flashing green eyes. Gorgeous head of chestnut-colored hair. Superb, athletic figure. An eye-catching, mouth-watering sight. — *And she was my responsibility.*

The moment we walked into the room, every young officer in the place descended upon my charge vulture-like. I only managed to dance with the girl twice, and one of those times some officer cut in.

What a night!

•

•

Being only miles from Penzance, you might think we visited there often. But that was not the case. In all the many weeks I was stationed in Marazion, I made only two visits to Penzance.

The first was during the day, and I spent only a couple hours. Like so many towns in Cornwall, Penzance was steeped in historical lore. There were many beautiful gardens to admire, as well as lots of older buildings.

But beautiful gardens and picturesque old homes really wasn't my thing. Anyway, we were in England on official duty, not touring on some family vacation. Pubs attracted us more. One thing Penzance had over Marazion was that it was larger and pubs abounded.

The other time I went in, it was with another officer. We had heard that the Queen's Hotel was the place to be, with a nice cocktail lounge and plenty of interesting guests. So we decided to check it out.

Sure enough, the lounge was grand. While we were sitting there, enjoying our drinks, another officer walked by, told us of a party going full blast on the fourth floor. My buddy and I decided to have a look-see.

The Queen's Hotel was a big enough place to have an elevator. We rode it to the fourth floor. After exiting the elevator, we paused for a moment, trying to decide which way to the party.

Right about then, we heard a young girl's giggle. We turned in the direction of the sound and, suddenly, here came a pretty, young thing — naked — laughing her head off and running past us down the corridor.

Right on her heels was a short, round man — also naked and also laughing — chasing her. Even without his clothes, we recognized the man right off, Colonel So-and-So from the Engineers Battalion stationed outside of Helston.

I turned to my friend to check his reaction and nearly had to pick his jaw up off the floor.

We didn't even say a word, but turned and got back on the elevator.

I punched the down button and back to the lobby we went, laughing all the way.

We got out of that hotel as fast as our legs would carry us.

10 APRIL 1944

The former Division Commander, when he was promoted and left the Division, had promised us that the 29th would be in on the invasion. Now, as we entered the final phases of our training, that promise was always in the back of our minds.

Changes in command occurred frequently, and at all levels, as the Army strove to find the best and most effective combinations of commanders and men. Some changes worked. Some were less than ideal.

When the 2nd Battalion was given a new commander — Lieutenant Colonel Shellenburger — this was not one of the better changes. Shellenburger was a former paratrooper. On first glance, that would seem to be a good fit for an infantry unit. Paratroops, after all, were considered among the most elite soldiers the Army had to offer.

But this fit like a pair of old underwear. Shellenburger was a NUTCAKE. The paratroops must have been happy to be rid of him.

Oh, Shellenburger was gung-ho alright. And, he was a true believer in physical conditioning, as well as strict discipline. That part was fine.

But the man had no brains. He had a habit of showing up for activities unannounced — which was his prerogative, of course. But it would be at strange times. On one occasion, he showed up just as we were heading out for our daily morning calisthenics.

On the morning in question, as we marched out of town toward the field where we did our daily hour of calisthenics, I glanced back along the ranks. Sure enough. There was Colonel Shellenburger stepping out

161

of his jeep and falling into line behind the last rank. *Fiddles! It was our day to put up with him!*

At first, Shellenburger put on a good show. Everyone knew the Colonel was a reject from the Airborne. Even so, the man gave the impression of being just as well conditioned as any other paratrooper.

I paid the man no attention and continued to march the Company. My men were sharp. They were marching with perfect alignment and marvelous precision, just as they had been taught. The word that the Colonel was back there, worked its way slowly and quietly forward through the ranks.

Perhaps his presence prodded the men to show off a little. But I wasn't happy to see him, not one little bit. So, that morning I really poured it on. In no time at all, Shellenburger was sweating profusely. His breathing became noticeably labored.

Shellenburger did not finish the session. He left the training ground with about ten minutes remaining on our hour of calisthenics. The men were aware of his difficulties keeping up, and loved it. Me, I was delighted.

The Colonel left the exercise field. He never checked in to his own office that morning, the so-called Orderly Room. Captain Singleton was not even aware the Colonel had been in the area. Shellenburger never came back for exercise again as long as he remained with us.

•

•

In late December 1943, we began the first in a series of full-scale amphibious exercises in preparation for the upcoming invasion. We did not know, yet, when the invasion would actually be taking place. Nor did we yet know where we would eventually be landing.

But, as trained infantrymen, we knew. We knew there was no other way to drive the Hun out of France except to invade. We knew a difficult and dangerous invasion lay in our future, probably sometime early the following summer.

Unfortunately, such large-scale exercises made a hash out of the lives of the locals. Thousands of British civilians in the area of Slapton Sands, near Dartmouth, on the southern coast of Devonshire, had to be expelled from their homes so that their beaches might be used by American Forces as a final rehearsal area for the D-Day operation. Many of these people had nowhere familiar to go. Many had never left their villages before, not in their entire lives. Now they were banished to who knows where.

Dartmouth was, by the way, home to the Royal Naval Academy, the British equivalent to our Naval Academy at Annapolis, Maryland. It was located some seventy plus miles east of Helston. In preparation for our arrival, engineers had cleared the beach of mines the British had laid earlier against the very real threat of a German sea invasion by way of the French coast.

By virtue of its location, as well as its physical layout, Slapton Sands was an ideal beach for us to practice our landing maneuvers and subsequent thrust inland. High ground backed part of the beach, and the tides were nearly the same as those we would find at Normandy. But, as I said, we had not yet been told that Normandy would be our objective.

Since the beach was somewhat protected, the surf was not too heavy, even in winter. The ports of Plymouth, Falmouth, Torquay, and Weymouth were all to become loading points for units involved in what would eventually be called "Operation Overlord," though this name was not yet known to us. We used these same four ports as points of embarkation for our exercises at Slapton Sands.

"Exercise Duck," as our first big exercise was called, began in late December 1943 and ran into the early days of January 1944. At the time, I was still with H Company. This was a full-scale amphibious exercise that involved elements of the Navy, the Army Air Force, Army Infantry, as well as Supply.

Because of a shortage of ships, only the 175th Combat Team and Division headquarters were actually loaded onboard ships. H Company went on an LCI, a Landing Craft Infantry ship. We departed from Falmouth and pushed out into the Channel. Then we proceeded on water up the coast to Slapton Sands. This was more dangerous than it sounds. German E-Boats (like our PT Boats, only larger) swarmed the Channel ports every night. Some were still there in the morning. Their possible presence was always before us. We held much concern about them.

That first exercise turned up any number of poor practices that had to be remedied before the actual invasion. These were the types of mistakes that could get men killed. Let me give you but one example, an example that centered around a failure on the part of our truck drivers.

In combat, each driver was to follow the truck in front of him, but at a distance of fifty yards. Proper spacing between vehicles helped to avoid traffic jams, which made the convoy an easy target.

After leaving our landing craft, the trucks were to go up the sandy hills beyond the beach. There was but one road out of the landing zone. All of a sudden, in the middle of the exercise, the long line of trucks and equipment came to a stop on the winding hill. The vehicles were bumper to bumper.

I saw this happen while still in my jeep. So I worked myself up the hill to the point of trouble. A truck hauling an anti-tank gun had broken down and the jam-up had built backwards from there to the beach.

Earlier that morning, we had noticed an artillery spotter plane hovering over the landing zone and the hills beyond. Sure enough, now, as I approached the point of trouble on the road, a jeep came barreling down the hill from the opposite direction. In it sat the Division Commander, Major General Charles Gerhardt. He had been observing the entire sequence from the overhead spotter plane.

He jumped, now, from the jeep, beet-red in the face. Apparently, because I was the officer closest to the action, he asked me, "Son, who's in charge here?"

"I don't know, Sir," I replied.

"You are now," he snapped. "Clean up this mess!"

"Yes, Sir!" And I saluted.

Then the General spun on his heels, climbed back in the jeep, and tore off in a hurry.

I turned to the Lieutenant who was in charge of the anti-tank gun and began giving orders. I told him to drop the gun off the hitch, then to have his men push the gun and truck off the road.

The man objected. I asked him for his name, serial number and unit. As I did, I took out my pen and pad to write it down. He got the message, dropped the attitude and gave my orders to his men.

It took about three minutes to get the obstructing equipment to the side of the road and out of the way. I waved the column through, and it again began to move.

But with each truck that passed, I yelled at the driver to maintain a fifty-yard gap between vehicles. This was, after all, supposed to simulate an actual combat situation.

It took about forty-five minutes to clean up the traffic jam to my satisfaction. That was my first brush with the General. I didn't want a second.

This was not the only exercise of this nature. After the first one in December 1943, there were others. We kept on making practice landings, mostly in smaller unit configurations, until mid-April. By then, every Combat Team had completed at least one assault landing.

Then came "Exercise Fox," a full-scale assault on Slapton Sands by the 1st and 29th Divisions with full Air and Naval support. It went well.

But the biggest exercise was yet to come. One, in late April, was called "Exercise Tiger." It went badly off the rail.

14 APRIL 1944

When the 1st Infantry Division returned from the fighting in Italy —
and after their successes in North Africa — they were billeted near the
port of Weymouth, another hour further east still from Slapton Sands,
along the English coast.

These were proud men. The 1st was the first. It was the oldest
Division in the United States Army. The "Fighting First." The "Big Red
One," after its shoulder patch. These were seasoned fighting men. They
had seen much combat and suffered many losses. They were in England
to rest up before the invasion.

I was sent there, to Weymouth, to act as a Unit Commander while
the 1st Division's regular officers were being instructed on the Division's
part in the upcoming invasion. Along with five other 2nd Lieutenants,
I reported in at Headquarters and was temporarily attached to the
2nd Battalion of the 16th Infantry Regiment. As the ranking officer,
I became temporary Battalion Commander. The other five became
temporary Company Commanders, except one who was assigned as
Adjutant.

The men of the 1st had been in almost constant combat, first
across North Africa, then into Sicily and Italy. As temporary Battalion
Commander, my orders were to keep these men busy doing close-order
drill and reviewing with them basic subjects.

What an assignment! These soldiers were combat veterans. I was an
unseasoned 2nd Lieutenant. These men were tired and war worn. No
way were they going to take orders from me. And no way was I going to

try and impose "chicken shit" upon them. So I called my four Company Commanders together and laid down the law.

We would hold everything to an absolute minimum. We would designate a period each afternoon for athletics. Participation would be mandatory. But it would be athletics of their choice, played by their rules, their way. In short, these soldiers were to do nothing except rest and unwind. Mornings, after *First Call*, the only duty we would perform was to march the men to the end of their Company streets and back again, one time only. That took care of their close-order drill for the day. We would hand out passes to the maximum allowed. We would stand *Reveille* and *Retreat*. That was it.

The detached service lasted eight days and then the regular officers returned.

•

•

Upon my return to G Company, we dug — literally — into the ground, into the very earth. This was to be our final phase of training before deployment. How to instill into the men a love of ground.

By ground, I mean terrain. The men had to learn how to use the ground to their advantage. They had to learn how the ground, the landscape, actually dictates a plan of battle. Above all, they had to learn how to live on the ground, how to live on it for days on end without being impaired or suffering a loss of physical efficiency. How to find food and water. What to use as shelter. How to see folds in the ground no civilian would notice.

We launched into exercises learning how to attack a town, how to approach a hill, how to enter a woods. We had live-fire exercises with artillery, with mortars, with machine guns. We crashed into our objectives, walked into them, fell upon them. Attack, attack, attack. That's all we did. Attack, attack, attack. We marched, spent nights in open fields, slept in foxholes.

We were schooled. We were schooled in the making and using of ordnance. Satchel charges and Bangalore torpedoes (a metal tube filled with explosive) were excellent explosives for blowing holes in barbed-wire entanglements and for neutralizing fortified bunkers.

We were schooled yet again in the use of bayonets, how to kill the enemy in one blow, how to use a bayonet to probe for landmines.

There were drills. Drills with gas masks to avoid being poisoned. Drills on the proper use of first aid. Drills on airplane and tank identification, both of the enemy and of Allied Forces. Drills to detect booby traps. Other drills on how to use them. Adrenaline was running high. The Company was getting ready for action.

But before long, the men needed some release. The drills were getting to them. They requested permission to hold a dance.

The Captain readily agreed. They could and they should. He placed First Sergeant George Ingersoll in charge.

Ingersoll jumped right in. He had the men transform the old ballroom in the hotel into something more appealing. An extreme makeover, as they say nowadays.

Somehow, the men came up with multicolored crepe paper. Plus, we still had balloons left over from our target practice weeks earlier. Several sturdy tables were set up to hold barrels of beer. Ingersoll had the cooks prepare hundreds of simple hors d'oeuvres, even arranged for a small band of local musicians to play for the dance.

The only missing element was the most important one — girls. Many of these men had been in Marazion for more than a year. There were not that many women they did not know. Plus, the women themselves were scattered across all of Cornwall in the many villages, on the farms, and in the town. We had limited transportation. *How to get all these women to the dance?*

The only automobile I had seen since I arrived belonged to the local doctor. The only other motorized equipment were a few trucks owned by this or that local business. Gasoline (petrol) was in very short supply and strictly rationed. Which left the Army. We had the only rolling stock of consequence.

By my count, we had only four "legal" vehicles at our command: the Mess Sergeant's kitchen truck, the Company's supply truck (a 2 1/2 ton GMC), plus our two jeeps. We might be able to use these four vehicles to make runs to a number of designated assembly points, where they could pick up loads of young women, along with their chaperones, and transport them all back to the hotel where we were holding our dance.

(I said "legal" instead of legal because, as I'll explain in a minute, we had one vehicle in our possession which we weren't supposed to have.)

The cost for the barrels of beer and the band was covered by us officers. Hard liquor was not part of our deal. But Ingersoll had a bar set up and saw to it that there was an abundance of booze. I'm guessing he put the arm on "Red" McDonald, who was still having an affair with the widow. In case you've forgotten, the "widow" had inherited from her husband the largest wholesale liquor distribution network in the district.

Army regulations specified that an officer be present at such affairs to act as a chaperone and to be responsible for maintaining good order. Captain Singleton decided that two of us should share that duty. He gave the assignment to me and Lieutenant Lister. But I knew that really meant me, as John was always on the prowl. He could only be counted on until such time as he met the next, new lovely young thing.

I made two trips in the kitchen supply truck, picking up scads of women in Trevenner Square, about one mile north of Marazion, and again at the Surgery (the doctor's office) which was also at the edge of town. This made sense because the doctor's wife had volunteered to be one of the official chaperones.

John Lister made a number of trips as well, and before long the hotel ballroom was filled with girls. *Perfect!* Lots of men, lots of women, plenty of drink, everyone in a happy mood.

I wouldn't have expected anything less. When one considers the long period of deprivation and upheaval brought on by the war, good times were hard to come by and in short supply.

There may have been a mismatch between the somewhat more puritanical moral code of the American serviceman and the more relaxed attitude towards sex among the British women we met. — But it was only in degree.

These women were starved for affection. Their men had been away for a long time. Lonely women and lonely soldiers far from home, found each other, often with instant, almost explosive results. It is safe to assume that at any given moment many, many liaisons were under way. I suspect that that night, as on any other night when an opportunity presented itself, there was lots and lots of hanky panky going on.

A half hour into the dance, Sergeant Ingersoll came by with a real pretty little woman. He suggested I dance with her a time or two then take her to my quarters. He said she would do things that would "stand your hair on end." I gracefully declined and spent most of my evening talking with the doctor's wife.

Lister disappeared partway through the evening, just as I feared he would. In fact, I had been afraid of this from the start. Later, when things started to wind down, the problem of returning all those women to their homes presented itself. John was supposed to be one of the drivers.

The other drivers were all in various states of intoxication. That alone wouldn't have been a problem, but English roads are notoriously narrow. I shuddered to think of those big trucks barreling around the countryside in the nightly blackout with a drunk behind the wheel. I let the men arrange the trips.

More trips were needed to return the women home than were first required to bring them to the dance, and for one simple reason. Each returning truck had men as well as women onboard for passengers. No one wanted to say goodnight. The only trip I made was to the Surgery, where I delivered the doctor's wife safely home, as well as a handful of girls plus the guys they were still hanging onto.

My misgivings were unjustified. The only mishap during the return operation was when one of the trucks failed to fully make a sharp turn and crashed into a hedgerow. But even "crashed" might be too strong a word. The truck was moving very slowly at the time, and there was no damage to the vehicle.

But the accident did make me reflect upon an earlier incident, one that will explain my prior use of the word "legal."

Back in March, shortly after I joined up with G Company, one of our drivers crashed a jeep and bent the frame. It was still drivable if somewhat less roadworthy.

There was a depot in Devonshire where we could procure a new jeep, but only if the damage to the old jeep was considered severe enough by whatever sergeant looked it over. In the Army, this process of looking things over is called "I & I," which is to say, "Inspection and Inventory."

But I wasn't going to the depot unprepared. I knew how such things worked, and I wasn't sure how this would turn out. So I packed a musette bag full with a number of "inducements" — a ream of typing paper, a dozen pencils, a supply of carbon paper, two typewriter ribbons, a bottle each of scotch and gin, plus a few cigars thrown in for good measure.

Then the driver and I set off for the depot with the old jeep to see if an exchange would be in order. Our intent, as I said, was to get the jeep I & I'd and to get a new one to take its place.

But then something else occurred to me. *Maybe we could have it both ways, keep the damaged jeep and get a new one on top of it.* Maybe that bag of inducements wasn't such a bad idea after all.

As I talked with the Master Sergeant who, for the moment, seemed to be in charge of the depot, I casually reached into my musette bag. I started with something simple, a few pencils. Then, every so often as we talked, I would reach into my bag and pull out another goody. He was beginning to get the idea. I wanted him to issue us a new jeep but let us keep the old one.

The man was a tough sell. But when the bottles of booze came out, it was game over. While we waited, he filled out a set of papers authorizing the transfer of a new jeep to us, plus another set of papers to cover the "scrapping" of the old one. But he warned us — We had thirty minutes to get both vehicles off the base before his Major returned, or else. We shook hands and promptly left with both.

Because we were G Company — and because "G" become "George" in the military's phonetic alphabet — our Company was issued two jeeps, appropriately named "George" and "Georgia." The names were painted in the middle of the front bumpers. Our Company was authorized two jeeps, and two jeeps only. Now we had three.

The damaged jeep had been a "Georgia," so we painted that name on the new one as well, making two Georgias. No doubt about it. It was darn handy having an extra vehicle at our disposal. And, aside from having to hide one of them from time to time, there was also the small matter of having adequate gasoline and oil for all three vehicles. Our gasoline allotment was figured on the number of vehicles we were authorized, not the number actually in our possession. But I did have a way around that.

While scouting potential locations for the rifle range we eventually built near the airbase at Lizard Point, I discovered that I could gas up at the U.S. Navy's Falmouth Harbor installation. As an officer, all I had to do was sign for any gasoline I pumped.

Each jeep had a gas can mounted on the rear. Three jeeps meant three gas cans. So, about once a week, I would chance it. I would have a driver take me over to Falmouth, along with the two extra gas cans. I would sign for the petrol as "Lieutenant William Schultz," and then we'd hightail it out of there.

Sometimes, a little confusion would occur. The Battalion Commander would see Georgia in or around Helston, especially when he was on his way to Marazion. We'd salute in passing, sweet as you please. But then upon arriving back at home, he'd see Georgia parked outside our Orderly Room. The man never said a thing, but I bet the Commander thought he was cracking up.

27 APRIL 1944

I mentioned earlier our ever-present fear of German E-Boats. These boats were a menace to our safety and we were afraid they might ambush us during one of our amphibious landing exercises on the beach at Slapton Sands. Make no mistake about it — the dangers were real.

The risk posed to us by these enemy gunboats was brought home to me in crushing detail during a D-Day rehearsal the Army called "Exercise Tiger." Tiger ended in disaster.

But before I go ahead and tell you this story, let me first put you on notice. At the time, back in late April 1944, when this disaster struck, I was sworn to secrecy — as were all the survivors of that dreadful day. We were to reveal nothing about what happened.

But now that these events have been declassified and have been written about by others, I can tell you my story, perhaps unburden myself of the awful truth.

Exercise Tiger was scheduled to run from 22 April until 30 April 1944. It was to take place at the Slapton Sands beach. As part of that exercise, thirty thousand troops were loaded aboard nine large tank-loading ships, the so-called LST.

"Landing Ship, Tank" was the military designation for naval vessels fashioned during the Second World War to support amphibious operations all around the globe. They were especially designed by the Army to carry significant quantities of vehicles, cargo, and men directly onto unimproved shore. Very hardy, very versatile, with shallow draft and a complex ballast system to keep the ship stable in high and uncertain seas.

As Tiger got underway, the men were keyed up and prepared for a mock beach landing. Slapton Sands had been selected for this exercise on account of its similarity to Utah Beach; namely, a gravel beach backed up by hills and a strip of land beyond.

Perimeter protection for the exercise was provided by the Royal Navy. Three motorized torpedo boats, two destroyers and a like number of motorized gunboats. This small flotilla patrolled the entrance to Lyme Bay just beyond the Sands. Other torpedo boats kept watch across the Channel, especially the area around Cherbourg, France, where the Germans normally docked their E-Boats.

After extensive preparations, the first set of practice assaults took place on the morning of 27 April. These proceeded successfully and according to plan.

But, early in the morning of 28 April, disaster struck. German E-Boats that had left Cherbourg on patrol the night before spotted a convoy of eight American LSTs floating in Lyme Bay. These ships were carrying combat engineers from the 1st Engineer Special Brigade, along with their vehicles and gear.

The Germans attacked. One of the giant transports caught fire immediately and was abandoned. A second sank shortly after being torpedoed. A third was set on fire but eventually limped back to shore. The remaining LSTs, and their escort, returned fire, scattering the E-Boats who retreated and made no further attacks that day.

More than six hundred servicemen were lost in the attack, including many who drowned in the cold sea waiting rescue. The men had a problem staying afloat, for they had never received proper lifebelt training. These were combat soldiers. They were unaccustomed to being at sea. They were certainly unaccustomed to being dumped in the sea weighted down by full battle gear. The servicemen panicked and put on their lifebelts incorrectly.

In some cases, what this meant was that when these men were flung from their landing craft into the water, the weight of their combat packs flipped them onto their backs, submerging their heads beneath the water and drowning them.

Of the two heavily-armed British destroyers assigned to protect the convoy of landing craft, only one was present. The second boat, a vintage World War I destroyer, had checked into Plymouth for minor repairs. The American forces had not been informed of this.

Nor had they been told that British ships sighted the line of E-Boats earlier in the night. This was an act of omission, not commission, as the British Commander thought they *had* been told. The problem was agonizingly simple — British Naval Command and the radio crews of the tank-landing ships were operating on different frequencies. *They couldn't actually talk to one another.*

But the carnage wasn't over. When the remaining LSTs landed on Slapton Beach, the blunders continued. A further three hundred plus men died from friendly fire. *What a horrible thing!*

On orders of General Dwight D. Eisenhower, the Supreme Allied Commander, no less, a British heavy cruiser began to shell the beach with live ammunition.

Why would the highest-ranking Allied Commander order such a terrible thing, you ask?

Because he felt the men needed to be hardened, that they needed to be exposed — if even a little — to actual battle conditions. Ike himself authorized the British shelling.

But men weren't supposed to die, and certainly not at the hands of friendly fire. According to the only military log known to have survived the incident, there was to be a white tape line on the beach, a line beyond which the Americans were not to cross until the live-fire exercise had ended.

But, according to that same log, the Americans did not stop behind the line. They kept going straight through the demarcation line, and they kept on getting blown up. Perhaps, after the German E-Boat attack, people weren't thinking straight. Perhaps they panicked, thinking they were under actual attack.

Official embarrassment, not to mention concerns over possible leaks just prior to the actual invasion, led to what nowadays is called a cover-up. It wasn't really. Nevertheless, all survivors of the incident were sworn to secrecy by their superiors.

A further complication arose, because ten of the missing officers had sufficiently high clearance to be considered security risks. These men knew intimate details of the invasion plans. If the Germans were to capture them alive, the invasion could be compromised. D-Day was put on hold until all ten bodies were recovered.

If there was any good to come from this fiasco, three things stand out. Radio frequencies were standardized between all landing craft and their escorts. Remedial life-vest training was promptly put in place for all troops scheduled to participate in the landing. Plans were initiated to make additional small craft available to pick up floating survivors on Invasion Day.

Maybe these measures saved lives on D-Day, I do not know. But surely not as many lives as were senselessly lost that April day at Slapton Sands.

The casualty statistics from Tiger were not released until August 1944. But the numbers were not listed separately; they were lumped in along with the casualties from the actual D-Day landings themselves. By then the incident was old news, conveniently forgotten rather than covered up. In any case, they went largely unnoticed in light of the larger events occurring that August as the battle for control of Europe raged on.

17 MAY 1944

On 17 May 1944, the 175th Combat Team moved into a marshalling area near Falmouth, Cornwall. Concurrent with this move, the entire south of England was sealed off from the rest of the country.

By the time of our move, we had gotten rid of Lieutenant Colonel Shellenburger as our Battalion Commander. Our new commander was Major Millard Bowen. He had come to us from 1st Division. Unlike Shellenburger, Bowen knew his stuff.

Security was tight. No one moved into or out of the marshalling area without permission. Any pretense of fun and games was now over.

Our marshalling area was not pretty, one big tent city and plenty of mud. Meanwhile, all of southern England had become a huge supply depot.

I can't quote you chapter and verse. But everything a man could possibly think of to support the upcoming invasion — medicine, supplies, ammunition, armor, artillery, etc. — was being stockpiled alongside roads and in every vacant field. It was a massive buildup of materiel, and the stockpiling was well under way even before we left Marazion behind and redeployed to the marshalling area.

From this point forward, no further passes of any sort were allowed. We were under tight, military control. All unit officers were briefed. Each was given detailed instructions.

We were told that our Division, along with the 1st Infantry Division, would be the two assault units assigned to storm ashore on OMAHA BEACH. Objectives were specified for each unit. The invasion target was identified. — It was to be Normandy.

As officers, it was our responsibility to brief our own men and to lay out for them their assignments in detail. This was an extraordinarily important task. To accomplish this task, we were assisted by any number of teaching aids — large maps, aerial photographs, and most important of all, a large scale-model of the landing zone and of OMAHA BEACH. The scale-model, as well as the maps and aerial photographs, were set up on tables or else on upright easels inside special tents. Grandstand-style benches gave everyone in attendance a clear view of the model and maps.

The large scale-model was made of stiff rubber. It was incredibly detailed. Every structure known to our war planners was easily identifiable on the model. The hedgerows, which in reality averaged some five feet in height, were actually there, each measuring several inches high on the model. Trees, roads, lanes, buildings — all easily identifiable.

After studying the model and the accompanying maps and photographs for several days, hours at a time, I knew the terrain as well as my backyard back home.

But one thing did surprise me. I never knew photographs could be made so large or so detailed. Such map details are commonplace today, perhaps, with satellites and the magic of computers, but not so common back then. The aerial photographs, huge, some taken by low-flying aircraft, were updated every day as new intelligence flowed in.

We were instructed on every facet of the entire operation. Every man knew exactly what was expected of him and what his part in the invasion would be.

Meanwhile, the entire Company was reorganized. Instead of being organized by platoons as before, now we were organized by Assault Boat Teams, thirty men to a team. Each team included a contingent of men armed with rifles, another with Browning Automatic Rifles (B.A.R.), plus machine guns, Bangalore torpedoes, pole and satchel TNT charges, as well as flamethrowers.

Each assault team was organized and designed to disable one concrete "pillbox." It was a name we picked up from the Brits. That's what they called these small, fortified bunkers for housing artillery. Apparently, the Brits thought these concrete bunkers resembled the cylindrical boxes in which medical pills were once sold.

Every day, often at night, I would spend one or more hours in the Headquarters tent studying the relief map setup to gain a sense of the lay of the land. Where were the hills? The bridges? The ravines?

I did not engage in this study alone. I was always in the company of my Sergeants. Together, we became intimately familiar with the beach and with the areas just beyond. Soon we knew by heart every building, every hamlet, every lane, every hedgerow. We knew where each line of bushes began, how long it ran, where it ended.

It wasn't enough to simply know the details of our intended route. We also had to become familiar with our other alternatives. What if we were thrown off course? In what other direction could we go? What if we were diverted from our primary objective? How could we double back and get back on course?

Battles rarely go as planned.

THE PLAN

Directly across the English Channel from Portsmouth, on the northern coast of France, is the Cherbourg Peninsula. A few miles east of the base of this peninsula is a crescent-shaped stretch of sandy beach. It extends from right to left for some seven thousand yards.

Along and behind each end of this long stretch of beach sits a line of rugged cliffs. A small road runs behind and parallel to the beach. Nowadays, that road affords easy access to a number of picturesque summer cottages clustered at the base of these abruptly rising bluffs. In those days, the bluffs were marked by pillboxes and other concrete-hardened defenses. At the top of the bluff sits a charming little village, Vierville-sur-Mer.

Extending back from the beach is typical French landscape: grain fields, apple orchards, cattle and pasture lands. Tall hedgerows separate one farmer's field from the next. These hedgerows stretch, row after row, across the Normandy countryside in jigsaw-puzzle-like fashion.

Also spread across this region are countless small villages. Vierville-upon-the-Ocean (its literal translation) is just one of many quiet, unimportant farming villages. Vierville was then known — but only slightly — as a haunt of second-rate French artists.

But other than that, Vierville-sur-Mer could not lay claim to any particular distinction among a hundred other similar Norman villages. And yet, it was about to become a major war objective in the greatest amphibious invasion in the history of war.

By 1943, the Germans had turned that seven-thousand-yard-long beach below Vierville and its neighboring little town of Les Moulins, into an integral section of Hitler's Atlantic Wall of Fortress Europe. The beach was guarded by every conceivable weapon and blocked by every possible obstacle of military capability. Allied war planners, after they selected this sandy, crescent-shaped stretch of beach as their prime target, designated it OMAHA BEACH.

In all, there were five beaches — UTAH on the right, then OMAHA, then GOLD, JUNO, and SWORD. The Americans had UTAH and OMAHA. The British and the Canadians, along with the Free French and Poles had responsibility for the other three.

The 29th and 1st Divisions were assigned to land on OMAHA. The 29th was to be on the right, the 1st on the left. Everything we knew about the beach and its defenses was gathered from intelligence reports, aerial reconnaissance, and aerial photographs.

"H" hour, the time when the first wave of men was due to land, would be early in the day. The idea was to take advantage of low tides, so as to avoid the negative consequences of riding over and into the underwater defense obstacles set up by the Germans.

But low tide carried with it some negative consequences all its own. At low tide, those landing in the first wave would have that much more sand to cross before they could reach relative safety at the base of those imposing bluffs. More men would likely die as a result.

On the other hand, massive air bombing ahead of time, as well an equally large artillery barrage, would hopefully soften up the German defense line. Big guns were mounted on all naval and landing craft.

On that part of OMAHA BEACH assigned to the assaulting 29th Division, the ground rises abruptly from a narrow, flat shelf into dominating bluffs, some as high as one hundred and seventy feet above the water.

At low tide, firm sand extends some three hundred yards from the high-water mark down to the edge of the sea. Unfortunately, strong tides frequently sweep across this stretch of beach. At their height, these treacherous waves cover the low-tide mark with some eighteen feet of water. Very dangerous for a man weighted down by a heavy pack and under enemy fire.

Shingle covers the narrow shelf of sand at the high-water line. In places, these egg-sized round stones form into little ridges and hollows. Hard to traverse on foot. But also some small protection against enemy rifle fire. A man in a prone position might find limited cover from flat trajectory fire.

One other notable landmark is the seawall. It extends from the western edge of the beach eastward across to a draw. A road rises from the beach, through that draw, and on up to the little town of Vierville.

Originally, the seawall was built to protect the promenade from crashing waves. To a landing force, that seawall presented a challenge all its own. Plus, the Germans had improved the wall into a serious, concrete obstacle. In some places, the concrete wall rose as much as twelve feet. It was a formidable barrier for tanks, one that was almost impassable for ordinary wheeled equipment or half-tracks.

But, for a foot soldier, that seawall would prove to be a godsend. It provided the only strong cover along the entire beachfront short of the bluffs.

The enemy had sited his weapons and planted his obstacles with typical German thoroughness and efficiency. The Germans had but a single aim in mind, to annihilate an invader while he was still in the sea and before he could storm the beach.

But, should the invader manage to penetrate the sea-obstacles, the enemy intended to annihilate him on the beach, deny him so much as a temporary toehold on the Continent.

Underwater obstacles were laid out in three bands between the high and low-water marks, and they stretched the entire width and length of the beach.

The first band, about two hundred and fifty yards out from the high-water mark, consisted of gate-like structures about ten feet tall. They were irregularly spaced so that a landing craft could not possibly avoid them or maneuver around them. A boat attempting to land on the beach at high tide would likely ram its bottom on one of the elements. The collision would likely explode the Teller mine lashed to the steel uprights.

(As a point of interest, a "Teller" mine was so-named because the explosive mine was plate-shaped. Teller is the German word for plate. To allow for easy placement, a Teller mine came equipped with a built-in carrying handle.)

Closer in, on the tidal flat, was the center band of defensive obstacles. These consisted of a series of heavy logs driven into the sand. They were angled seaward, spaced at irregular intervals and topped with explosive mines. Should a landing craft strike one of these "loaded logs," the mine would detonate and the landing craft would be blown up.

The final band of obstacles was set about one hundred and twenty-five yards below the high-water mark, the so-called "hedgehogs". Each hedgehog was formed of three or more steel rails, crossed at the center and strongly imbedded into the sand. They were designed to puncture holes in the bottoms of any landing craft that attempted to ride the waves over them.

On the beach shelf itself, the Germans had buried thousands of explosive mines and strung miles of barbed wire. Plus, there were machine-gun nests everywhere, in pillboxes as well as out in the open.

By virtue of their position atop the cliffs and bluffs, the Germans enjoyed observational command of the entire beach. Beside machine-gun nests, there was also any number of mortar emplacements.

Aside from the small arms just described, the Germans had big guns as well, some placed behind concrete easements, others in open-field emplacements beyond the beach proper. These big guns — 75 mm and 88 mm — covered the entire length of the beach. They, too, were protected by minefields and barbed wire.

Further back still were larger guns, 155 mm and up. These gun batteries could be found atop the rocky cliffs. Some were set back as much as several miles inland. They were large and capable of hurling shells at the shoreline, even at boats still out to sea.

On the section of OMAHA BEACH, where the 29th was supposed to come ashore, the Germans had sealed off the natural beach exits with thick concrete walls. Wind, rain, and storm had conspired to form these natural breaks, or draws, that led up from the beach to the bluffs behind.

One draw led up to Vierville, another to Les Moulins. Both were blocked with tank traps and other obstacles. Both were heavily mined, the mines stretching a quarter mile up the roadway.

Possession of these exits was vital to the German defense. They were equally vital to our advance. If the Germans could deny us the use of these roads, we would have no other means for moving tanks, trucks, and heavy equipment inland.

We had absolutely no choice but to take them.

1 JUNE 1944

For planning purposes, OMAHA BEACH was partitioned into three sections — EASY, DOG, and CHARLIE. Each of the three sections was further broken down into subsections — RED, WHITE, and GREEN, as seen from left to right when approaching the shore from the ocean.

G Company's objective was DOG GREEN, at the extreme right of DOG BEACH. That would place it to one side of the cliffs adjacent to CHARLIE BEACH. The 2nd Rangers were to attack CHARLIE.

Flanking movements were next to impossible. The cliffs at each end of OMAHA BEACH saw to that. If there was to be an assault, it would have to be from the front, the ocean.

The entire 175th Infantry Regiment — G Company included — had a landing timetable that placed us ashore at H+27 (H hour plus 27 hours). We couldn't help but hope that, by then, the first waves of men would have cleared the beach, providing us safe passage. In case they had not, our initial objective was to be the Vierville exit.

On 1 June we loaded onto trucks and were transported from our tent city to Falmouth Harbor, a few miles away. The harbor was jammed full with boats and ships of every sort. Our conveyance to Normandy was to be LST 266 (Landing Ship, Tank — Number 266).

An LST carries men as well as their equipment. The roster of equipment includes such things as tanks, bulldozers, trucks, anti-tank guns, munitions, and spare parts. The men were almost an afterthought.

Once loaded, our landing ship motored out into the harbor and anchored. This was no cruise ship, mind you. Not like the *Mauritania* had been anyway. No, this was seriously rough living under the most cramped of conditions.

We had no cabin space in which to sleep. Instead, we had to find suitable spaces on deck or alongside vehicles to bed down. Remember: the inside of an LST is mostly a large, open area. Only, now it was filled to overflowing with trucks and armored vehicles. Thus, our choices for places to sleep were on — or under — trucks, tanks, or anti-tank guns.

But inside the LST, things were extraordinarily cramped. Even before we men were loaded onboard, the interior space of the LST was completely jammed full with equipment.

And there were lots of men. All of G Company, all of 2nd Battalion Headquarters Company, as well as the entire Regimental Anti-Tank Company. This legion of soldiers mostly cluttered up whatever available space there was to be had on deck.

I use here the term "cluttered" to describe the situation, as I can think of no better word. Try to visualize our setup:

For each man, who was trying to find a comfortable niche in which to sleep, there was also the small matter of stowing his weapon and everything else he was expected to carry with him into battle.

As a platoon, my men were carrying between them any number of TNT pole and satchel charges, explosive mortars, machine guns, Bangalore torpedoes, spare ammunition.

Each rifleman carried two extra bandoliers of ammunition in addition to his ordinary pack and weapon. Plus, there was his gas mask, his trenching tool, light pack with raincoat, two days' K-ration, and two days' chocolate ration.

(As a point of interest, let me only say this about K-rations. A single K-ration was simply too small a meal to keep a man alive for long, only to keep him from starving. The calorie content of a K-ration was at least a thousand calories short of what a highly active man required each day, especially if he was working in extreme heat or bitter cold. The ration may have been named for Dr. Ancel Keys, the man assigned by the U.S. War Department to design a non-perishable, ready-to-eat meal that could fit in a soldier's pocket as a short-duration, individual ration.)

Each man also had his bandage and medical kit, including syringe and morphine syrette. These were mounted on his web belt along with his canteen, spare clips for his M1, and bayonet. Every soldier carried three or four hand grenades.

Then there was also the stuff we didn't need to have but had along anyway, like cigarettes, pictures of loved ones, the random lucky rabbit's foot.

Each officer, in addition to carrying his conventional equipment and his walkie-talkie, also carried three extra bandages on his web belt plus ten, morphine syrettes. The morphine syrette was a true battlefield innovation, a device for injecting precious liquid through a needle. The design was similar to that of a syringe except that it had a closed flexible tube like that used for toothpaste instead of a rigid tube and piston as in most hospital applications.

After breaking the seal on the syrette and removing the wire loop pin, the hollow needle inside was inserted under the skin at a shallow angle and the tube flattened between the thumb and fingers. This pushed the morphine into the wounded soldier's body. After injection, the used tube was pinned to the receiving soldier's collar to inform others of the dose administered. Too much morphine could kill.

•

•

The night of 1 June passed quietly and without incident. I slept amazingly well considering. After we moved out to our anchorage in the bay, we watched with great interest as ship after ship was loaded with men and equipment, then moved away from shore out to an anchorage position nearby. Falmouth Harbor was quickly becoming very crowded.

The next two days and nights passed quickly. We had very little in the way of official duties to perform. So each man occupied his time by checking and rechecking his ammunition, his weapons, and his equipment.

Before long, fine tooth-files surfaced and began to make the rounds. The men put these files to work sharpening their bayonets and trench knives. When they weren't doing that, they were busy cleaning and re-cleaning their weapons.

The men discussed the invasion. How many Germans would still be there, still defending the beach? How hard would it be for us to break through, to break through and reach Vierville, our first objective?

It's not that my men were unprepared. It's just that it was difficult for any of us to accurately judge how hard the coming fight would truly be. To a man, we had each spent untold hours studying that huge rubberized relief map while still back in the marshalling area. These men — my men — knew every road, every river and stream, every farmhouse, every hedgerow, every wooded tract. They knew every rise, every narrow, every draw. In short, they knew *where* to go, but not how hard it would be getting there.

The men reminisced. They reminisced about the good times they had had here or there in any of several locations the Company had been stationed while in England.

They reminisced about home, so far away. They reminisced about this or that girlfriend, this or that fight they had had with one or both of their parents, about other roads not taken.

They read pocketbooks, traded them off for others they had not yet read or wanted to read again.

Card and crap games sprang up here and there around the ship. The men knew this was "it," that moment when they could no longer look back, only forward. Morale was high. Talk ranged from anticipated furloughs after D-Day plus 3. Would they be able to go directly home after the invasion?

•

•

After that first night, sleep no longer came easily. We were kept at anchorage in that harbor, day after punishing day. LST 266 was beginning to take on the dimensions of an over-crowded prison with limited toilet facilities.

Constantly checking weapons and other equipment had kept the men busy for a while. But now, they were rapidly becoming bored.

Nerves were on edge. Occasional scuffles broke out. There was a lot of pent-up adrenaline that had to be burnt off.

Regular and vigorous calisthenics might have helped solve some of our problems. Or perhaps a game of tackle football. But there was no room on deck for such shenanigans.

Fatigue, not boredom, helped a man sleep. Without proper exercise, it was physically impossible for a man to tire himself out enough to fall asleep. The Division battle cry — "29 LET'S GO!" — had diminished in volume until it became a mere statement of frustration.

These men truly wanted to go. They were highly trained. They were mentally ready to get "it" over with, no matter what the outcome.

Even if spoken only in whispers, each was sure he would come through it unscathed. If anybody got hit, surely it would be the other guy.

A soldier had to think that way. He had no choice. Not if he didn't want to lose his mind. The other guy might lose a limb. — But not him.

Finally, late on the fourth of June, we slipped anchor and cruised out of Falmouth Harbor along with everyone else. *Yes! Here we go!* Guys were smiling. *Finally!*

After about two hours, two hours in which we pushed further and further out into the English Channel, we suddenly reversed direction and returned to the harbor. *False start?* We did not know, and no one would tell us a goddamn thing.

Faces darkened. These men — these infantrymen — were primed to kill — or be killed. *Is that such a callous thing to say?* No, not really, not if you think about it. We drill it into these men's heads every waking moment. The mission of the Infantry. TO SEEK OUT AND DESTROY THE ENEMY. Waiting around listlessly isn't exactly part of that code.

Consider an athlete who, after years of intense training, has been benched without explanation. Now he has to sit there on that cold bench night after night, heart pumping, mind racing, body ready to jump into the fray on a moment's notice — but never being tapped nor told when his turn would come. Frustrating.

•

189

•

Then, in the afternoon of the next day — 5 June — we set out from Falmouth Harbor again. This time, we did not return. This time, we kept on going.

Afternoon passed into evening — but only slowly. At this time of year, days are long. As night fell, most of us curled up in whatever small space we had become accustomed to and drifted off into a restless slumber, just as we had done for several nights running.

But who could sleep? The sea was rough. But then again, nobody expected it to be smooth as glass.

For those of us who could not sleep, those of us who wandered the decks aimlessly for hours, nighttime brought its own demons. In the dark of night we could just barely make out several dark shapes in the water nearby. Every ship was running without lights.

6 JUNE 1944

It was now early morning on 6 June. The sun was barely above the horizon. I had not slept well. I propped myself up, now, on one elbow, tried to make sense of what was going on.

The ship seemed to have stopped dead in the water. Off to one side of me, I sensed noises, unfamiliar noises. Still in a half-awake daze, my mind tried to sort things out. *What were those noises? Where the hell was I anyway?*

"CRA-A-ACK!!"

A tremendous broadside let go from the battleship *USS Texas*, a few hundred yards north of us. The sound blew away the last vestiges of sleep, and I was instantly alert and awake.

Now the symphony of artillery began. Booming cannon fire. Banks of deadly rockets. Shells launched from armored tanks on deck. All together and all at once from an entire menagerie of Navy ships positioned all around us in the sea.

"CRA-A-ACK!!" Again from the *Texas*.

I looked at my watch. It was 0547. Cruisers, destroyers, and destroyer escorts all firing, and all at once. The *Texas* heeled over following each loud "CRACK!"

The thundering cannonade was deafening. It became next to impossible to speak or to hear what was being said, even from a buddy sitting next to you. If you sat close enough, shouting might work.

During the night, as we all tried to sleep, the entire flotilla of landing vessels and their escorts had moved much closer to the Normandy coast.

Now we lay about three miles off the coast, surrounded by any number of naval ships.

In the half-light of early morning, the shore was a distant blur, close, but shrouded by fog and smoke. Around us, the relentless thunder-like percussions of big guns continued.

By 0600 hours the sky had lightened appreciably. But the shoreline remained barely visible. All we could see was voluminous smoke. All we could hear were ceaseless explosions. Our shells were raining down on that beach in an unending stream of fire. When we did talk, which wasn't often, everyone agreed that we were giving the Jerrys hell.

Then, suddenly, the tenor of the shelling changed. No longer were our gunners blasting the beach and shoreline. Now they had begun directing their fire more against the top of those menacing bluffs.

Our troops will soon be landing, I thought. *Please, Lord, don't kill our men with friendly fire.* The thought popped into my head before I knew it was there.

We couldn't see much. But it didn't seem as if the Germans were returning our fire. *What were they waiting for?* I wondered.

I picked up my binoculars, put them to my eyes. I had a clear view of the water. It seemed entirely clear of any detonations. All I could make out was thick smoke, thick smoke lit up here and again by incessant flashes, these the product of American shells detonating near the high-water mark. The beach itself was completely hidden from view.

Meanwhile, LST 266 was inching ever closer to the shore. By 0700 hours we were little more than two miles out.

Rocket-firing ships unleashed bank after bank of deadly rockets. Tanks sitting on deck, as well as cannons mounted on the landing craft, began to lay down fire.

This was a critical moment. The close-in support fire had begun. This meant that the first wave was only a couple hundred yards from RAMP DOWN.

The din, already loud, increased tenfold. Through my binoculars I could see geysers erupting from the water with each explosion that hit. *Just as I thought* — the Germans were firing back.

The first wave was getting closer to the shore now. Support fire shifted up the bluffs.

Again I wondered whether I would measure up to the job. My training could not be called into question. Nor could my confidence in my own abilities. *But my courage?* It had yet to be tested under fire.

Would I perform well, or would I fail? I silently thanked the war planners for having scheduled our unit for H+27. Maybe — just maybe — things would be well under control on the beach by then. The first waves seemed to now be meeting their share of opposition, if not a little more.

•

•

All that day, as the second and third waves slugged their way onshore, I could see through my binoculars that our men were under nearly constant heavy explosive enemy fire.

The sound of explosions on shore reached our ears, even as far out as we were, and they never seemed to decrease in intensity. Many, many fires were raging onshore. I supposed they could be vehicles or other combustibles that had caught fire when they were targeted and blown up by the Germans.

Details were hard to make out. The shroud of smoke along the coastline made sure of that. But one detail I *could* make out was the church steeple in nearby Vierville. For some reason or other, it was still standing. The church was only about four hundred yards inland from the beach proper.

Although our planned landing site was to be on DOG GREEN just below Vierville, I was very much aware that we could easily be ordered to come ashore anywhere. If things went badly anywhere along OMAHA BEACH, we would most assuredly be sent in where they needed us most.

But, for now, it was more hurry up and wait. And wait, we did. Throughout that entire day, while the battle for control of the beach raged on, LST 266 held its position some two miles out from the shore.

But we were not alone in our vigil. Something on the order of five thousand Allied ships, of all shapes and sizes, now lay off the Normandy coast.

In every direction, as far as a man could see, there were ships, ships, and more ships. Many of them sported barrage balloons. This was to discourage low-flying enemy planes that might zoom in and strafe us.

A barrage balloon, by the way, is a large, lighter-than-air balloon tethered to a ship or building with metal cables. On some versions, a small explosive charge was affixed to the cable. The idea was to destroy any low-flying aircraft either by entangling them in the metal cable or by pulling the explosive charge up against their wing or fuselage.

The waiting was taking a toll on us all. The men were getting antsy. A hundred times an hour, they would glance toward the beach, look down at their weapon, check their ammo, inventory their medical kit, sharpen their trench knife, examine the business edge of their bayonet. It soon became a labor of love.

I, myself, had already sharpened my trench knife to such a keen edge, a man could literally shave with it. When not in use, I kept my trench knife mounted down in my right boot, where I could easily reach for it.

Conversation, already made difficult by the incessant noise, now took on a different tone.

There was the hopeful — "Boy, oh, boy, I can't wait to see the mademoiselles of Paris."

There was the gloomy — "Give my love to my girl (or my wife, or mother) if you get home and I don't."

There was the infuriated — "Damn it to hell. I can't wait to kill some of those bastard Nazis."

Some men read the little pocketbooks they had received with their rations. Others just stared blindly at the pages.

No matter what the men did or what they said, they were all trying not to think about how things were going onshore. Hard to do. No information was coming to us from the beachhead, not one little bit.

Darkness crowded in upon us, as yet another day of waiting drew to a close. As night fell, the noises of battle subsided to a degree. Fewer sounds of high-explosive detonations. Spotty bursts of small-arms fire.

In the darkness, we could see fires burning at multiple locations along the beach. German planes soared over our heads followed by anti-aircraft guns from our boats scaring them off or bringing them down. When our guns fired, it looked to us like luminous rain streaming upward. It sounded to me like every Fourth of July I had ever known all rolled into a single, unending set of fireworks.

Sleep did not come easily or quickly. My thoughts ran through my fears. Everything I ever dared hope for in my life, now had to be put on hold. I missed my folks, wondered what they must be thinking. I talked to the God I rarely talked to, prayed that I would be up to the job of leading my thirty-man boat team ashore, that I would not fail.

At last, sleep overcame me.

7 JUNE 1944

"The rifleman fights without promise of either reward or relief. Behind every river there is another hill, and behind that hill is another river. After weeks or months on the line, only a wound can offer such a man the comfort of safety, shelter, and a bed. Sooner or later, unless victory comes first, this chase must end on a litter or in the grave . . . "

. . . . . . from the writings of General Omar Bradley

LST 266 was positioned about two thousand yards offshore DOG GREEN BEACH at dawn when I woke up. Visibility was much improved from yesterday, even though morning clouds still hung low in the sky.

All the men of G Company were now either awake or just waking up. The heavy shore bombardments that had accompanied the landings of the previous day had now given way to more nuanced tactical firing on the German positions above and beyond the beach.

The lion's share of the action had moved from the beaches to the overhanging bluffs. This is how it was supposed to be. The intense smoke which had obscured our view of the beach yesterday had now mostly dissipated. Even so, many fires were still burning and visible.

We were all keyed up. This was the day we had been waiting for, the day we had been training for. This was IT.

But, we had our doubts. What was it like on the beach? Had the first waves made good progress? Had they punched through the German line, the so-called "Atlantic Wall"?

Thoughts were running rampant. But conversation had all but ceased. The men were checking their equipment, their weapons, their ammunition, all for the final time.

Dead bodies drifted past our ship. It seemed like everybody saw them. Young, broken bodies, some already bloated. *Could there be a harder reality?* Men were getting killed out there. The war was coming home to us. No more talk of Paris or furlough after D-Day plus 3.

Suddenly, off to our port side, as if by magic, a Destroyer Escort slid abreast of our Tank Landing Ship only a hundred feet away. It was the Beach Master. Loudspeakers blared:

"RIFLE TROOPS NEEDED ON THE BEACH! 175th COMBAT TEAM WILL COMMENCE LANDING IMMEDIATELY!"

That was us, the 175th Combat Team. We quickly assembled by assault boat teams. In no time at all, it was over the side, down the cargo nets, and into the LCM (Landing Craft, Motorized).

My team was first over the side and first into our boat. In the bobbing LCM, I glanced at my watch. 0540 hours. More than three and a half hours ahead of schedule. To me, that spelled trouble. The motors were already running full-tilt. As we pulled away from LST 266, some officer hanging over the side yelled out instructions — "Go to EASY RED."

The order surprised me. EASY RED was on the rightmost edge of 1st Division's half of OMAHA BEACH, not at all what I expected. This was some three thousand yards left, which is to say, east of our planned put-in point on DOG GREEN. — But if that's what they wanted, that's where we would go.

As we had been laying off DOG GREEN all night long, at the right edge of our Division's Sector, we now had to veer far to the east to reach EASY RED. It took us about twelve minutes before we were abreast of that part of the beach.

But it was a difficult twelve minutes. The water was uncommonly rough and several of my men got seasick in transit. They promptly puked all over themselves, as well as their neighbors.

No matter. We turned toward the shore, now, and began our run. The tide was rising rapidly and most of the underwater obstacles were submerged and could not be seen. Earlier boats had cleared a small, safe lane through the obstacles onto the beach.

But the "lane" wasn't very wide, and only one or two boats could make it safely through to the beach at a time. When we arrived to make our run, twenty boats were already ahead of us in line.

As far as I was concerned, waiting was not an option. All we had done for three days now was wait, wait, wait. I was impatient to get in the fight.

So, I turned to the boat's coxswain and issued my first combat command of the war, "Take us back! Go to DOG GREEN!"

The Navy man nodded, turned our LCM around. We started back along the beach, much closer than before. I worked myself forward to the bow of the boat, where I could see better what was going on.

That three-thousand-yard run was frightening. More bodies in the water, lots of them. Bodies. Half-sunken landing craft. Half-submerged mechanized tanks, trucks, bulldozers.

And not just in the water, on the beach too. Bodies. Heavily damaged equipment. Wreckage of every sort. Damaged and blown up. *But nobody was shooting at us, thank God.*

Off DOG GREEN, we found only six boats waiting to make a run through the narrow lane that had been cut through the underwater obstacles. Only six! I had made the right decision after all.

The last-minute change in orders as to which beach to go was a fine example of the confusion that reigns in almost any combat situation. Intelligence is always spotty and incomplete. Messages come in garbled, particularly by radio. Mistakes are made.

We got in line. The minutes passed. Boat after boat started down the lane. When we were the number two boat in line, we came under fire. *Ping! Ping! Ping!*

We were being hit by small-arms fire emanating from somewhere onshore! Bullets began bouncing off the sides of our landing craft!

Instinctively, we ducked. But we weren't actually in that much danger. The firing was spasmodic and unsustained. Plus, at this range, it was highly unlikely that a small calibre slug would have sufficient energy to penetrate the metal sides of the boat. Nerve-racking nonetheless.

Just ahead, a boat similar to ours started to sink. My best guess was that it must have struck an underwater obstacle. Off to our right, another blew up. A brilliant flash of yellow and white, then body parts and shrapnel everywhere.

I suddenly realized something about myself. I had been singing silently to myself. Trying to calm myself, perhaps. But singing nonetheless.

" . . . Mine eyes have seen the Glory of the Coming of the Lord. He is trampling out the vintage where the Grapes of Wrath are stored . . . "

The Battle Hymn of the Republic. Over and over again. First silently, then in quiet whispers, then outloud.

" . . . He hath loosed the fateful lightning of His terrible swift sword. His truth is marching on . . . "

All of a sudden, we were there, at the shoreline, motor idling. The boat stopped. The ramp went down. I stepped forward onto the ramp, began issuing commands.

"FOLLOW ME, BOYS!" I yelled, as I leapt off the ramp into waist-deep water.

Bullets were peppering the water all around us. *Scared?* You bet your life I was scared. *But I had no fear.* How strange is that?

We had seen films, back when we were training, films of Marines landing on TARAWA BEACH in the Pacific the previous November. The Marines were put off their landing craft in chest-deep water. Many died, and for all the wrong reasons. When Jap artillery shells burst in the water near them, the concussions knocked the men off their feet. They fell backwards and drowned under the weight of their own heavy packs and equipment.

What a way to die, I thought. *I would rather be shot dead!*

Now here we were, in the precise same situation, wading in waist-deep water, loaded down with equipment, under fire and still some distance from dry land. *No way was I going to let my men perish this way.*

I ordered my men to lean forward, to make like motor boats in the water, and to keep on moving forward, no matter what.

Machine-gun fire danced all around us as we pressed rapidly for the shore. Then the mistakes began.

Time and time again, throughout our training, the Cadre had drilled one theme into our heads. It was repeated over and over again throughout our many practice landings —

ONCE YOU LAND, MOVE DIRECTLY OFF THE BEACH. WHATEVER ELSE YOU DO, DO NOT HIT THE DIRT, NO MATTER WHAT!

So, what did my men do? You guessed it. No sooner had they exited the landing craft, than every single one of my men hit the deck.

Cursing and swearing, the Sergeants and I had to physically drag our men to their feet and propel them bodily across the rock and sand. At least we had one good thing to be thankful for, and that was the level of the tides. Not only were they high enough to have covered the underwater obstacles, the amount of exposed sand was narrowed appreciably.

Moving quickly now, and still under fire, we all made it safely across the shingle to the base of the seawall. The seawall gave us some cover in which to regroup. The small-arms fire, mostly from machine guns, was relatively light but persistent.

Sometime during those first few minutes, I got creased on my upper arm. It probably happened while I crisscrossed the landing zone getting my men up and running again.

Funny thing is: I never felt the damn thing. Too much adrenaline, I guess. I only discovered the gunshot wound moments later, when my right hand felt sticky as I went to grab hold of my carbine. I looked down, saw the blood. It had run down my arm from where the bullet dug into my flesh and into my hand.

Beneath the relative safety of the seawall, I dropped my web belt and pack, then removed my field jacket. I had one of the guys cut open my shirt sleeve, sprinkle some sulfa powder into the wound, and apply a bandage. That would have to do for now.

I slipped my field jacket and pack back on, pointed my men in the direction we had to go if we wanted to connect back up with the rest of the Company.

Ever so cautiously, now, I started to work my boat team slowly to the right, in the direction of the Vierville draw. My walkie-talkie had been pierced by a bullet so I discarded it. Up to this point, I was the only one who had been hit.

As we moved forward, we occasionally looked back, back in the direction we had come. The wounded had been evacuated. The dead had not. They were still there, on the beach, some in pieces, all rotting.

God, there were a lot of dead bodies! A lot of *parts* of dead bodies. *Who could possibly make sense of a beachfront filled with shattered body parts?* Heads, torsos, arms, legs. Everywhere. Blood mixed with sand, sand dyed dark brown by blood.

Earlier, as I crossed the beach, before I was shot, I saw something I would rather not see again, a body with a squashed head. Some tracked-vehicle, probably a half-track, had rolled over it. *Did the driver of that half-track know what he had done?* I wondered. *Did he care?*

Half-tracks were widely used as armored personnel carriers, although they also saw duty as mortar carriers and self-propelled anti-tank guns and armored fighting vehicles. They were easy to operate. Anyone who could drive a car could manage a half-track.

The physical devastation on that beach was as widespread as the death. Everywhere we looked. Shattered and burned out tanks. Wrecked field artillery pieces. Flattened trucks. Every type of equipment in the Allied arsenal lay on the beach somewhere, either wrecked or broken.

The conclusion was inescapable. The men in those first waves had been punished severely. They had paid a terrible price for their success, and the paying wasn't over.

So far anyway, the battle to gain a tiny foothold in Europe had been tough, real tough. *But think of those men!* What guts! What magnificent courage!

A battlefield possesses a stench peculiar unto itself. Spilt blood. Burnt gunpowder. Seared flesh. Smoldering oil. Vomit. Urine. Human feces.

For the moment, that's all we could smell. The stench of battle hung thick in the air, unmoving, that whole lousy revolting sickening smell.

It hung there, like the death and dismemberment around us.

It violated our nostrils in a way few things could, an unholy smell none of us were likely to forget any time soon.

It didn't take long before we, too, had added some of our own vomit to the mix.

What an awful, bloody horror!

7 JUNE 1944

We had come ashore on DOG GREEN BEACH at approximately 0645 hours. It was now two hours later and we were presently making our way off the beach, along the base of the seawall and over to the Vierville draw.

I had my doubts as to what we would find once we reached the draw. We knew the Germans had sealed off the natural beach exits with thick concrete walls backed up by tank traps and other obstacles.

What we did *not* know was whether or not the exit to the draw had been cleared of obstacles. If the beach exit was still blocked, we were in for a peck of trouble.

Yesterday, around three o'clock in the afternoon, while we were still at sea, our boat team had had a front row seat to an awesome demonstration of U.S. naval firepower. The Navy had shelled the draw repeatedly, trying to knock down the concrete impediments the Germans had erected to block us from exiting the beach.

Before the shelling ceased an hour later, there had been a giant explosion at a spot that now lay just ahead. I took that explosion to mean the Navy had cleared our path up the draw.

Now, as we approached the base of the draw, I hoped my interpretation of events was correct. — By God, Yes! It was.

With our senses now set to their highest setting, we edged cautiously up the draw. A short way up, we began to breathe easier. We found the Division Command Post. It had been set up within the confines of a small stone quarry the locals must have cut into the bluff at some point in the past. Division was using the rocky recess as a temporary Command Post.

I led my men further up the draw, past the Command Post. That's where we found the rest of our Company. They were busy reorganizing, piling ordnance beside the road, calling roll.

We were met there by Captain Singleton. He was real happy to finally see us. Singleton had feared the worst, that my entire boat team was either dead or lost. I explained what had happened.

The rest of G Company had been ordered to DOG GREEN, as per plan. Only my boat, of all the boats, had been ordered to EASY RED. Singleton agreed. My decision to change course and land at DOG GREEN had been the right one.

The pile of ordnance beside the road grew with each passing minute. Bangalore torpedoes, flamethrowers, pole and satchel charges. We had all carried more explosives onshore than we actually needed.

Boat team by boat team, we each stacked our extra munitions at the roadside along with the rest. Instead of thirty-man boat teams, we now reorganized ourselves back into our regular Company configuration.

By midday I had reassembled my entire thirty-nine-man platoon. The Captain gave me my orders and, at my command, Third Platoon picked up their weapons and gear and we moved off in the direction of Vierville. The village had been taken by our boys during the night.

As we moved cautiously up the road — and even before we reached the little village of Vierville — we maneuvered around remnants of several tank traps that had been recently neutralized by our Combat Engineers. The Germans called these obstacles "Dragon's Teeth," on account of how they looked.

Each "tooth" was between three and four feet tall, a truncated square-pyramidal fortification of reinforced concrete. The teeth were topped with Teller mines and staggered and spaced in such a way as to prevent a tank from simply driving through the maze undamaged. Landmines were often laid between individual "teeth," as well as barbed wire to impede infantry.

The idea was to slow down and channel enemy tanks into specific killing zones, where they might be more easily dispatched by an anti-tank weapon. In practice, though, our extensive use of Combat Engineers enabled us to dispose of these impediments relatively quickly. I think the Dragon's Teeth proved to be more of an inconvenience than an actual obstacle to our advance.

We worked our way around what was left of the concrete stubs in the field of "teeth." Half an hour later, when we slipped into town and past Vierville church, I noted with some dismay that the top half of the church steeple had been blown off. As recently as yesterday morning, it still stood proud up there. Now it was gone. *To save the nation we first had to destroy it.* Or so it seemed. Shame.

From the center of town, we swung right and pressed west, which is to say, parallel to the shoreline, about five hundred yards. That placed us outside Vierville proper and in the fields beside a small, no-name hamlet. Evening was already upon us as we dug in.

I looked at my watch. 1830 hours. Evening, but not yet dusk. At this latitude, with the longest day nearly at hand, the sun set late.

We had landed on DOG GREEN BEACH about 0645 this morning, some twelve hours ago. Would it be an exaggeration to say that that heady moment already seemed an eternity ago? Or that I was still haunted by the brutal reality of having stumbled across that flattened human head in the sand?

Working our way along the seawall to the Vierville draw had been agonizingly slow. Our safe passage along that treacherous stretch had been a matter of utilizing every last bit of natural cover as well as taking advantage of the active fighting at the top of the bluffs. We were now all of five hundred yards into France and — although we had been shot at plenty of times — we had yet to fire a single shot.

Now it was time to eat a little something. Each of us carried a light pack. It included our mess kit, raincoat, and what was considered by the Army to be food for four days — two K-rations plus two chocolate rations. Most everybody had crammed cigarettes and candy into their packs as well.

On my web belt, I had my canteen, four bandage packets, an extra canteen cover containing four hand grenades, plus two sleeves of ammunition. I carried my carbine in my hand, had my gas mask slung over my shoulder.

Around my neck, suspended on a leather strap, were my binoculars. Earlier that morning I had discarded the case. It was just in the way. Now I dumped the gas mask as well. Also in the way. My walkie-talkie had gone by the wayside earlier, back on the beach, when my arm was creased.

On another strap, I carried my map case. In one of my shirt pockets, I had pinned ten morphine syrettes. In my other shirt pocket rested a copy of the New Testament of the Bible.

I opened my ration, took a morsel of food. From nearby Vierville we could hear artillery shells exploding. The Germans were punching back at our positions. Forward movement looked to be slow and painful.

As we dug in, we heard lots of small-arms fire near our position. Shortly after 2000 hours, Captain Singleton assembled his platoon leaders. The order had come down from Division Headquarters. The 175th Infantry Regiment was to advance from our assembly area, then seize and defend the town of Isigny without delay. I looked at my map. Isigny lay about ten miles south and west of our current position.

We moved out in a column of Battalions, with the 2nd Battalion leading and G Company up front. Third Platoon, my platoon, was on point. Our job was to probe and clear out resistance.

It was pitch-black darkness when we fanned out. 2130 hours 7 June. Silently, we crossed the fields, worked our way through and over the hedgerows. The first town we entered, Englesqueville, we entered unopposed.

We ignored the buildings, as if they weren't there, and made our way to a small road which ran more or less due south. This road would eventually lead us to the main road, the Isigny-Bayeux Road. That main road ran roughly parallel to the coast, about three miles inland, between Bayeux and Isigny.

We reached the junction with the main road sometime after midnight, which is to say, very early in the morning of 8 June. Here we stopped and rested four hours until daybreak.

The Germans did not bother us while we slept, thank God.

8 JUNE 1944

0600 hours. Daybreak. Four hours of blissful sleep. We had been dug in just north of the Isigny-Bayeux Road. Time to get up and moving.

My platoon was still on point, so we were first to move out. We pushed west along the main road. We didn't get far though, when a sniper opened up on us from his lair somewhere in a grove of trees across the field to our right.

I guess my men were trigger-happy. They hadn't yet fired their weapons in anger. So perhaps this seemed like the perfect time.

To a man, they ducked behind the closest hedgerow alongside the road and promptly began returning fire. *But what a grand waste of ammunition!* They didn't even know where the sniper was or even which tree to shoot at.

"Cease fire!"

I yelled it in frustration. Then I called out to ask if anybody had actually seen the bloke.

Nobody had.

"Okay, guys, keep your eyes peeled."

I told them I was going to stand up, walk along the wall of bushes, draw the sniper's fire. Then I shouted:

"But, for God's sake, when the bastard does fire, spot the son of a bitch and take him down!"

Talk about your bonehead plays. What was I thinking? That a trained sniper would simply shoot at me and miss?

I stood up, walked about fifteen feet. Then I heard the "POP!" that a bullet makes when it narrowly misses your head as it goes whizzing by.

I dropped to the ground, asked if anyone had seen the sniper fire. One man saw him work the bolt of his rifle. I told that man to load tracer bullets into his M1 and to fire at that spot. I left a Sergeant and a pair of binoculars behind with him. They were to direct our fire after we identified which tree the sniper was holed up in.

Then, using the wall of bushes for cover, the rest of us started to move forward again. Our first shot missed him. The second one hit him, though perhaps not squarely.

The sniper had lashed himself to the tree, probably to steady his aim. Now he tried to cut himself loose of his moorings. A third shot hit him dead on. We left the area with the man dangling upside down from the tree. *So Endeth The Lesson On How To Deal With Enemy Snipers.*

A little further on, we came to a crossroads. We probed the area carefully and found it undefended. But then all of a sudden, we heard a vehicle approaching from our right.

Using hand signals, the very same hand signals we had practiced so often in our training, I got everyone down. Instantly, my platoon melted into the tall grass.

The unknown vehicle drew closer. I could see it now through my binoculars. It was a jeep.

Christ! It was an American jeep!

I stood up, raised my hand, ordered the vehicle to stop. I like to have filled my pants. It was the Division Commander, General Gerhardt, and his driver!

I was not amused. We had just taken out a sniper. Who knew what other dangers lay lurking beyond the next row of trees?

But I did my best.

With the biggest grin I could manage, I told the General to please get the hell back where he belonged. Then I pointed.

General Gerhardt looked like he was about to dress me down, when I added that it made my men nervous, him being out here.

The General took it okay. With a jovial wave of the hand, he instructed his driver to turn the jeep around. The two headed back the way they had come.

A short while later, we were ordered to stop and wait for 3rd Battalion to pass us and take over the lead. This was a welcome break, as nearly a thousand men passed through our position while we rested at ease.

Forty minutes later, we fell in behind the men of 3rd Battalion and continued west down the Isigny-Bayeux Road into the tiny village of La Cambe. The village was not defended, not a German in sight. So we passed through La Cambe and headed on toward Isigny, still some miles away. So far, we had not met the enemy in force.

We were still a couple hundred yards east of La Cambe, on the main road, when we witnessed two Allied fighter planes wingover to make a strafing run down the very road we were presently standing on.

Back in England, our trainers had warned us of such dangers. Pilots could make mistakes, and we had to be on our toes. We had specific instructions what to do in the event of a strafing run by our own fighters. Protocol called for us to throw out two yellow smoke grenades to mark our position. That was the order in force. Then we were to scatter and took cover off the road.

The fighters seemed oblivious to our signal smoke. They dove full bore into La Cambe, guns blazing. First, they dropped their five-hundred-pound bombs, trying to take out two tanks (ours). Then, they strafed a column of ground troops passing through town (also, ours). These were soldiers from the Army's 1st Battalion.

Like the earlier disaster on Slapton Sands during "Exercise Tiger," the strafing run at La Cambe was another gruesome example of death by "friendly fire." So far as I know, it was the only incident of its kind anywhere on the battlefield throughout the entire Battle of Normandy.

Minutes later, as we pressed into and through La Cambe, 3rd Battalion began to meet strong resistance from their left. Our Company was still to their rear, but we could hear the firefight from our position. The firefight expanded rapidly and they left the main road to engage the enemy. 2nd Battalion again picked up the lead and continued to press west toward Isigny. My platoon once again took point.

A couple of hundred yards further on, we were suddenly under heavy machine-gun and mortar fire from our right front. If I haven't told you already, let me tell you now. The Germans had the best machine gun in the war. Their MG 42 fired twelve hundred rounds per minute.

Our best gun fired less than half that number. Plus, their mortars were heavier — 100 mm versus our 60 mm and 81 mm. And they packed a much bigger wallop.

So, when I say, we were under heavy machine-gun and mortar fire, you must recognize this as a potentially lethal situation. We immediately jumped off the road and sought cover.

Moving defensively, I had my men take up positions along the nearest hedgerow. I unslung my binoculars and peered ever so cautiously over the top of the hedgerow.

I could see that the Germans had machine guns dug in at the far corners of the adjoining field. A dash by us across that open space would be met by murderous crossfire as well as a barrage of mortars.

Then again, we couldn't exactly sit still. The Jerrys were already lobbing mortar shells in our general direction. *We had to do something, and we had to do it fast!*

Norman hedgerows were different from those of England. The hedgerows in Cornwall stood four to five feet tall. They were almost two feet thick and were "clean" on top. That is to say, they were straight across on top, as if they had been shaved smooth with a blade. Easy for a normal-sized man to see across.

In Normandy, the hedgerows were much larger and not nearly as cleanly kempt. A Norman hedgerow often stood five or six, even seven feet tall. They were upwards of three feet thick, with small trees or bushes protruding from the tops. It was almost impossible to see the enemy over them.

Wherever the Germans dug themselves in, they bored machine-gun holes through the thick growth of the hedgerow. The holes were perfect camouflage for their guns, and they fired at us through those slots.

Generally what the Germans did was to position their guns at the corners of two hedgerows. This setup afforded them a vicious crossfire should anyone inadvertently enter that farmer's field.

Each Norman field had but one entrance, and the entrances seemed to be randomly arranged within the length of the hedgerows. Plus, the fields themselves varied sharply in size. There was no rhyme or reason to it. One field might be two hundred feet across and the next one only a hundred, or three hundred, or four hundred feet across or larger.

And, to make matters even more hazardous for us, adjoining fields were not positioned symmetrically. Oftentimes, they were arranged at peculiar angles, not always ninety degrees. The physical layout made it exceedingly difficult to accomplish a flanking maneuver. A platoon or squad might get lost, or turned around. Perfect for a defender. Confusing and murderous for an attacker.

As far as military tactics go, there is really only one way to defeat such a defense, and that is to try and flank the enemy. But it is a risky maneuver.

I called over my best squad sergeant, Sergeant Shackleford. He knew the score. I told Shackleford to take his squad and to try and work himself around to the right of the German position. The idea was to place his squad where they might hit the enemy with fire along the enemy's own hedgerow, what we call "enfilade fire." Under cover of a blaze of enfilade fire from Shackleford's squad, the rest of us would cross the field and close ranks with them.

By the way, the term "enfilade fire" means sweeping gunfire along the length of a line of troops. A trench is said to be enfiladed if the opponent can fire down the length of the trench. A column of marching troops is said to be enfiladed if they can be fired upon from the front or the rear in such a way that the projectiles are able to travel down the length of the marching column.

Shackleford's squad took off. I crossed my fingers. If his squad couldn't get on the Germans' right flank, I was sending them to their death. To the rest of my men, I called out, "Fix Bayonets!" Things were about to get bloody.

Fifteen minutes went by. My men were picking away at the enemy, but with only minor success, shooting at what they could see. Jerry was still doing his best to drop in mortar rounds right on top of us, and the explosions were getting uncomfortably close. A couple of my guys had already been hit by shrapnel, and so far I had heard absolutely nothing from Shackleford. I was beginning to worry.

Suddenly, the fire from across the field stuttered. *Shackleford's squad was in position and had begun strafing the German line!*

I jumped up and yelled to my men, "Follow Me!"

Then I climbed over the hedgerow and started across the field in the direction of the German fire. My men followed, bayonets extended out on front of them

Even with Shackleford's squad bearing down on their position, the Germans kept on firing at us as we charged forward. Then the firing abruptly stopped and a couple mortar rounds fell in among us. We hit the dirt.

The mortar fire stopped and up we went again, resuming our frontal charge. *This time, there was no resistance!*

By the time we reached the hedgerow, Shackleford and his men had come boring in from the right. *It had worked! The Germans had skedaddled!*

We probed to the other side of the hedgerow, the side where the Germans had just been. Even a lone German on the other side of the hedgerow could still lob grenades at us. Even a lone, wounded German could still fire a machine gun.

As we came around the side of that first hedgerow, we were suddenly again under fire, this time from the far side of the adjoining field. The Germans had withdrawn one field further back.

We were now in the exact same position as before, only one field further on. As my men began to return the enemy's fire, the terrible thought popped into my head:

If the enemy was going to surrender France only one hundred feet at a time, this was going to make for a very long war.

8 JUNE 1944

" . . . *War binds men more tightly together than almost any other branch of human activity — to undergo shame, fear, and death with scores of others of your age and mental coloring. Who, indeed, would trade these comrades of the battlefield, for friends made in time of peace? . . . "*

. . . . . . *from the writings of General Omar Bradley*

With our first skirmish over, I began to take stock of our losses. We had gained all of one field and had suffered mightily for our tiny success.

I called in my squad leaders to see where we stood. We had lost two men who were wounded and who we had left behind at the last hedgerow before our desperate charge across that field. We had lost another three men wounded crossing that field. *Five good men down.* Our first firefight had cost us dearly.

We collected our wounded and brought them up to the hedgerow, where they had good protective cover. Once the wounded were safe, we popped them with morphine, bandaged them as best we could.

It was now late afternoon. Daylight was fading fast. The problem was, we were presently facing west. The sun was low in the sky. What sunlight there was, was in our eyes, blinding us. I peered over the hedgerow.

From this vantage point, I could see the enemy firing from the same type of setup as before, machine guns in the corner. The only thing different from before was that there was no longer any mortar fire raining down upon our heads. I wondered why. A moment later I thought I had my answer.

An hour earlier, when my platoon first surged forward to take out that machine-gun nest, the rest of our Company swung to the right. Even now, they were still engaged in a vicious firefight a short distance away. The way I had it figured, the Germans must have relocated their mortars to their own left in order to meet the larger threat.

It only made sense. Plus, there was a constant booming of explosions coming from that direction. Maybe, if the German mortars were busy over there, that might work in our favor.

The overgrowth of trees and bushes on top of the hedgerow made it very difficult for us to see anything clearly. Our fire at the enemy was therefore not voluminous, but selective. The men pretty much stuck to my admonition that they fire only at targets they could clearly see.

Each length of hedgerow had but a single entry point cut through its width into the field beyond. These entry points were randomly positioned, sometimes at the end of the row, sometimes in the middle. I assume their arrangement made sense to the farmers who owned them. But they made no sense to us.

The field we presently faced had an entry point positioned roughly halfway along the hedgerow on the side directly opposite us. Jerry had a machine gun placed at each corner of the hedgerow, as well as one on either side of the entryway. That made for a total threat of four machine guns facing our way — twice as many as before — plus who knows how many riflemen.

I considered our options. They weren't particularly good. The field that lay in front of us was simply too darn wide for us to make effective use of rifle grenades. Which left me only one choice — and a bad one at that — yet another frontal attack.

Sergeant Shackleford's squad had done such an effective job flanking the German line the first time around, I decided to chance it again. Only this time I would send him around to the left. His orders were as before. Work his men into position, establish a defensible stance, catch Jerry in a flurry of enfilade fire.

At Shackleford's signal that his men were in place, I had my other two squads begin to fire heavily as the rest of us scrambled over the hedgerow and started across the field. It was a deadly game of bullet tag, as we advanced rapidly, then hit the ground, then dashed forward, fired our weapons, dodged bullets, then hit the ground again.

The incoming German fire was heavy, much heavier than I could have possibly imagined. Bullets were snapping past me, some tearing at my clothing, none striking flesh.

It was a reckless dash, and we had barely made it to the middle of that large field when, all of a sudden, artillery shells began to drop in on us like flies. Now it all made sense. *Who needs to toss in mortars when we have artillery shells to cut them down with?*

What was left of my shattered platoon hugged the ground, now, in sheer terror as a murderous concentration of high explosives detonated all around us. The shelling seemed to last an eternity though the actual duration was under ten minutes.

I pressed my body and soul into the ground, prayed to God that I wouldn't get hit.

By now, Him and me were in pretty regular contact. I asked God to spare me, to not spill my guts in this lousy place, to not strike me down this early in the war.

So far, He seemed to be listening. In fact, God and I talked together quite a bit that day. Funny how religion and faith take on a whole new meaning when Death is staring you right smack in the face.

A piece of shell casing hit the guy next to me. It struck him in the head, shattered his helmet, sprayed pieces of skull and brain matter all over me. I could hear another man screaming for his mother, some crying out in pain, others calling to GOD.

Suddenly the shelling stopped. It stopped as abruptly as it started. Those of us, who could still walk, moved as quickly as we could up to the hedgerow. The Germans were gone. We had lost contact. *They had pulled out under cover of their own artillery fire.*

I looked around. Blinked my eyes. Could hardly believe the devastation. What ought to have been some peasant farmer's quiet pasture had become a killing field.

The guy who had been calling out for his mother was now silent. Probably dead. The men who had been screaming out in pain were still screaming. Countless others were just lying there, moaning. *Was this my fault? Or was this just the way it was?*

Not all of my men were hurt. I had some of the uninjured ones set up a defensive perimeter. The rest I took back into the field. Together, we dragged those men who were wounded, yet still alive, forward to the safety of the hedgerow, where we tried the best we could to treat their injuries. My stock of morphine syrettes and sulfa powder was disappearing fast.

My Platoon Sergeant and friend, Harold Kinkade, was dead. He had taken a machine-gun burst full-on in the chest. When I found Harold, he was still alive. But just barely. His chest was just a mass of bloody pulp. He died quickly. In my arms. That hit me hard. Harold was a good man.

Corporal Zuber was wounded through his inside upper right thigh, close to his privates. The man was positively certain his testicles had been shot off. The wound was giving him a lot of burning pain. But he didn't want to look, just in case he had lost his balls.

I ordered Doc, our aid man, to peel back Zuber's bandage, so I could see the damage for myself. Everything was intact, just as it should be. The wound — a bad one — was in his upper leg, not his genitals. The family jewels were unscathed. Zuber was damn near ecstatic.

With my men now safely behind the hedgerow, I took reports from my squad leaders. The numbers were devastating. Since the day began, we had lost fifteen men — Sergeant Kinkade, plus fourteen other soldiers killed or wounded. This, out of a platoon of thirty-nine.

Among the dead was a nice kid from North Carolina named Leo Holden. Leo was my best B.A.R. man. He had died quickly. A large piece of shell casing had struck the man broadside, torn out the front of his abdomen. It also bent the barrel of his Browning Automatic Rifle.

During our many months of training, I had developed a real liking for Leo, and for his skills and attitude. Leo would surely have been in line for the next promotion I handed out. Sad thing was: About the time we went into the marshalling area in Cornwall, Leo had received a letter from his sister telling him their mother had died. I figured Leo was with his mother now.

And then there was Davis, the oldest man in the platoon. And Casale. And the others . . . .

After training them all, after getting to know them so well, the losses hurt, badly. There were tears in my eyes. But I did not cry.

As for me, I had had several close calls. A shell fragment or bullet had sheared off one of the eyepieces from my binoculars. When you consider that my binoculars hung from a leather strap around my neck, that makes for a particularly close call. I was now the proud owner of a monocular — and in almost constant communication with the Fellow upstairs. Like I said, me and God were keeping up a regular conversation right about then.

I had Sergeant Bill Kazanza, the Platoon Guide, take over Harold Kinkade's position as Platoon Sergeant. We would have to operate without a second-ranking Sergeant until replacement troops arrived.

Afternoon was well gone by now and evening was fast approaching. By the time we had gotten our wounded attended to, it was beginning to get dark.

I tried to remember what day it was. *Had we landed just yesterday? Yesterday was what?* — 7 June? That would make today . . .

Oh, well, the math was too damn hard and I was too damn tired to add one to seven.

The field we faced was a grain field. It was June and the crop was almost knee-high. We were tired. No, make that exhausted. We didn't have an ounce of strength left in our bodies.

Those of us, who could stay awake, were propped up like zombies against the hedgerow. We kept looking across the field to see if the Germans would return. We had no strength left to fight them.

Through heavy eyes I thought — *the tall wheat would conceal them. Enemy soldiers could creep up on us, and we would never even see them.* That thought scared me. Small, intermittent breezes rustled the grain. It made it look as if someone or something was moving out there.

Me and God started talking again. He kept telling me to stay awake. I wouldn't listen.

My eyelids were so heavy, I would fall asleep momentarily then jerk myself awake, terrified, heart beating rapidly, head cocked upright, listening intently. *How long had I dozed?* Then I would fall right back to sleep.

I cycled through this process several times. Then I got up, worked myself along our position, checked both our flanks, found a few others also managing to stay awake. It was dark now. Sergeant Kazanza and I took turns, prodding enough of us to keep watch so we wouldn't be overrun by the enemy.

Scary.

9 JUNE 1944

A runner dispatched from our Company's Command Post made his way into our little corner of the world. I don't know what time he arrived. I was dead asleep. It was pitch-black night. I jerked awake at the sound of his voice.

I think I told you I discarded my walkie back on the beach when it was destroyed by a bullet. That's why Captain Singleton sent a runner. He wanted to talk to me and couldn't raise me on the radio. I followed the runner back the way he had come.

While my platoon was bogged down in this treacherous field fighting our little fight, the rest of the Company had neutralized the balance of the enemy's strong point. They, too, had been ravaged by a brutal artillery barrage as the Germans withdrew and were now in Battalion Reserve.

My orders were to move my men in behind the other Companies in our Battalion. They were presently engaged in a horrendous firefight alongside a big radar installation outside of Cardonville. Opposition was apparently heavy and strong. Cardonville, by the way, lay north of the Isigny-Bayeux Road. Two more hard miles of fighting lay between us and Isigny proper.

After my meeting with Captain Singleton, I returned to my platoon and briefed my Sergeants. Minutes later, we moved out, leaving behind our dead and wounded.

For us, the Battle of Cardonville was a snap. Our Company was in Reserve and we weren't even committed. And it was a good thing too, as we were beat up and tired. My men and I caught catnaps wherever we could.

Despite all that had happened, the goal remained unchanged — seize and hold Isigny. We passed through Cardonville about dawn, took this or that small road south, then briefly headed west across hedgerow country before turning south again. Shortly thereafter, this second small road junctioned with the main Isigny-Bayeux Road. We swung hard right onto the main road and moved cautiously the last quarter-mile into Isigny.

At first, we met no resistance. Then, at one street corner, a few blocks in, machine-gun fire put a stop to our advance.

We had adequate cover and used it our advantage. From behind doorways and rubble, we shot back. There were two machine-gun nests, one on each corner. That made the street a fine killing zone. As far as I could see, no fire was coming from upstairs in the buildings.

The idea now was to move quickly from doorway to doorway, firing as we went, each time drawing closer to those guns. One nest was set up just beyond the corner of a bombed-out building.

I had a bazooka team set up behind a pile of rubble. To give them time to get their weapon ready, my riflemen kept up a steady fire directly on the machine-gun positions.

Finally, the bazooka team let one fly. *Bingo!* It hit right square on top of one of the two machine-gun nests. Much to my surprise, the other gun, across the street, also stopped firing. The Germans, still hidden, waved a white handkerchief.

What the hell? I thought. We took three of them prisoner. In the other nest, the blown-out nest, two Jerrys were dead, a third only slightly wounded.

Well, here I was, the proud owner of four enemy prisoners. *But what to do with them?* My first instinct was to kill them all and be done with it. I could even the score. An eye for an eye and all that. Harold Kinkade, dead. Leo Holden, dead. Davis. Casale. Yes, that is what I would do.

But then three American MP's approached and offered to take the four prisoners off my hands. I couldn't very well say no.

Our work in Isigny wasn't done. We continued to press inward toward the city center and swept out two more machine-gun nests along the way. Finally, we reached what seemed to be a town square. Here, three major streets came together.

Although I didn't know it at the time, two other Battalions had taken the southern half of the city while our Company was occupied on the north side. What seemed to be a town square wasn't actually the town center. We continued to push inward.

Other platoons ran into the same sort of trouble as we had. But, little by little, we vanquished the enemy's various strong points until we had eliminated them all.

The town was ours!

•

•

Once Isigny was secure, we were ordered to take up a defensive posture. Our Company moved back out beyond the edge of town, where we crossed two bridges and were soon back in hedgerow country. We pulled off the road and dug in. The men, dog tired, just leaned back and fell asleep.

At first, I couldn't sleep. My arm hurt like the dickens where I was creased that first day. So I made my rounds, woke up a few men, had the Sergeants rotate who would stay awake when and who would sleep.

Then we all hunkered down for some shut-eye. Aside from the four hours we stopped outside Englesqueville, we had been living on catnaps for two days now, ever since first landing on the Normandy beach the morning of the seventh. It was now somewhere past noon on the ninth. We were tired, very tired.

We weren't asleep long when K Company moved through our position and we were booted out. Other elements of 3rd Battalion took over our foxholes.

We moved, now, into two open fields further off the road all the while hugging the hedgerows. An ammunition truck came by and each of my men drew three or more bandoliers of rifle ammunition. A second truck dropped off a pile of K-rations, which we grabbed for hungrily, two or more rations per man. Then, about fifty men came shuffling up the road. Their boots kicked up a lot of dust. These were replacement troops to replenish our losses.

I was happy to see these men. They were fresh and unhurt. More to the point, I had trained with every last one of them back in Cornwall. I knew these men. They fit in perfectly with the rest of us.

I had one man take over as Platoon Sergeant, the others I assigned to open positions within the squads. Staff Sergeant Bill Kazanza once again became Platoon Guide. I had a new B.A.R. man and several new riflemen. *My platoon was back at full strength!*

Rest time was over, short as it had been. With my platoon again at full strength, Singleton ordered us to establish a strong point on the Division's exposed flank. This was to be at a place called Neuilly (one of several French towns with similar names), a small village on an equally small but important river — the Vire River — south of our present position. An important rail line ran past Neuilly. Several key bridges crossed the river nearby. We moved out.

Maybe I should explain what I mean by a "strong point." In the parlance of the Army, a strong point is any fortified position. My platoon was to be beefed up with explosives, as well as a section of 60 mm mortars from the Fourth Platoon and a section of heavy machine guns from H Company. My platoon was so far to the front, we waited more than three hours for Supply to find us.

Finally, at about 0200 hours, we had in hand everything we would need to fortify our position and to move into place. That would put us now at two o'clock in the morning — the next morning — 10 June. Still, no real sleep.

It was slow going getting down to the river, and not just because of the dark. Near as I could determine from the maps, we were slipping into territory still held by the Germans. Last thing I wanted to do was to wake the bastards up — or run into them.

Finally, around dawn, we reached Neuilly. We probed the area carefully but did not turn up any of the opposition.

The river was a natural obstacle, thus it made sense for us to use it to our advantage in establishing a strong point. I laid out our fortified embattlement on the townside of the closest bridge over the Vire River.

We refrained from using any of the buildings as part of our defense perimeter though we did use them as observation posts. From the second floor of one building I could see across the low, soft ground for at least twelve hundred yards.

The men began to set up their guns and dig in. We wanted to be ready for whatever the Germans threw at us.

But the truth of the matter was different. With only one bazooka team we didn't offer much resistance to armor.

Oh, we could slow them down alright — we had mined the closest bridge, after all — but stop them? Not hardly.

The one thing we did have in our favor was this. Any approaching armor would have to stick to the road coming across the river. The ground in the fields was too soft and mushy, and the river itself was too wide to cross easily.

Then too, we had a radioman assigned to us. He had with him what we called a 300 radio. If the Germans tried to come our way, I could always try and radio for artillery support to take out the enemy armor. That was of some comfort.

I should point out here that portable, battery-powered voice radios were rather a new thing. They were quite heavy and quite bulky, not something a platoon normally carried. This particular unit had a range of some three miles over level ground.

Once we were in position, I could see perfectly well why Captain Singleton dispatched us to this location. Neuilly-la-Forêt, as the locals called it, was a perfect place to mount such a defense.

Neuilly was precisely at the one spot where an important east-west road came across the lowlands, crossed the river as well as the railroad tracks. The nearest similar road lay at least a mile away, to the north.

Plus, the topography suited us. The ground rose slightly behind the town. We were set up on that ridge. We could see across the low, mushy ground a long distance. No way were enemy troops going to sneak up on us and take us by surprise.

By 0800 hours 10 June, we were dug in, machine guns placed, B.A.R.'s positioned, fields of fire laid out. Everybody crept into their holes and promptly fell asleep, me included.

10 JUNE 1944

We were in position at the edge of town and dug in. After fighting our way ten miles into lower Normandy, we were now worn out and tired. Our bodies were dirty, our faces unshaven, our minds numb. My men were hungry, their bellies empty. But they weren't complaining. The addition of replacement troops had helped reinvigorate our spirits.

I was proud of my men. They had fought well. But, to a man, we were all thankful for a lull in the fighting. Our unit had been on the move, without any real rest, since just after sunrise on 7 June, when we first landed on the coast at DOG GREEN BEACH. It was now 0800 hours 10 June, and we were deep inside German-held territory.

Even our replacement troops were fatigued. Their journey these past several days had been one of almost constant movement, from England, across the Channel, now across France. Sleep had not come easily to them, not even aboard ship. Concerns and misgivings about what lay ahead would keep any man awake. Except now. We were all dead asleep in our foxholes.

Suddenly, a noise startled me awake. My eyes popped open. I was instantly sitting up and on high alert.

A German command car was sitting on the road just across the way. Four German officers had gotten out of the vehicle and were moving onto the bridge, probably to check for mines, our mines.

Driven by a sudden surge of adrenaline, I leapt into the unmanned machine-gun position, swung it their direction, and started to fire at them. The noise woke up my entire platoon.

My other machine-gunner also swung into action and began to fire in the same general direction. Riflemen quickly grabbed for their guns and a hail of bullets followed.

But the Germans were too far away. Our bullets were not hitting them, and they ran back in the direction of their command car.

Although our blaze of gunfire did not knock down any of the enemy, it appeared as if at least one officer got hit. He had to be helped back into their vehicle. They backed out of there fast, turned around about five hundred yards down the road and sped off into the distance, no longer worried about searching out explosive mines.

I yelled "Cease fire!" and glanced around nervously. Everyone was certainly wide-awake now. I looked at my watch. 0925. We had been asleep a little more than an hour.

I kicked myself for the mistake. *How dumb could I be? — letting everyone fall asleep at the same time?* If the Jerrys were in staff cars, checking out the road, they were looking for a secure route to advance their men and armor along.

I tried not to show how angry I was with myself when I turned, now, to my squad leaders. Together, we set up a rotating schedule of observation. The idea was to allow the rest of the unit to get some much-needed sleep even as we kept a constant lookout for Germans.

I should have done this before we dug in. But, at the time, I had been too tired to think. Now the realization flashed through my head. *Fatigue was every bit as dangerous as the enemy.* I wasn't about to make that mistake again.

An hour and a half later, my worst fears about those command cars were confirmed. While I was scanning a patch of higher ground in the far distance, I saw what appeared to be trees moving slowly north along a major road. This particular road ran north through the forest, north being in the direction of the coast, north being where they could endanger our re-supply lines.

My binoculars had been reduced to a single monocular thanks to that earlier close call, so I borrowed an undamaged pair from one of my Sergeants. Now I could see more clearly. The "trees" were actually camouflaged artillery pieces. *Jerry was on the move!*

Immediately, I yanked my map out of its case. I determined our current coordinates while my radioman raised the artillery unit that had been deployed as support for the Regiment. I was well versed with map reading. I knew my map would be printed at a different scale than theirs would be. So I gave them the coordinates as they appeared on my map, as well as the map scale so there would be no mistakes. Moments later, they radioed back — *A round was on its way.*

I heard the shell sail overhead, watched carefully where it landed. The round fell a little long. Without even needing to look again at my map, I called in an adjustment, hoping I'd judged the miss correctly. *Bingo!* The second round was right on target.

Now I called in the order. "Fire for effect! Traverse along the road!"

Moments later we could hear the barrage of shells as they soared over our heads and into the enemy position. Then, all of a sudden, there was a large explosion along the road.

One of our shells must have struck an ammunition truck because the big explosion was followed by several more right on the same spot.

It took a moment before the smoke started to clear. But once it did, I could clearly see a number of wrecked artillery pieces beside the road as well as several destroyed trucks.

I called in a second adjustment and had them unleash another five-minute barrage of concentrated fire on the roadway. More dead-on hits. Our boys had inflicted a great deal of punishment on some German artillery unit.

I let our artillery guys know their firing mission was a success. I felt good. I had made up for my earlier mistake falling asleep. Plus, my Forward Observer training at Okehampton had paid off handsomely in the field.

Nobody else came along that road or across the flatland the rest of the morning. About 1300 hours two American tanks arrived and took up positions on the small hill behind the town. A regular Artillery Forward Observer Team arrived and took up positions above and below us. The original strong point I had chosen was even stronger now than before.

Late in the day, we were relieved by a platoon from K Company. We set out, now, to find and rejoin the rest of our Company. G Company had moved on to La Forêt, a village two miles due east of our present position, on the main road south of Isigny.

By midnight we had found our people. A short while later, we were in our holes dozing off. G Company was in Battalion Reserve.

But, as we were so close to the front, perimeter security was tight. The troops were in a high state of readiness. Everyone was nervous. 1st Battalion had been jumped by a German unit the previous night while they slept.

Two hours later, which would now put us about 0100 hours on 11 June 1944, Captain Singleton called his platoon leaders together. Things were getting dicey and we were to move our various units closer to the Vire River near Neuilly.

One thing dawned on me in that middle-of-the-night meeting. The faces around that circle were somewhat different than before. Some of the officers, who had come ashore with us on OMAHA BEACH, were no longer with us. Several of the platoons were now under new leadership.

The leader of one boat team had been shot dead outside of La Cambe. The leader of another boat team, Lieutenant James Flanagan, had been shot dead on the beach. Flanagan, you may remember, was the guy I replaced when I first came to G Company. My friend and drinking buddy, Lieutenant Tom Lombardo, was still leader of First Platoon.

Two hours later we moved out and by 0600 we were in our new positions. My platoon was still on the exposed flank of the Division. But fortunately, G Company was still in Battalion Reserve and we were not bothered by enemy activity the rest of the day.

11 June proved to be a relatively quiet day. We spent much of it in our foxholes, sleeping.

12 JUNE 1944

Before dawn on 12 June, Captain Singleton again called his platoon leaders to the Company Command Post. Easy Company was engaged in a vicious firefight two miles due west of us, outside the town of Montmartin-en-Graignes. We were to cross the Vire River a mile south of town and swing into position to support their effort.

It took us about an hour to get underway. But, by late morning, we were at the crossing point. Battalion had managed to come up with a couple small rowboats to get us across the river.

But the number of boats was completely inadequate to the job. There weren't nearly enough seats onboard these little boats to transport the lot of us across, barely enough to get one platoon from shore to shore at a time. I took this as a bad omen.

The Captain didn't like it either. With just a few small boats, the Company would have to go over piecemeal. But he had his orders — and he gave me mine.

My platoon was to lead the way. Intelligence was scarce. We were told that there had been no sign of German activity opposite the point of crossing. I wasn't so certain.

The spot where they had chosen for us to cross would land us in a large flat field, a field some one thousand feet across. I had had some experience with the dangers of crossing large fields. We would have to cross this one fast. No cover, no cover-fire, no cover of darkness. *Oh, boy.* We took quickly to the boats and paddled over.

Things went better than I expected. We got on shore and I moved my men quickly across the field. There was no resistance.

On the opposite end of the field was a farmhouse. We made for it. An irrigation ditch curved around the edge of the field. That included the house. I had the platoon take up positions in the ditch to cover the rest of our Company as they crossed that same big, wide-open field. The water in the ditch was refreshingly cool and about three feet deep.

But then things started to go wrong. Just as the next boatload of men was about to begin making their way across the river, a strong German force started down the slope under cover of mortar fire. *For God's sake, they were advancing in the open!*

My men fired, and they fired again, and they kept on firing. This put a stop to the German advance but not to their mortar fire. It was raining down upon us.

Singleton pulled the second load of men back from midstream. Now we were in trouble. A runner came in, told us to withdraw. We would be covered by fire from the other side of the river.

It took everything G Company had to protect us. Mortar fire, machine-gun fire, rifle fire, you name it. Weapons Platoon unleashed it all. Fast as our legs would carry us, we withdrew to the Vire River bank. 60 mm mortars were flying over our heads at the enemy.

You never seen boats move that fast. We hopped back in them and dashed back across the river. Enemy mortar rounds chased us all the way to the opposite shore. The amazing thing is — *not one of my men got hit in the entire debacle!*

Under heavy fire, now, from our entire Company, the Germans stopped in their tracks. By late afternoon they had pulled back up the rise and melted away into the woods.

The skirmish was over but so too was our aborted attempt to cross this key river in boats. Now we were mired in a sort of frustrating stalemate, with the Jerrys holding one bank of the river and our Company holding the other.

We were dug in and waiting for new orders from Regimental Command. They weren't long in coming.

We were instructed to move further south along the Vire River — maybe a mile — to a point where intelligence had determined the river to be only two feet deep. We were to traverse the river at this shallow point, move cross-country, then seize and hold the several bridges where a major road crossed the Vire-et-Taute Canal.

This road, the Saint-Jean-de-Daye Road, crossed the canal maybe three miles southeast of Neuilly. Even after all these many days of fighting, we would likely traverse the river but a couple thousand yards from where we started.

It had to be done though. This road was the only route Allied armor could use to push further inland. But, in crossing the river at that shallow spot, we would end up several miles behind known German lines.

The Company was beefed up with the addition of a section of heavy machine guns from H Company. In total, our force now numbered more than two hundred men, including our Regimental Commander.

It seemed an unnecessary risk, him joining us. *Did the man feel responsible for our earlier failure not getting across the Vire?* Maybe.

Moving out now in a column of platoons, we soon arrived at the point where we needed to cross. It was now 2300 hours and it was dark, very dark. No moon, no stars, no light whatsoever.

An hour later, at 0003 hours 13 June, I was in the black water leading my men across the river. The information was correct, at least in one respect. The water at that spot was only about two feet deep.

But, beneath the black water was more than a foot of gooey mud. This made for a rather messy crossing. Plus, it slowed us down.

To keep our weapons dry, we held them over our heads as we quietly slogged and slopped our way through the muck and water to the other side.

Half-covered with mud now, we fanned out on the opposite bank and positioned ourselves to move quietly cross-country. My platoon was on the left, Second Platoon on the right, First and Fourth Platoons in the rear behind Second. Fourth was our Heavy Weapons Platoon.

We edged forward. Everything we did now, we did with extreme quiet. We were behind enemy lines. No conversation. As little sound as possible.

We passed by a tiny, no-name hamlet, my platoon still on the left as we advanced. The rest of the Company passed through the village. Less than a mile further on we ran into trouble.

Reading maps and plotting our exact position had become a practical impossibility in the black of night. We relied instead on our compasses and our intuition, a near-perfect recipe for making a mistake.

Moments later all hell broke loose. My Third Platoon had stumbled onto a German patrol bivouacked for the night. Most of the enemy was asleep. Even so, a short but vicious firefight ensued. It didn't last long. Conditions favored my men. In short order we permanently put out the lights on a lot of sleeping Germans without any losses to our own forces.

Success in hand, I rapidly disengaged my men and we continued toward the bridges. At least I hoped we were headed in the right direction, as we were still traveling somewhat blindly in the dark.

In the minutes ahead, the sky began to lighten as dawn approached. I broke out my flashlight and buried myself under my raincoat. Hidden this way, with just a modicum of natural light, I was finally able to check our position on my map.

What I discovered made my heart skip a beat. We were south and east of that little no-name hamlet. That meant our connecting file was gone. This was dangerous. *We were advancing without contact with the rest of the Company!*

I needed a moment to think and decided this might be a good place to stop for a short rest. We had been on the move for nearly twelve hours now.

13 JUNE 1944

That we had lost contact with the rest of the Company couldn't be helped. We were behind enemy lines, and we still had a job to do — *Get to those bridges.*

By 0700 we were up again and moving. I was determined to push my men until we reached our stated objective.

We continued to observe complete and total silence. I controlled my men's movements almost entirely with hand signals. Going was slow, though not as slow as it had been at night.

Each hedgerow represented a new danger, every hidden spot a possible German position. Each field — as well as the hedgerow beyond — had to be thoroughly scanned before risking an attempt to move out into the open and cross it.

Caution, caution, caution. Those were our watchwords.

In the dark we had moved in a tight group, fairly well bunched up. Each man followed closely behind the man in front of him so as to not get lost.

But, as the sky lightened, our tactic had to change. I decided to employ a skirmish line, with two squads in front, the third holding back. This way, the platoon was spread out. Any enemy resistance would not have a single concentration of men to fire upon.

My men understood my motives, even if they were cold and calculating. It was simple economics. The more spread out we were, the less chance an exploding mortar had of taking out the entire platoon. The fewer men that were taken out, the more men left alive to carry on the fight. We moved forward slowly and carefully.

About 0800 we came upon a small farmhouse with what appeared to be an upstairs loft. Two of my men spoke fluent French, so I kept them both at my side as we entered the house. An older French man and woman — probably husband and wife — stood inside the door. They held on to one another, obviously frightened. I couldn't blame them.

Who among us wouldn't be terrified if a contingent of foreign soldiers brandishing automatic weapons and drenched in mud, sweat, and blood entered their home?

Even if these people did recognize us as being American, even if they did recognize us as being allies in common cause to expel their Nazi occupiers, we were still fierce looking men — and we were still present in their home without invitation. That would scare me too.

I could see the fear in the old man's eyes. He and his wife were at once frightened and excited. We were liberators, yes. But we were also destroyers. Our armies were about to tear up their fields and their homes and their towns as we drove relentlessly toward the heart of Germany. In our wake we would leave behind stinking corpses and dead bodies for them to clean up after, as well as mountains of rubble and debris.

I turned to one of my translators. "Ask them if there are any Germans in the area?"

He did and they quietly whispered "Non."

But even as they answered, they pointed nervously toward the ceiling over their heads. We got their meaning and proceeded to immediately fire a clip apiece into the ceiling.

Plaster fell everywhere. At the sound of gunfire, the old woman began to scream. Her husband clamped his hand over her mouth to keep her quiet. I could imagine my own wife in the same situation. She would have fainted, I am sure.

At the corner of the room was a ladder-style stairway to the loft overhead. I poked my head up through the narrow opening, spied two German soldiers lying on the floor badly wounded and moaning. Our wild firing had hit them.

I climbed up through the opening in the floor, holding tight to my weapon. Several of my men followed. On a table in the corner of the loft we found a field phone. Now everything was clear.

This was an outpost. These men had probably seen us approach, undoubtedly warned others in the vicinity.

I instructed my men to pull up the phones and cut the wires outside. I had Doc, our aid man, shoot up the Germans with morphine and bandage their wounds. Then we were out the door and again on our way. — *But I was troubled.*

Despite our every effort, silence had most definitely now been broken. There was a remote chance that the sound of our guns being fired had been muffled because we were inside the house.

But that was a big maybe. Plus, those Germans had probably alerted their unit of our approach. Maybe, just maybe, if we moved fast enough, we might be okay. We crossed the next three fields at a run.

Once I felt we were out of immediate danger, I stopped my platoon in the shadow of the closest hedgerow to check my map and verify our position. We were almost to the Saint-Jean-de-Daye Road. It crossed the Vire-et-Taute Canal further along.

I didn't want to remain out in the open for long, so I decided to stay off the road and to confine our movements to the fields that ran parallel to it. The bridges were close. Probably only a couple hundred yards off. But we couldn't see them yet. Maybe if we crossed another field or two.

Because the Saint-Jean-de-Daye Road was as important to the Germans as it was to us, I knew we had to be extra careful now. It was the only major road either army could use to move their armor.

Binoculars in hand, I scrutinized every inch of the field ahead of us, as well as the hedgerow beyond it. No sign of the enemy. I signaled my men to climb over the hedgerow and to start across the field in the direction of the road.

But we only got about ten feet into that field when the Germans opened up on us with rifle and machine-gun fire. They had been well hidden behind that next hedgerow and I hadn't seen them. They had probably been alerted to our presence by their comrades when we knocked out the outpost in that farmhouse loft.

"Back! Back! Back!"

I shouted it urgently to my men and we beat a hasty retreat. Back over the hedgerow we had just crossed.

I was not at all happy with what had just taken place. I looked anxiously about, did a quick headcount. All the men in my command seemed none the worse for the wear. It was a close call, but none of us had been wounded or knocked down by enemy fire.

Now we responded in kind. We started firing back. I ran along the line of bushes shouting to my men, "Shoot only at what you can see!"

Soon we were in a full-blown fight. Within minutes, a couple of my men caught bullets. Doc, our aid man, sprang into action, quickly bandaged the two men. They took up positions again, beside the hedgerow.

But we had the same problem as before, the problem common to all Norman hedgerows — the bushes were tall and the vegetative growth on top blurred our sightlines. We were shooting blind. On the other hand, the overgrowth across the way was very sparse.

Our tactical position was simple enough. We were pinned down in a smaller field with larger and wider fields on each side of us. A flanking attack would almost certainly meet with stiff resistance. For the moment, the enemy was firing at us in great volume with machine guns and rifles. Thus far, no mortars had been flung our way. I thanked God for that one. He and I were talking quite a bit again.

To hold the Germans off, I moved B.A.R.'s to each flank, keeping one gun in the middle. These were Browning Automatic Rifles, and they were very effective guns. The Browning had a high muzzle velocity and was accurate out to about six hundred yards. Our Brownings were the newer models, the ones with a skid-footed bipod fitted to the muzzle end of the barrel, as well as a redesigned magazine guide. My B.A.R. men were crack shots. So was I.

The enemy continued to fire and we continued to return fire. With the B.A.R.'s in place, we were being more effective at knocking them down. Even so, several more of my men got hit, one badly.

The opening from the Saint-Jean-de-Daye Road into the field in front of us was at the middle of a long hedgerow across the way. Suddenly, four Germans swung open the gate and set up a machine gun right there in the opening. I was amazed. It was as if they were going through the motions of a parade ground exercise rather than lethal combat.

Right about then, my B.A.R. man in the center of our line got hit in the left upper arm. I saw him go down and grabbed for his gun. I had no problem taking out the four enemy machine-gunners busy setting up their gun at the opposite gate.

In the minutes ahead, we kept picking away at the enemy. The moment we would spot someone stick his head out or see a weapon protrude over the hedgerow, we would shoot.

About ten minutes later, another set of four Germans began to set up a second machine gun at the same spot, right smack in the middle of that opening.

I couldn't believe my eyes. I was still at the B.A.R. and I promptly dropped the four of them. I thought they must be nuts. *Why didn't they just set up the gun over top of the hedgerow?* I couldn't figure it out. They had now lost eight men in a stupid move.

It was at about this time that I decided we needed reinforcements. I'm not sure what made me come to that decision. Maybe I reasoned that any force that could withstand the loss of eight men in rapid succession without withdrawing had to be much larger than my own.

I called over my Staff Sergeant. Kazanza was a good man and I trusted him implicitly. Like me, his first name was Bill. I told Bill to work his way back and to the right.

"Find the rest of the Company," I said. "Find Singleton. Tell him what we're up against. Ask him for support."

Bill left as ordered. But I never saw the man again. Official records show Staff Sergeant William Kazanza as having died in combat that day. We didn't know it at the time, but the rest of our Company was fighting a losing battle some six hundred yards up the road to our right.

No sooner had Kazanza taken off, than there seemed to be a sudden, large increase in volume of fire from across the field. Jerry had brought two 40 mm anti-aircraft guns into position. The explosive rounds were now hitting the hedgerow, spraying us with small but deadly shrapnel.

I was still manning the Browning when I suddenly noticed that my men on the right flank had started to increase their rate of fire. The enemy was trying to sneak along the hedgerow, trying to outflank us on that side. So far, rifle and B.A.R. fire had them pinned down. To drive them back we tossed in a couple fragmentation grenades. That tore them up badly, knocking down perhaps eight of them at one time. The rest beat a hasty retreat.

By now, my bazooka men had only two rounds remaining. I knew we had to use them judiciously. I gave the men orders to aim for the location where the 40 mm rounds seemed to be coming from and then crossed my fingers.

My men fired one round. It hit the hedgerow near the top. A miss. *Damn!*

My men moved a little to one side to keep the Germans off-balance, then fired a second time. This time they aimed just a bit higher so that the round would clear the bushes. *Bingo!* The second round — our last round — exploded just beyond the hedgerow. That AA gun fell silent.

Now, yet a *third* enemy team set up a machine gun in that opening beside the Saint-Jean-de-Daye Road. *These guys must be absolutely crazy,* I thought, as I quickly dropped the four of them with my trusty B.A.R. They had now lost twelve men trying to set up just that one gun.

My original B.A.R. man was now bandaged and back in the line of fire. I gave him back his piece. He had replaced Leo Holden. I don't remember his name.

The volume of fire from across the field seemed to lessen, if only for a moment. Then, another machine gun started up, this time from over top the hedgerow. *They had finally gotten smart.*

Again the fire from my men on the right flank got heavier. The Germans were trying yet another sneak move along that hedgerow. This time they didn't get far at all. My third B.A.R. man had moved to where he could fire his Browning from the opening and spray bullets across the entire field. Three of my riflemen were there alongside him. The opening was only about twenty feet from the corner of the hedgerow.

I figured the Germans had only recently moved to their current position. They were probably called back from defense of the bridges and were therefore not well dug in at all. *This might work to our advantage,* I thought. Plus, the absence of mortar fire indicated they were likely a rifle company not a full infantry company. That meant they were armed with lots of machine guns and Schmeisser MP 40 automatic guns but no cannons. I had seen at least four machine guns so far, and a typical German infantry squad had at most two.

But then the situation changed drastically. We were suddenly under sustained fire from heavy cannon, my worst fear.

Based on what I could see through the bushes, the Jerrys had moved in two 88's, probably self-propelled. The big guns were positioned just behind the hedgerow. The 88 mm gun was a German anti-aircraft gun.

It was used widely throughout the war and could be found on just about every battlefield, where it was often used as an anti-tank weapon. This particular pair of guns was about two hundred yards out and firing instantaneous detonator shells, very dangerous stuff.

With this new weapon now in place, a murderous barrage began to run the length of the hedgerow as their fire systematically traversed our position from one end to the other. *The results were devastating.*

With nearly every explosion, now, my men were getting hit and hit hard. One of my two men who were fluent in French went down with a big hole in his leg. I went over, cut open his pants, tore open a packet of sulfa powder and sprinkled it over the man's wound. I bandaged him best I could and shot him full with morphine using the syrette in his bandage pack. Then I laid him back against the hedgerow.

I moved to the right and found my B.A.R. man dead from a wound to the head. His assistant now manned his gun. Everyone else was hunkered down. One of my Sergeants was dead. Another had half his right arm gone, plus a big, gaping wound in his abdomen. He, too, was dead.

There was a brief pause in the cannon fire. I glanced along the hedgerow counting heads. Some of the wounded were moaning in pain.

It looked as if I still had ten, perhaps as many as twelve men in line and still firing spasmodically.

But the firing was sporadic and accomplished little. The men fired only at what they could see, which wasn't much. Ammunition was low. So low, we were almost out of it. Whenever a man went down, we would take his ammunition, refill the B.A.R. magazines and distribute the rest. We had already fought for hours, stretching out what little remained.

From where I was situated, near the center of our position, I started left to check on my men on that side. I was in a crouch, running.

After about two steps, there was an explosion on top of the hedgerow beside me. Something that felt like a rod of hot steel rammed into my left leg just above the knee.

I knew I had been hit. But the sensation of pain was short-lived. A moment later I was lifted violently into the air. I guess I must have passed out before I hit the ground.

I don't know how much time passed before I came to, perhaps minutes, maybe only seconds. But, through a fog, I heard one of my men yell, "The Lieutenant's dead!"

Me, I was dazed, not dead. I raised myself half-up on my arms and answered his frenzied call.

"In a pig's fuckin' whistle, he is!"

But my bravado didn't match my condition. I was splayed out on the ground about ten or twelve feet from the base of the nearest hedgerow, lying in a pool of my own blood. The explosion must have flipped me through the air.

Pushing back now against the pain, I rolled onto my side. I dragged myself across the ground in the direction of the hedgerow using only my arms and hands. I was exhausted by the effort.

I cut open my pants leg where it hurt, and sprinkled the last of my sulfa powder into the wound. It cooled the fire of pain down a bit, but the damn thing still stung like hell.

I had no bandages left, nor any morphine. I had used the last of it minutes ago on another man. I thought to call our aid man, Doc, for help. But from where I lay, I could see that he too was dead. There would be no relief for my pain, nor any bandage for my wound.

My B.A.R. man was dead. He had been in the center of our line near where I lay. So I rolled over, picked up his piece, and propped myself against the hedgerow.

I was hurting badly but I wasn't yet defeated. I selected a few targets, managed to squeeze off a couple bursts. Our fire had dwindled to almost nothing. We were badly beaten down. It was over.

At about this moment, thirty plus Germans came pouring through the opening in the hedgerow to my right.

I yelled, "Cease Fire!" to my men and threw down the Browning in defeat. I raised my hands best I could and said, "Kamerad!" I was surrendering my command, what little was left of it.

My men followed suit. Those who could raise their hands did. We'd all been hit, every last one of us.

The German nearest me looked as mean as I looked scared. He raised his gun, pointed it at my head. But he did not fire.

Perhaps out of respect to my rank, the Germans carried me off the battlefield. My other men followed closely behind, but on foot.

We were taken to their aid station, which had been set up alongside the Saint-Jean-de-Daye Road at the opposite end of the field. As they carried me across that field, the field we had both been defending so vigorously, I counted the Germans who were down, either dead or wounded. I stopped counting at one hundred and twenty-seven. There were more.

I thought to myself how amazing that was. I had all of thirty-nine men with me. We had neither self-propelled cannons nor anti-aircraft guns. A few bazookas and that was it. — *And yet we had taken them down by a ratio of more than three to one!*

I felt good about that. I felt even better after the war, when I learned who we had fought that day: a heavily armed unit from the formidable 12th SS Panzer Division.

They say God fights on the side with the artillery. Not that day. Yes, we had lost that one battle. But in losing, we had won something just as important: our pride.

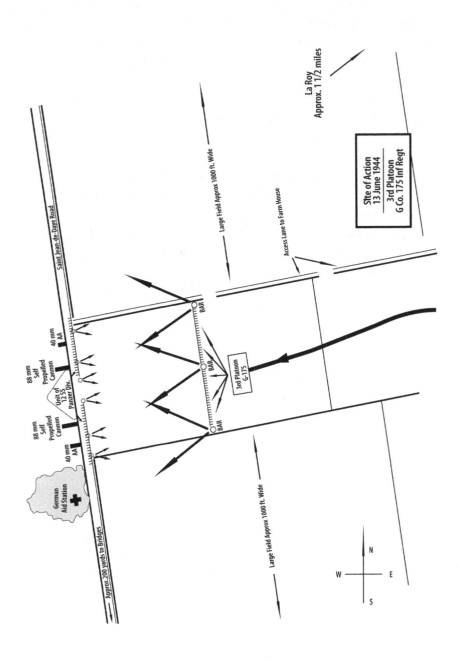

13 JUNE 1944

The German aid station was in a small wooded area next to the Saint-Jean-de-Daye Road. The medics immediately swooped in to tend to my wounds. But I raised my hand and said:

"Nein. Erste meine Soldaten." ("No. First my soldiers.")

That earned me a few raised eyebrows, though they did as I asked. Apparently, their Army operated on a different philosophy from my own.

While the medics were busy patching up one of my men, one of their junior officers cut down a tree branch and fashioned me a crude crutch.

But as far as medical care went, it wasn't much. All they did was wrap my wound with a bandage — and a lousy bandage at that. It wasn't really gauze at all, but some low-quality tissue paper more akin to crepe paper.

And you can forget about any painkillers or sulfa powder to prevent infection. This was the most rudimentary of medical care. I knew that unless I got to something more sophisticated soon, I would be in deep trouble.

On the other hand, it's not like I could complain. They didn't shoot me dead when they could have. I could take some solace in that.

The soldier, who was wrapping the bandage around my leg, looked up and said in broken English, "Fur you der var ist ofer, Herr Leutnant."

I nodded and gave the man a weak smile. "Ja, danke." I was thanking him for the bandage, not for telling me my war was over.

The makeshift crutch allowed me to stand propped up on one leg. The other leg hurt like hell. I offered the two aid men a cigarette from my next to last pack. They eagerly lit up.

Then I handed the rest of the pack to the soldier who had made my "crutch." They were not at all antagonistic. These guys seemed young. But they also seemed as if they had been in lots of other fights. Probably veterans of the Russian front.

The soldiers separated me from the rest of my men. Enlisted men were treated one way, officers another. A Duesenberg touring car drove up, and I was told to get in. It was a convertible, if you can believe that, with the top down. I was taken aback that such a fancy car should be sitting here in the middle of a war zone being used as a sort of pseudo-ambulance to transport wounded.

A German guard draped himself across the mudguard that covered the right front wheel. His rifle rested on the hood. It was pointed directly at my head. I sat in the seat next to the driver. We took off.

No sooner had I gotten comfortable than I began to feel woozy. Moments later, I went into shock. I felt cold, began to tremble all over. It was to be expected. A wounded man should never be transported head-up. The blood rushes from his brain and he passes out. I did.

The driver stopped the car, got out, took off his coat. He knew enough to wrap me up in it. From then on, until we arrived at wherever we were going, I was half out of it. One second I was awake, the next I was out.

Wherever turned out to be a fairly large farmhouse. The Germans had apparently commandeered the place as their Division Headquarters.

I was taken upstairs, given a towel, some warm water, a razor and a bit of soap. I guess they meant for me to wash and shave. They fed me some black bread and a small amount of cheese. I got to sleep in an actual bed that night, something I hadn't done in a good long while.

So ended my first day as a prisoner of war. My wounds had yet to be properly attended to.

14 JUNE 1944

In the morning, after they gave me a breakfast of weak coffee and some strange gruel, I was ushered into an interrogation room. Four German officers, all SS, were seated at a long table. They were seated according to rank — a Hauptmann (Captain), two Majors, and an Oberst (Colonel). At a separate smaller table to the side was an interpreter and a clerk, who took notes.

I stood in front of them and assumed — as best I could — the position of attention.

Then I said, "I am Lieutenant William Frodsham. My serial number is 0-1313234."

The Colonel spoke, in German. The interpreter translated, "You fought well."

I said nothing but nodded and thought: *Damn right we did. We cost you nearly a full Company before you got us.*

Then the questions started to fly. "What is your unit? Why were you so far into our lines?"

I did not tell them, but reminded them that according to the Geneva Convention all I was required to give them was my name, rank, and serial number, which I did again.

"William Frodsham. Lieutenant. 0-1313234."

"Are you a professional soldier?"

"No, I'm a student." (A lie.)

Then I made a mistake, a stupid one. I answered before the interpreter translated the question for me.

Immediately, the Colonel pounced. "So, you speak German?"

"A little. My mother's parents were German."

"Ah . . . . What was their name?"

"Schultz." (A lie. My grandmother's maiden name was Weiss, and my grandfather's was Brickner.)

"Where were they from?"

"Someplace in Baden, I think." (Not a lie. My grandfather was from Baden.)

Then came more questions. — *What unit was this? What type of soldiers were we? Why were we where we were? Where had we been? When and where did we come ashore?*

This kind of stuff went on for about twenty minutes. Always polite, always professional. But I evaded each and every question. Finally, they gave it up. I had told them exactly nothing.

Then they took me outside, and it was back in the Duesenberg. We exited the farmhouse lane onto the Saint-Jean-de-Daye Road and turned south. We drove quite a while, maybe twenty miles, then turned west.

Our destination was a holding camp at a place called La Chapelle sur Vire. There were other prisoners here, mostly Airborne. They had been taken at nearby battles, either at Sainte-Mère-Église or at Carentan. La Chapelle was apparently a collecting point for our sort.

(As a point of interest, many of these wounded captives were from Easy Company, the Army unit later made famous by the hit HBO miniseries "Band of Brothers" based on an earlier book of the same name by Stephen Ambrose.)

I walked amongst the prisoners, searched the throng for familiar faces. There were between sixty and eighty prisoners being held here, most of them paratroopers.

Then suddenly I spied the Colonel, my Regimental Commander. He had decided to accompany our unit after the botched river crossing two days back. The Colonel was a big guy, probably two hundred and forty pounds, hard to miss, even in a crowd. Stretched out on the ground beside him was Captain Singleton. I worked my way over in their direction, still heavily favoring my wounded leg.

The Colonel did not seem to be badly wounded. But I could not say the same for Captain Singleton. The Captain seemed to be in bad shape. The bullet that struck him had entered his body from the rear, on his right hip. The exit wound was on the front of his right thigh. He said the bullet had torn out a hunk of flesh from his leg the size of a tennis ball. Plus, he had a second wound. It was in his shoulder aside his clavicle. The bone was likely broken.

I sat with them, and we briefly talked. The three of us compared our experiences. But I could see that Singleton was not up to it. The man was in a very bad way. Pretty soon thereafter, he and the Colonel were led away. To where, I had no idea.

Soon the lot of us were walked over to an old monastery nearby on the property. I was getting more use out of that crutch than I would have liked.

Inside the monastery was nothing. Absolutely nothing. It was just a big, bare room. No beds, no dressers, no toilets, no chairs, no wash sinks. Nothing.

There were sixty or seventy of us stuck in that room. We lay down on the cold, stone floor. It was hard. My leg hurt like hell, and I was glad to be off it. *But this?* This was unconscionable. We each got a bowl of crappy soup and that was it. Good night.

So ended my second day as a prisoner of war.

21 JUNE 1944

We were held at the monastery in La Chapelle sur Vire for six days. It was not an easy nor pleasant six days.

The food was nearly nonexistent, mainly some kind of cold "soup." Hardly the sort of food a wounded man needed to help his body heal.

I don't know which I enjoyed more. The cow soup with a drop of horse blood mixed in? Or the horse soup seasoned with a little cow blood? The cow soup, I guess. Who could tell?

Bread was equally scarce. In the course of those six days I think we twice got one slice apiece.

There was no facility for washing or bathing. None of us smelled that good on Day One. Guess what we smelled like by Day Five?

At least there was a crapper. But it was an old crapper. Barely flushed. It was at one end of the building. It stunk pretty bad.

My last shower had been on 31 May, three weeks ago, the day before we loaded up the boats and set off for Normandy. Inbetween I had washed my face only once, at the farmhouse the SS commandeered for their Headquarters, the night before I was interrogated. So, right about then, I wasn't looking — or smelling — all that civilized.

Then, on the sixth day, 21 June, we were woken up at dawn and told we were moving out. Four old trucks, obviously of civilian origin, pulled up outside the monastery and we were loaded — or rather crammed — into them.

But we were crammed into them *standing* up, no seats. And they were open trucks, no tailgates, no canopy over top of us. Then we took off accompanied by a pair of small, German Army jeep-type vehicles

246

full of guards. I think they called these jeep-like things Kubelwagons. I learned later that the Kübelwagen was designed by Porsche and built by Volkswagen.

I hope you can appreciate how utterly dangerous a trip like this was. We were in enemy territory but close to the frontlines. The Allies were bombing everything in sight, including sometimes us. Me and God had a long talk about that one the first day.

I believe our initial destination after leaving the monastery was to be Alençon, a hundred miles to the southeast. But we only got as far as Bagnoles, barely two-thirds of the way, when the trucks pulled over to the side of the road.

Apparently, Bagnoles had something worth bombing, because we were quickly herded into an old barn. Minutes later, a six-box of medium bombers came overhead and dropped their eggs.

I couldn't see too much, so I don't know for sure. Either we were very near their target. Or their gun sights were not all that accurate.

One of their sticks came walking right toward us. The last bomb in the stick hit just short. One more bomb in that stick and it would have been curtains. The bomb would have hit the barn. We would have been dead, another victim of friendly fire. GOD was with us. I knew it. And I thanked him profusely.

A combat "box," by the way, was a tactical formation used by the United States Army Air Forces during World War II to organize and protect its heavy (strategic) bombers. Three groups of aircraft would fly together as a "combat wing." All three groups would be organized in the same triangular design — a leading bomber (or group of bombers) in the center, with two bombers (or groupings) immediately behind in a V-shape, one group at an altitude above and one group below, all in close proximity to one another for mutual defense.

The "six-box" formation consisted of forty aircraft, with the group divided into two units of twenty B-24s, one behind the other. Each unit consisted of three squadron boxes. Because the grouping was laterally wide, the six-box formation was not a compact formation. It was cumbersome to fly and frequently less efficient in its bombing accuracy.

That's how we almost got hit. A "stick" of bombs was a cluster of bombs dropped from an aircraft in quick succession in order to spread them out over a target area. Accuracy be damned.

Like I said, our prisoner group amounted to some sixty-plus men, mostly paratroopers. Their attitudes were poor, and that near miss in the barn didn't help. Emotionally, some of them were very down. They were suffering mightily from the ignominy of having been captured.

I quickly got fed up with their constant bitching. So I propped myself up on that rudimentary crutch of mine and chewed them out but good. For about five minutes I let them have it. My theme was simple: YOU ARE THE CREAM OF THE ARMY. ACT LIKE IT. ALL YOU SHOULD BE THINKING ABOUT IS HOW TO ESCAPE. FROM THE MOMENT YOU GET UP IN THE MORNING, UNTIL THE VERY MOMENT YOU FALL ASLEEP AT NIGHT. FIGURE OUT HOW TO ESCAPE. NOW STRAIGHTEN UP!!!

They showed signs of buying it. Yes, the Germans had us now. But some of us would figure out how to slip away, that was for sure.

Our trucks were not the greatest. Nor were they marked in any particular way. So far, during our single day of travel, we had been strafed three times by Allied aircraft. That is why we only made it as far as Bagnoles.

Late that night, we moved out again. A few hours later — morning now on the twenty-second — we arrived in Alençon.

And yet, our trip wasn't over. They dropped us beside the road and pointed. We still had a six-mile walk ahead of us to the camp.

I'm not sure how, but somehow I made it. My leg was still killing me, and I was generally weak. That crutch, as well as my arms, were getting quite the workout.

Night travel was better. During the day, each time an airplane approached, it had been out of the truck, into the ditch, head down and pray, bullets flying everywhere.

God was certainly with us every step of the way. I don't know how many times those old trucks were struck by .50 calibre strafing bullets.

But somehow, the trucks kept running and none of us were hurt, not one.

At the POW camp in Alençon, we were greeted by the senior Allied officer being held, a Canadian by the name of Captain Phillips. We got a hot meal — our first since being captured — soup plus a slab of bread. And we slept on a cot, also a first. A straw mattress and two blankets, both clean.

The next day I was finally able to wash up, yet one more in a series of firsts. When I did, I found that I had two other wounds, both slight, where small fragments of shrapnel had penetrated my clothes and hit me in the right shin and left ankle. I probably did not feel them, as the greater wound, just above my left knee, was nearer my brain and took precedent.

An opportunity to wash up also meant an opportunity to shave. While still in England, I had placed a double-edged razor blade in my wallet. The Germans had never searched me and I still had it. What I lacked was a razor to hold it. No matter. I used it that way, slowly and carefully, like one might a straight razor. It wasn't easy, and it took me like two hours. I left myself a moustache, already well grown in. But at least I felt civilized. At last.

7 JULY 1944

We were held at Alençon for seventeen days. On the seventh of July, a truckload of prisoners — all officers — departed Alençon for points further east. It was the same as before. Ride awhile then into a ditch when somebody saw a plane wing over to make a strafing run at us.

"Flieger! Flieger!" They would yell. Then it was off the truck, into the ditch, hunker down and pray to God once again.

As we pressed deeper into France, away from the frontlines and away from actual combat, fewer and fewer Allied planes went after us. We breathed a sigh of relief. It was a curious metamorphosis, as our former comrades-in-arms now posed the greatest danger to our lives. Now, when we heard the unmistakable "coffee grinder" beat of a German plane's motors, we would say, "It's okay. It's a friendly."

We finally arrived at Chalons-sur-Marne, over three hundred miles from Alençon and on the far side of Paris. Here, we were delivered to a new gulag, a Processing and Interrogation Camp.

The food was little better at Chalons than it had been at Alençon. There was a daily ration of bread, as well as the standard ersatz coffee and soup made from whatever moldy greens happened to be available. The amount we got each day was small, and I was already losing weight.

The trip to Chalons had taken us through Chartres. Had it not been wartime, and had I not been a prisoner of that war, I might have stopped for the day. Chartres is home to one of the most beautiful cathedrals in the world. We did not see it. Our truck plowed right through the center of the city without stopping.

I was sitting on the truck bed, on the right side of the truck, when we reached the city-center. There were a lot of people in the streets of Chartres, both soldiers and civilians. We prisoners were a sort of public spectacle, like slaves paraded through the Forum in ancient Rome. The people were yelling and gesticulating at us all along the way.

Suddenly, out of nowhere, one fanatical young soldier reached up and rapped me across the skull with a stick grenade, what we called a "potato masher." For a moment, I saw stars.

At the front, where we first encountered the enemy, our adversaries had been real professionals. They would shoot us dead in battle, yes. But they did not exhibit hate, not of a personal nature.

These townspeople were different. These rear-area troops, still far from combat, were all pumped up, adrenaline boiling. I thought — *Wait 'til they get shot at a few times . . . . Then we'll see what passes for bravery . . . .*

A potato masher, by the way, was the standard hand grenade of the German Army throughout both World Wars. It had a very distinctive appearance — explosive head on top, pull cord inside, hollow throwing handle twelve inches long.

That distinctive shape is what led to its being called a "stick grenade" or a "potato masher," in British Army slang. Even today, it is one of the most easily recognizable infantry weapons of the twentieth century. The stick provided a lever, significantly improving the throwing distance. But that stick did something else, almost as important. It nearly eliminated the risk of the grenade rolling back downhill towards the thrower when used in urban areas or hilly terrain.

Brilliant design. But hard on the head. I still had a headache an hour later from that whack on the noggin. And a nasty bruise to match.

On the way to Chalons, we also passed through Versailles, just south and west of Paris. This piece of history we actually got to see, the beautiful Palace of Versailles. Our truck had to pull off the road directly across from the Palace, so that a convoy of German troops and equipment might pass. Thus, for about ten minutes, we had a perfect view of that beautiful building and the surrounding grounds.

On the evening of 11 July, I was placed in solitary confinement. I'm not sure what I did to deserve this. Except for one small window, the four walls of my confinement cell were completely lined with Celotex, a sort of insulating composition board. The only furniture in the room was a tiny wood-frame bed with a straw mattress and blanket, a three-legged stool, and a bucket for a toilet.

Each day, long about noon, an Interrogator who spoke perfect English would come strutting into my cell. He would bring with him a little table and chair, sit down and have his lunch.

It was always the same. A series of questions. A series of taunts. He would snack on jelly and crackers, smoke half a dozen cigarettes, sip his hot tea.

Over and over he would tell me. If only I would answer his questions, I could enjoy the very same things he was enjoying. Tasty jelly, hot tea, a good cigarette.

This little routine of his was performed day after day. A series of questions. A series of taunts. Oh, I would talk to the man alright. But not about the things he wanted to talk about. I told him nothing of the war or of our Army.

The man thought he was softening me up with all his sweet talk. But he was not. He was making me harder and more determined.

Because of the Celotex lining, the room was very quiet, eerily so. The only noise I ever heard came through the window. I was able to observe the almost nightly air raids. The bombs were getting close, some as close as a mere two hundred yards away. That bucked up my spirits.

Aside from the daily visits of the Spook, the only other time I saw anyone was when a guard brought me my food. I got three squares a day, just like at home.

Sorry. Now I'm being sarcastic. My meals consisted of a cup of ersatz coffee and a bowl of gruel at dawn, a lunch of some kind of soup, and a slab of black bread for supper. That's it.

Oh, and I also got regular exercise each day. I was allowed to empty my waste bucket. For this, the guard would escort me to a latrine at the opposite end of the building where I could dump out the contents of my waste can. Such fun.

The rest of the time, I played with my flies. *Is that pathetic, or what?* Originally, there were four of them. Their food was some crumbs that fell to the floor when I ate my bread. I would try to catch them on the fly. But I would take care not to crush them in my hand. Then my fun would be over. Once caught, I would release the little buggers for another time. During my stay in that room, I "lost" only one.

Actually, I had several forms of entertainment. I would count the number of nail heads in the Celotex walls. There were 496 of them. The counting was something that had to be done systematically. I didn't want to be interrupted, or else I would have to start all over.

Then I could always read the Bible. It got regular use. I had a copy of the New Testament in my shirt pocket when I arrived. They let me keep it.

These three things — counting nail heads, catching flies, and reading the Scriptures — kept me from going bonkers. Oh, and watching the air raids. Taken together, these mind-numbing activities strengthened my resolve and reinforced my ability to remain strong when the Spook came in every day to harass me.

Now, about that "ersatz coffee." I've mentioned it several times already, without really telling you what it is. Ersatz coffee, or just plain "ersatz." The synonyms run from lifeless to bogus to imitation to poor-excuse-for. In other words, very watered down. At least compared to what I was used to drinking back home.

Home? Yes. There, I said it. Home. I had suppressed all thoughts of home until this very moment. No use to think about it. No *time* to think about it. Home might as well be on the far side of the moon. I wasn't getting there any sooner.

But of course now, between catching flies and counting nail heads, I did think of home. Then I quickly would file it away in the footlocker marked "DO NOT OPEN UNTIL AFTER THE WAR."

Finally, on 17 July, after six days of bloody hell, I was released from solitary confinement. But I was not returned to my former pool of inmates. Upon release, I was placed with a different group of captive officers. These men had all endured varying lengths of solitary, as I had.

On 19 July we were marched as a group five or six miles to a rail marshalling yard. Here we were loaded onto boxcars, like cattle. These boxcars were of the 40/8 variety and had been in use since at least the First World War. The boxcars were rated that way, as the Army deemed them capable of carrying either forty soldiers at a time or else eight horses. We had about that many prisoners onboard each car.

Once again we had luxury accommodations. No furniture, no chairs, no beds, no mattresses, no blankets. A small window on each side at opposite ends of the car, about five feet up from the floor. One crap bucket for the lot of us. It went unemptied the entire trip.

I positioned myself at one of those two windows, both for ventilation and for view. It was a position I was willing to fight for, if necessary.

24 JULY 1944

Our trip by rail took us five nights. Much of that time was spent sitting in rail yards, not moving. We traveled mostly at night.

Consider, if you will, our living conditions. It was summer, the hottest part of the summer, warm even in Northern Europe. We were housed in an unventilated boxcar. Little food, not much water, no way to clean ourselves, only a bucket to poop in. Forty of us, none of whom were in high spirits.

We traveled mostly at night because daytime travel was dangerous. Allied fighter-bombers were in the air almost constantly. Daytime movement would bring the aircraft down to strafe us, sometimes drop their bombs. Hell, I couldn't blame the pilots. We could just as easily have been enemy soldiers onboard those boxcars as prisoners of war.

In those five days, we traveled all of two hundred miles, not much if you think about it. We didn't follow the most direct route. Allied bombing runs had knocked whole sections of track out of service.

As before, when we were traveling by truck, we were given little to eat, usually just some bread and water. We were all getting progressively weaker. Not good.

On 24 July, at night, we arrived in Germany. Limburg an der Lahn, to be exact. Limburg is an industrial town that lies some twenty-five miles due east of the much larger and more important city of Koblenz. Koblenz lies on the Rhine River, a major artery flowing through the heart of Europe. The Lahn River as well as the Mosel River join the Rhine just below the city.

We disembarked our train in a switching yard near the Lahn River in Limburg. From there we marched uphill to a prisoner-of-war camp located just outside town. This was our new home — STAMMLAGER XII-A, or STALAG XII-A, for short.

After our miserable days locked in those boxcars, it was good to get out and stretch our legs. But what came next was even better — delousing.

At XII-A the first thing they had us do is go through the "entlausen." Here we got a shower and some slimy green soap to wash our bodies with. Our clothes were taken away and baked in some kind of oven to kill lice. I was issued a pair of OD (olive drab) pants as well as a British officer's shirt. Where they got them, I had no idea. But odds were, these clothes were formerly the property of a now-dead soldier. I didn't want to think about that. I was clean, and I felt almost like a new man.

Now came time to be officially registered as a prisoner of the Third Reich. Each of us were issued our Prisoner Serial Number. I became KRIEGSGEFANGEN Number 80810. That long German word literally means "war captured."

Each man's serial number was stamped on a dog tag that we had to wear on a length of rope around our neck. The dog tag was square with several slits cut across it. The idea was that it could be broken in two if you died. One half would stay with the body, the other would go to their "Graves Registration Unit." I don't know what they called that unit in German. I had no intention of increasing their flow of business.

After the delousing, we also had a chance to attend *Sick Call*. With nearly everyone suffering from acute diarrhea, that was a busy place for quite a long while.

Food improved some. In addition to the standard, small German ration of ersatz for breakfast, we also had a bowl of soup for lunch and another for dinner. Surprise! Now our soup had color. It was made from cabbage or collard or other kinds of greens, sometimes used-up sugar beets, very occasionally some boiled potatoes.

But one thing we missed was salt. There was no salt whatsoever in our soup or on our greens. Anyone who has ever tried to eat collard greens without at least some salt sprinkled on can appreciate its taste. The stuff adhered to our teeth, leaving behind a thick film of gunk that later had to be physically scraped off.

Each day, along with our bread ration (one slab one-inch thick) we were given a small amount of oleomargarine. At least that's what they told us it was. This glop had the consistency of cold cream, and tasted just as good.

Occasionally some jam was issued along with our bread. Twice that I can remember. We usually got this around noon.

While at STALAG XII-A, we received three Red Cross parcels, two Canadian, one British. These were a godsend, and I picked up some much needed strength from them. My weight loss was getting worse. Each parcel had four packs of cigarettes, which were also very welcome. I've already told you of my fondness for tobacco.

The second Sunday we were there, a group of us decided that some sort of religious service would be in order. Like many of the men, we felt indebted to God, that we had to somehow thank God for sparing our lives. I, myself, had had enough close calls with bombs, bullets, and strafing runs to convince me that the Lord had been watching out for me personally. I didn't exactly know why He was protecting me. But He was. I intended to show my appreciation.

I still carried with me my government-issue, pocket-sized edition of the New Testament. I knew it well, having read it several times cover to cover. We had no chapel, so our service — whatever else it turned out to be — would have to be held out-of-doors. Nor did we have a Chaplain. One of us would have to step forward to play that role. I was elected, this from a pool of some thirty officers ranking anywhere from 2nd Lieutenant right on up to Major.

It was overcast the day of our service, but not raining. We had no text or hymnal book or source of music. So any singing we did would have to be a cappella.

The service was very simple. We opened with the childhood hymn "Jesus Loves Me, This I Know." Then, after singing the hymn, "Reverend" Frodsham delivered a short sermon based on the faith expressed in the Twenty-Third Psalm, which we recited in unison.

That part about walking through the valley of the shadow of death held much meaning for me. *I will fear no evil, for thou art with me, thy rod and thy staff, they comfort me . . . .*

Then together we recited The Lord's Prayer. *Our Father, which art in Heaven, hallowed be thy name. Thy kingdom come, thy will be done .
. . .*

After a moment of silent prayer, we closed our service with a verse from the hymn "Rock of Ages." Most of us remembered enough of the words that it went pretty well. Thus ended our first group worship since first being taken prisoner.

With as much violence and hatred in our midst, let me only say this about my fellow soldiers. Within the Army's infantry units were those men whose battlefield lives were the most miserable, the very toughest soldiers, the soldiers whose job it was to kill, maim, and destroy. It is just those men who, in their ordinary lives, were often the most gentle, most considerate, most moved by feelings of sympathy for others. Certainly they were the most reverend people I ever knew.

Within a few days after that service, our lives changed again. Once more we were to be moved. I guessed without knowing that it might be to an "Officers Only" Camp.

As a general rule, stalags were operated by the Germans as prisoner-of-war camps for non-commissioned personnel only. Officers were generally held in separate camps called an Offizierslager, or Oflag for short.

Perhaps that is where they were sending us. We did not know.

10 AUGUST 1944

After two-and-a-half weeks of imprisonment at STALAG XII-A, it was back into the forty-and-eights boxcars again, destination unknown.

The train pulled out during the night and we spent several days moving slowly from rail yard to rail yard. I'm quite certain Berlin was among them.

The slow progress, punctuated with numerous layovers, was largely because ours was a low priority car. It was a cold fact that anything moving by rail or by truck was subject to air attack. As we got deeper into Germany, the number of such raids sharply dwindled until they eventually stopped. But that didn't mean we would move with any greater speed. Troops and supplies going out of Germany by rail ranked higher on the pecking order of importance than prisoners of war coming in. So we sat.

But, for me, there was an upside. Because I had once again taken command of one of the two windows, I got to see a lot of Germany. In some ways, I was impressed.

From what I could see, Germany was clean and very neat. When I say it was neat, what I mean is that the grass alongside the roads was cut neatly. The roads, as well as the streets and boulevards, were clean. No garbage anywhere. And, of course, there was no traffic, not a car.

In high school, back in Hackensack, my German teacher was a very nice lady, German-born but a U.S. citizen. I remembered her once telling the class that she was born and raised in Giessen, a university town in central Germany. Well, lo and behold, one day our train came over a rise and there, spread out in and along a beautiful, shallow valley was the town of Giessen. If I ever did get back home, at least I could tell my former teacher I had passed through the city where she was born.

The larger rail yards were not so neat. Or so clean. We could look out that window and see lots of bomb damage here and there, practically everywhere. Our bombers had been busy.

Days later — I don't know how many — our boxcar carrying thirty officer prisoners finally arrived at our destination deep in the heart of Poland. This was a small town that originally went by the name of Szubin. But, with typical German efficiency, the Jerrys had deemed it necessary to rename the town to one better of their liking — Altburgund. The prison camp we were going to was a couple miles outside of town. We were hungry and getting weaker.

By this time I was no longer using my crutch. It wasn't that I didn't need it. It was that pride had kicked in. I wasn't going to be seen as a cripple in the eyes of my captors — or my comrades. I had discarded the thing back at Limburg after our delousing.

Now they marched us from the rail yard out to the camp. It was quite a long distance and without my crutch I limped a great deal.

Also at Limburg I had liberated a spoon along with a table knife. The knife was actually a good one, with steel running all the way through the handle. Surprisingly, the guards never took it away from me. Machine guns and muscled guards trump table knives and starving prisoners, I guess.

The camp was OFLAG 64, short for OFFIZIERLAGER 64. When I saw the name I realized I had been right. The Germans actually did separate their noncom prisoners from their officer prisoners. Maybe this meant better food.

OFLAG 64 was perhaps the only POW Camp in all of Germany that had been established to exclusively hold American ground forces captured in Europe. Other camps housed prisoners from multiple nationalities. Having that common denominator of us all being American may have contributed to a certain esprit de corps. I don't know.

OFLAG 64 was built on the grounds of a Polish boys' school by adding a fence and several barracks. We were searched thoroughly upon arrival — though, like I said, I got to keep my knife and spoon. Then we were registered, both with the Red Cross and with the German prisoner-of-war department. From there we were assigned barracks. We were fed, handed a pack of cigarettes, told to bathe (cold water only) and ordered to bed.

So endeth Day One as a valued guest of OFLAG 64.

•

•

The next day we were marched into town where we had our pictures taken. These photographs were to become part of our camp ID cards. As each man's turn came to have his picture taken, they handed us an olive-drab enlisted man's tunic to put on over whatever else we were wearing at the time.

When we returned to camp, my first order of business was to become better acquainted with my cubicle mates. Each barracks was subdivided into several rooms or cubicles, and each cubicle had a small table as well as a number of three-legged stools, one for each occupant.

In my cubicle, there was Roger Whitehall, a native of Port Arthur, Texas. He and I first met in "Starvation Manor" at La Chapelle in Normandy. That is what we called the monastery where we were held for six days with nothing but cold soup to eat. Roger had been in the Army since before the war. His service included the Alaska Defense Command, 3rd Infantry Division, 36th Infantry Division, 27th Infantry Division, and, finally, the 82nd Airborne Division. The man started as an enlisted man, went to OCS and became an officer.

Then there was Steve J. Kochy, from New York City. Sidney "Sid" I. Frederickson, from Roseburg, Oregon. Don O. Graul, from somewhere in the Midwest (Detroit, I think). Don M. Chappel, from Buffalo or Rochester, New York.

That made for six of us. A cubicle was laid out for eight. We were two short at the start, so our daily bread ration was three-quarters of a loaf of ersatz black bread. Actually, this stuff was gray in color.

I use "ersatz" here and throughout the text as a pejorative because it absolutely was. *Ersatzbrot* was replacement bread. It was given to the POW's and much of the local population. But it was bread made from the lowest grade flour or sometimes potato starch and it was frequently mixed with extenders. Here I'm talking about things like sawdust or other things I don't want to think about.

Our group of eight was rounded out about two weeks later with the arrival of two new men, Tom Barclay of Charlotte, North Carolina, and Tom Pinkerton from New Jersey. Accordingly, our daily bread ration was increased to a full loaf. Germans kept careful count of everything. One-eighth of a loaf of bread per man per day, and not a crumb more.

Barclay was a newspaperman. Pinkerton, I don't remember what he did prewar. I do remember, however, that he was married to the daughter of the head of the Standard Oil Company, now known as ExxonMobil. Tom Pinkerton was a Captain in the Cavalry. His armored troop had been Eisenhower's personal guard all through North Africa. Like Tom Barclay, he had been captured in the invasion of southern France.

Now, back to the events of Day Two:

Even before my cubicle reached its full complement of eight, I set about trying to learn how the camp was run. The inmates — that is, the prisoners — had developed a small "country" behind these fences. As in any small country, there was a national currency. Actually, there were two, an "official" currency set by our captors in special Reichmarks issued by the German government, as well as a camp currency where the rate of exchange was in numbers of cigarettes.

We never used the official currency except to transact "official" business — printing the camp newspaper, printing theatre programs, purchasing supplies for the construction of theatre sets for our various stage plays, etc. The printing was done by a printer in town named Willi Krick.

In our new "country," we called ourselves Kriegies, on account of that long German word I gave you earlier: KRIEGSGEFANGEN, or "war captured." It was a term of endearment and pride among the men.

Any small country has its leadership, as well as the bureaucracy that actually runs the place. Our country was no different. Rather than explain it all, let me refer you to the Appendix at the back of the book. Our small country had a newspaper, *The Oflag 64 Item*. It was written in a breezy, chatty manner, typically four to six pages in length. Take a look at it. The January 1, 1945 issue contains an overview of how the camp was set up. Read it.

•

•

As you can see, our camp was organized by departments. We had an entire kitchen staff, a library with some seven thousand volumes, a medical service, a tailor shop to repair worn or torn uniforms, a church, a parcel store with tobacco and the like, a barbershop, a bookbinding operation to keep our many volumes readable, the Altburgund Academy school to advance our education, a large and active theatre group, a mail delivery service, a vegetable garden. Like I said: an entire small country.

Each of these departments was manned by volunteers, men who would work without pay in a pursuit or activity that interested him. Whether one participated in these various activities or endeavors was a matter of individual choice. Many times the available work slots were filled. Then you were put on a waiting list. Overwork was not a problem. Fighting boredom was.

In a typical stalag, where the prisoners were enlisted servicemen, the prisoners had more outlets to relieve their boredom than we did. In those camps, the Germans would organize what they called "work commandos." Men assigned to commandos were permitted (under guard) to leave their stalag to perform physical labor, usually on farms but sometimes on road repair or similar projects. Some men actually lived on those farms full-time and were trusted by the Germans not to run away or organize some form of resistance.

But officers were not eligible for such work, nor could they leave their camp under any circumstances. I'm not sure whether the Germans didn't trust us, or whether they simply feared us. Were we (in their eyes) too smart to be trusted? Either way the result was the same — we had to work damn hard not to get bored.

The leadership of our little country was strictly military and strictly by the book. The senior officer in camp was the Commander. Aside from his personal staff, the rest of us were organized according to a standard staff setup, same as you would find in a typical regiment, but without the enlisted men.

When I arrived in camp along with my group from Limburg, the camp population surged above five hundred, all officers. The first of these men had arrived long ago, at least a year, when they were captured in Tunisia, probably around the same time the U.S. took the Afrika Korps prisoners I met a year earlier at Fort Leonard Wood. And the total prisoner population kept on rising with each advance the American Army made. By mid-January 1945, the count exceeded fourteen or fifteen hundred.

The one thing you will not find any mention of in any issue of *The Oflag 64 Item* is the Camp Bird. The "Bird" was Kriegie code to describe the camp's secret radio receiver. It was smuggled into OFLAG 64 piece by piece over many, many months. Some parts were traded for, with the camp's guards. Some were stolen. Its assembly certainly predated my arrival.

Part and parcel with the radio receiver was a manual generator, powered by a hand crank. Pure genius. Electrical usage was closely monitored by our hosts. We couldn't exactly plug the darn thing into a wall socket. The hand-crank generator was also built by Kriegies in a machine shop they set up.

Unknown to the Goons, the Bird operators regularly listened in on BBC broadcasts coming out of England. After each broadcast, two men from the Bird operation would go from barrack to barrack to bring each building up to speed as to the progress of the war.

To avoid detection we used the simplest of methods. One man — our lookout — would choose a spot where he could view the grounds. Should one or more Goons approach the barracks where a briefing was taking place, that man would move to another location. Spotters inside the barracks would keep that man in sight. His movement was the signal: end of briefing. The gathered men would disperse. When the coast was again clear, the briefing would resume.

Each barrack had a large map mounted on the wall. On it was plotted the latest situation as announced over the camp loudspeaker system by way of German radio broadcasts or actual announcements by camp Goons. Each briefing by Bird operators was held in front of the map so that we could see and judge the *actual* situation. It goes without saying that we would only plot the German version of things on the official map. But their version was always well behind the facts, and more often than not, filled with lies and distortions.

17 AUGUST 1944

By my third morning in OFLAG 64 I began to learn the camp routine. We had to follow orders, of course. But our job was not to make Jerry's life any easier than we had to.

The morning began with *Roll Call.* We fell out in the camp's sportsplatz, where we lined up in six ranks. We never did this quickly or professionally. — This was by intent. We would goof up the process by doubling up in some ranks and leaving other files empty, thus making an exact count hard to come by. If someone did manage to escape during the night, this might be one way to hide their absence. Plus, nothing seemed to delight us Kriegies more than watching the Germans squirm as they tried their darndest not to get upset.

Once we were finally lined up, the German Commandant would take center stage to deliver us the nearly daily announcements. After that, we were free to go about our business. Some went to their jobs. Others did nothing.

Red Cross parcels were stored in a central warehouse building completely under prisoner control. Kriegies saw to their storage and distribution. The most recent shipment had arrived in camp the day before my group arrived from Limburg. I received my first parcel on that third morning.

I had lost a lot of weight since first being captured, and I was still very hungry. The temptation to scarf it all down in one sitting was almost irresistible. I tore my parcel open and dug into it.

A typical Red Cross parcel contained cheese, meat, and a host of other goodies. Here is a complete list of its contents, best as I can remember them:

eight-ounce package of American cheese
sixteen-ounce tin of oleomargarine
four, two-ounce D-ration chocolate bars (nasty tasting)
six-ounce tin of jam
two-ounce tin of soluble coffee
twelve-ounce tin of pork lunchmeat
twelve-ounce tin of corned beef
four-ounce tin of salmon
sixteen-ounce box of dried prunes
six-ounce package of Army K-2 dried biscuits
eight-ounce package of sugar
six-ounce can of liver paste
sixteen-ounce can of powdered milk
one package of ascorbic acid tablets
two bars of soap
five packs of cigarettes

Even when hunger stares a man in the face, your average Kriegie has his favorites and his not-so-favorites. We set up an Exchange Store where trades could take place. It did a brisk business whenever new parcels were distributed in camp. In place of currency, prices were set using a unit of relative value, the smallest denomination being one cigarette.

Although the Exchange Store provided a measure of value, many prisoners chose to bargain directly with their fellow Kriegies and to try and arrive at a mutually acceptable deal. Some men were better at this than others. Some men became "wealthy" as a result.

Even starving hungry, even with that first Red Cross parcel torn open and in my hand, I resisted the temptation to eat it all at once. I could see that things might soon be getting better for me.

Red Cross parcels were issued to the men weekly, even though current supplies were somewhat depleted. Still, another shipment was said to be on its way. With our Air Force going after everything that moved, even Red Cross supplies were sometimes delayed.

Now, with a little food in my stomach and a cigarette in my mouth, I continued my exploration of the camp. I began back at the sportsplatz where we had assembled this morning.

I could see right away where I might want to make frequent use of this place. My legs were weak and I needed to strengthen them. I used to play semi-pro ball, run Track & Field as a boy, ice-skate in winter and box in summer. Now I had been locked up for days on end inside a dust-filled boxcar. So I was ready to run. And run I did. Sometimes as much as three hours a day.

Before long I made an acquaintance of another runner, Captain Ed Berlinski. He was from Bloomfield, New Jersey. We were practically neighbors. Bloomfield lay no more than ten miles from Hackensack, where I grew up.

Back in the world, Ed had been a high school history teacher as well as head coach. I actually knew the man, and I told him so.

Berlinski had quarterbacked for North Carolina University. I even recalled the game with Boston College where he had taken a kickoff on the four-yard line and run the ball all the way back for a touchdown.

Officially, he had run back ninety-six yards. But, in all his scampering back and forth around the field like a pursued rabbit, it had probably been more like three hundred. That I knew this about him made us instant friends. Soon we were punting a football back and forth together.

Aside from the sportsplatz, I found that the camp had devoted a fairly large-sized plot of ground to a truck garden. I called it a "truck" garden, by the way, because that's what we called it back at home, any garden small enough to need but a single pickup truck to transport the crops to market.

As it was summer — late summer, at that — the garden was very mature. Whatever produce the garden yielded was taken directly to our kitchen, where it was combined with the meager daily German rations for the benefit of all us Kriegies.

But, of course, with summer winding down, the garden would soon be producing less and less. Within a few weeks we were down to where our weekly Red Cross parcels were the only source of calories we could depend on to supplement the daily German food ration. Food remained our main topic of conversation, ahead of sex, the war, or even escape.

During this time I was sharpening and reshaping the knife I had acquired earlier. I was transforming it from a round-tipped table knife into a more serious thing, with a pointed blade. I used a nice round smooth rock I picked up in the compound yard as a whetstone. Within a matter of days, the knife had become razor sharp.

Because the knife was so sharp, and apparently because I was good at using it, my cubicle mates appointed me bread "czar" and tasked me with the responsibility for dividing each day's bread ration equally. This was a weighty responsibility. With food so scarce, any perceived disparity could become a source of disagreement, something we all wanted to avoid. I accepted the appointment.

My cubicle mates followed my lead on something else as well. I had this huck towel. Each day, after cutting our loaf of bread, I had a habit of laying out my huck towel like a tiny tablecloth, either on the table or on my three-legged stool. Then I would proceed to neatly arrange my tin plate and cup — both of which I had fashioned from containers in the Red Cross parcels — so that I might enjoy, in civilized fashion, whatever little food was available.

This ritual seemed to make a mark on several of my cubicle mates. They soon did the same. Indeed, after the war, one of my mates mentioned this habit of mine to my father. This particular man got back home before I did, and he looked my father up. He told Dad that my mealtime sacrament had been profoundly inspiring to him.

A huck towel, by the way, is a small cotton towel with a honeycomb texture, very absorbent, often used in surgical settings, which is where I got mine, from the hospital.

After dinner, such that it was, I would clean my little table setting. Somewhere down the line, I had persuaded a fellow Kriegie to give me a musette bag. Now I used it to store my place setting until the next meal.

A touch of civilization. But one I needed.

AUTUMN 1944

In September we held our Track & Field meet, my kind of competition.

Each barracks entered a team. My barracks finished seventh overall. I did the high jump and took second. The guy who beat me was a West Point man and a collegiate champion at that. My left leg, the leg in which I'd taken two pieces of shrapnel, was my "takeoff" leg. Even so, I was able to high jump six feet, three-and-one-half inches. Pretty damn good. *My legs were back!*

Escape was always on our mind. I soon realized that a procedure — unwritten but strict — existed for such endeavors. If a Kriegie thought he had worked out an escape plan, he was required to submit the plan to the Escape Board for consideration. If the plan had merit and was accepted by the Board as feasible, it might be approved for action. But it would be the Board, not the Kriegie, who would implement the plan. The plan originator might not even be included.

One escape plan included a tunnel. Work had been underway for a while. Then, in October, an opportunity of a different sort presented itself. I thought it was a rather well thought-out plan. It included the use of decoys and look-alikes.

The Germans had taken our senior officer to observe the site of the Katyn Forest Massacre. Twenty thousand Polish Army officers had been systematically gunned down by the Soviets at this site and buried. Nazi Germany announced the discovery of the mass graves in 1943, contending that Stalin's secret police had been the perpetrators of the massacre.

The revelation led to the end of diplomatic relations between Moscow and the London-based Polish government-in-exile, a diplomatic nightmare as the two were supposed to be "allies." For the Germans, it was a propaganda triumph. They would take our senior officer to the site. He could help the Allies separate wheat from chaff.

But such a visit so far from camp also presented an opportunity for escape. *Perhaps our senior officer could shake himself loose from the delegation?* If so, he might be able work his way to Switzerland, where he might be interned and thus able to relate his story to our Embassy people.

The escape came off without a hitch. But the Colonel was picked up again within four hours, his decoys within half a day. Now there was a price to be paid for our audacity.

As punishment for this transgression, the Germans cut off our water supply. They did this whenever we misbehaved. For the next five days, not a drop of water was to be had by anyone in camp, not for drinking, not for bathing, not for cooking. As summer had passed, there wasn't even dew on the grass that we might collect as a last desperate source of moisture. Nothing.

Well, if you know anything about survival in the wild, you know a man can die in as little as three days without water. We made it five. Mouths and tongues became so dry, conversation ceased. When the water did finally come back on again, I drank at least a gallon in one sitting, as did just about every other man in camp.

But if you think that punishment broke our spirit, think again. It did not. During those five days, with nothing else to do, I took my knife and did a little surgery on my field jacket. Back in May, before the invasion, I had sewn a small, silk map of France into the jacket beneath the lining. Now I removed it, folded it, and placed it in my pocket to be used as a handkerchief. Another tiny little bit of civilization in a world gone mad.

No sooner did the water come back on than we ran into another crisis. Our reserve of Red Cross parcels stored in the warehouse began to run low. As the Allies intensified their attacks on the industrial heart of Europe, movement by rail movement became ever more difficult. Shipments did not arrive as scheduled.

Many of the men had diligently built up reserves from previous weekly parcels, just to cover such an exigency. But I hadn't been there long enough to build up much, nor had I benefited much from the summertime "harvest."

Stretching what little I did have did not make up for the utter lack of food. In the end, I had to rely on the meager German ration. Everybody was losing weight. My weight, which had been a trim one hundred and ninety-five pounds when I landed in Normandy, reached a low of one hundred and thirty-eight by 15 October. I was so thin and run down, it took me nearly ten minutes to rise from a prone position and remain standing without blacking out.

Now, to conserve calories, all physical activity was severely curtailed. *And it wasn't even winter yet!*

Food, as a topic of conversation, reigned supreme. In my barracks there were two doctors, both Captains, both paratroops, both from Oklahoma. It was their opinion that our periods of near-starvation would ultimately work to our benefit. They insisted that our extremely low calorie intake would ultimately have the effect of lengthening our lives by five to ten years.

I don't know if they were kidding us to make us feel good about our plight, or if they were serious, but recent scientific research has borne them out as being correct. Nevertheless, near-total deprivation coupled with unrelenting boredom left much to be desired.

With physical activities cut to a minimum, indoor activities became king. Cards, checkers, chess, you name it. I took up chess.

Among the population of Kriegies were some Free French. Two of them were avid chess players, and I soon became quite friendly with both.

One carried the regally sounding name of Louis Saint-Sauveur. We nicknamed him Frenchy. Frenchy was from Algeria and always seemed to be in good humor. The other man, Yves Poussier, also from Algeria, was the son of an important man loyal to the Free French government. I don't know all the politics, but both men considered themselves under the command of General Charles de Gaulle.

Yves was a crackerjack chess player, and he taught me well. I think I beat him once. Others, I beat often. Yves was a young man, slightly built, with blond hair. He possessed a gentlemanly attitude and a pleasing personality, always full of fun. Our many chess games helped relieve the incessant boredom.

Aside from chess, there was one other diversion — theatre. Now I have to tell you. Theatre isn't my thing. Or should I say, acting isn't my thing. I loved to watch the performances though, and so I thoroughly enjoyed what our little theatre group managed to put together.

How they did it, I'll never know. But sometime before the first snowfall, our little theatre group managed to put on a play, and a good one at that. The Man Who Came To Dinner. It ran for three days to a sell-out crowd. No sooner was it done than they went about preparing for their next presentation, an original musical to be entitled Full Swing.

EARLY WINTER 1944

In late November, near Thanksgiving, a large shipment of Red Cross parcels arrived. We had been without parcels for more than six weeks, now, and everybody promptly "pigged out" on their contents. It wasn't exactly Thanksgiving dinner, but close enough. At least bellies were full. This hadn't been the case for a very long time.

At about the same time a new senior officer arrived in camp. Actually, for me, it was my old senior officer, my former Regimental Commander, who was captured, same as me, in the 13 June action and who I had last seen back at La Chapelle sur Vire with Captain Singleton. He did not stay in our camp long. About a month later, he was taken away by the Germans and sent to Stalag VII-A at Moosburg in southern Bavaria.

Stalag VII-A was a very large camp, with some thirty-seven thousand American prisoners. From what I could learn, during my Regimental Commander's short stay at OFLAG 64, he thoroughly annoyed the Germans. And how did he accomplish this, you may ask? By playing his bagpipes day and night. He had petitioned to secure them under the Geneva Convention. But once the Germans let him have those noisemakers, he drove the Jerrys crazy with the sound. *Bully for him*, I thought.

In the first part of December, our little theatre group put on a show with two short one-act plays — Pot Luck and In The Zone. Meanwhile, outside, the weather got ever colder.

All our barracks were built entirely of brick. This was a good thing. They weren't drafty. But our supplies of coal and lumber were dwindling fast. Much of our lumber went to shoring up the walls and ceiling of our escape tunnel.

Work on the escape tunnel, which had been going on for more than one year, now slowed to a standstill. This was not strictly on account of the cold weather. We had a different problem. The dirt being dug out of the ground was of a different color than the dirt lying on the surface. Rather than risk spreading out the odd-colored dirt over the compound, where it might be discovered, it was packed into empty Red Cross parcel boxes and stacked in the attics of each building, between the ceiling joists and the roof.

Of course the Germans were not fools. Every so often they would circle the runs outside the barbed wire fences and blow up dynamite sticks every six feet or so to collapse any tunnels being dug underneath the fences. So far, they had not been successful in destroying ours. Our tunnel stretched for some one hundred eighty feet beneath the compound from the warehouse where we stored our Red Cross parcels. It would soon be used for a breakout.

At night, with it being so cold, we slept under covers wearing all of our clothes. Like many others, I was issued an Italian Army overcoat to help keep me warm. It was light blue in color and made of wool. But it was of a type weave that offered little resistance against the wind, perfect for winter in Sicily perhaps, but not northern Poland. When I wore my field jacket beneath it, the two together made the cold almost bearable.

Our only water was cold water. This was nothing new. There never had been any such thing as hot water. What little we heated for our coffee was heated over tiny burners we fashioned from tins in our Red Cross parcels. So we spent lots of time in our sacks trying to keep warm.

When Christmas arrived, we had a "special" meal. It was concocted with much ceremony from the contents of various Red Cross parcels. A "menu" was printed by our friend in town, good ole Willi Kricks. It was Christmas for the Germans too, so they somehow arranged for an extra shipment of potatoes.

The menu advertised an item cited as "Turkey Hash a là Schubin," which was actually just a slab of spam dressed up a bit. Someone in the kitchen had a sense of humor.

EARLY JANUARY 1945

As we went into January the cold intensified. New Year's Day was a non-event. Meanwhile, the Soviet Army continued their advance westward across Poland from the east. This worried our captors a lot. The Soviets, their enemy, were pressing ever nearer OFLAG 64. Mid-month, the Germans decided that rather than risk our liberation by the Russians, they would march us further to the west ahead of the advancing troops. Remember: It is January. It is bitter cold outside.

The warehouse was emptied of all its contents and everything that had been stored inside there was distributed among us Kriegies. That meant everything — food, supplies, books, bandages, everything. Suddenly, my musette bag was quite full, as was everyone else's. Some of it I would eat, some might be used later on for barter — soap, chocolate, cigarettes, that kind of thing. The Germans split us into two columns, though at the time I wasn't sure why.

The columns left camp separately and we never saw the other group again. I found out later, after I returned home, that this second group of men was in fact "liberated" by the Russians.

But I use that term loosely. In point of fact, these men actually became hostages of a sort. The Soviets wanted to hold American POW's captive until all Soviet POW's being held in German camps that were presently behind Allied lines were repatriated.

As I understand it, these men were taken to Moscow, then down the Volga River to the Caspian and finally to the Black Sea where they were transported by ship to American control. Part of this was a propaganda move. The Soviets wanted to "showcase" these American prisoners before their very own people. This is how my cubicle mate, who I told you about earlier, made it home to see my father before I did.

Actually, there was yet a third group of prisoners who never left camp in either column. Some medical personnel and patients were necessarily left behind, perhaps one hundred and fifty men in all. Plus, there were a few men who temporarily hid out in our escape tunnel. Finally, some two hundred men escaped from our marching column and returned to camp voluntarily. All these many hundred men were likewise held hostage by the Soviets for a time and suffered mightily at their hands.

I'm not certain of the exact date, but about 20 January 1945, the Germans marched most of us out of camp just ahead of the advancing Russian Army. Every man capable of walking walked. The word in camp was that the Russians were within twenty-three miles at the time. Our group numbered perhaps twelve hundred in all.

To begin the march we formed up into platoons of roughly fifty men each. It was blistering cold with a stiff wind. That first day, we pushed about ten miles almost due north. We crossed the Bromberg-Poznan Canal, then stopped on the heights overlooking the canal. They put us up at a large farm. We bedded down wherever we could find shelter from the cold wind. There were more than a thousand of us. I secured a spot next to the barn with about ten other guys. We huddled together like children to try and stay warm.

During the night, we learned from the farmer who owned the place that one of his mares was having a difficult time foaling. Two of the guys I was huddling with had experience with horses, so we three went into the barn to try and help the man. My part of the ordeal was to hold down the mare's head so she would remain calm and wouldn't try to get up. In the end, I actually had to sit on the poor girl's head to get the job done.

The foal was in the wrong position and couldn't be birthed. While I held the mare's head down, the other two fellows massaged her and attempted to manually shift the foal into proper position for delivery. After about an hour of hard work, they met with success. The foal shifted, then emerged from the womb just as it should. The farmer was beside himself with joy.

Now we were friends. The farmer quietly let us know that, if we wanted, he would hide us under the floorboards of his farmhouse until the column had moved on. The three of us couldn't believe our good fortune.

Without making a fuss, we gathered our stuff and slipped surreptitiously into the man's house. He pulled up a couple heavy planks from the floor as if he had done this before and beckoned us in. We slipped under the floorboards and he just as quietly replaced the planks. As tired as we were, we three promptly fell asleep.

I think it was the best night's sleep I'd gotten in a month. The three of us slept so soundly, we didn't even hear the column pick up stakes and move on. The farmer didn't disturb us until two o'clock that afternoon. We were still asleep when he lifted the planks and suggested we come up. We stepped outside and the sun was shining brightly, a glorious blue-sky winter day!

It was great. *We were free!* All we had to do now was head east and wait for our Russian allies to take us under their protection. *Hooray!*

We thanked the farmer on his front porch. We started around the corner of the building and ran right smack into a German patrol that had been left behind to pick up stragglers like us. *Damn! Double-damn!* (I used stronger words at the time.)

The German patrol wasn't kidding around. They made us move fast. We caught up with the main column in a matter of hours.

•

•

The second day we again covered about ten miles. The Goons put us up that night inside a quadrangle formed by a house, a barn, an equipment building, and a hayloft at one of the bigger state farms. To keep warm, we were allowed to build fires.

Someone — I'm not sure who — killed one of the farmer's pigs then proceeded to roast the thing over one or more of the fires. It smelled delicious, and my mouth flowed with saliva. But the closest I ever got to that roasted pig was its smell. I never got to eat any. The next morning the farmer was understandably livid with rage.

Warmed by the fires, many of us crawled into the loft and slept, warm and comfortable in the hay. In the morning, after the regular formation for counting heads, the count came up short. Some guys were missing. The Goons began to fire machine pistols into the hay, and sure enough, out came the missing men.

LATE JANUARY 1945

The day dawned overcast and threatening. There was a light snow on the ground when we woke up. The temperature outside was below zero. No matter. We moved.

The column continued pressing west. By now a heavy snow was falling. Soon we were slogging through half a foot of the stuff.

We weren't dressed for this weather. Nor were we taking in enough calories to march hour after hour in the cold. Our shoes became thoroughly wet. The snow would melt on them. Then our feet would become very cold. Before long, melted snow had refrozen over our wet shoes making them very slippery.

But, on the plus side, the icy crust around and on top of our shoes was actually somewhat of an insulator, a thin barrier against the cold. At least I thought so at the time. Maybe my feet were just becoming frostbitten, I don't know. I'm told frostbite feels "warm" as the skin starts to tingle before it dies. So long as we kept moving, it felt okay.

We covered about eight miles that day, and they again put us up at a large farm quadrangle. I had long ago lost my bearings, so I can't tell you where we were.

Fires were once again permitted, and we did our best to dry our socks and shoes. They had issued us tubs of oleomargarine when we left OFLAG 64. But rather than eating it all, I rubbed some of it into my now-dried shoes and socks. The fat might repel the water and keep me drier the next day.

That night I decided not to sleep in the hay. Something about the experience bothered me. When I would burrow down in the stuff, I would suddenly have this feeling of weightlessness, this feeling of not knowing which way was up. Give me hard ground to sleep on any day.

So that night I slept in the livestock barn, odors notwithstanding. First lesson of barn sleeping — Do not sleep with the horses. They are restless and roll around a lot. Cows are a better bet. They are warm and remain in one position until morning. They smell a little, that is true. But, boy, do those beasts throw off a lot of body heat!

The next day we were at it again, marching. This new road took us in a more northwesterly direction. The snow had stopped, and we moved out of it.

Now there was something new. *We must be nearing a town*, I thought. The road was crowded with refugees. They were fleeing the approaching Soviets. I guessed these people were either German or pro-German and had much to fear. They were all carrying something or else pulling some sort of conveyance piled high with personal belongings. But no horses or mechanized equipment. Just terrified refugees fleeing for their lives. And we had to walk among them. Not pretty.

With so many refugees jamming the roads, our progress was agonizingly slow. At one place, where we were stopped by some sort of jam-up, I stepped down into a roadside ditch to empty my bowels. Not five feet from me was a nice looking young woman doing the same.

We exchanged some pleasantries in German as we each did our thing. Nobody paid us any attention. It was a normal bodily function that had to be performed. Besides, she was only concerned with getting away from the Russians, same as us. Ships that pass in the night.

That afternoon we veered off to the right at a Y-junction in the road, moving more north now than west, and leaving the refugees behind. As darkness began to fall, we came upon a small town. The guards brought the column to a halt in the town square. This is where we were to spend the night.

No fires were permitted, nor was there any obvious shelter. It was very cold. So we hugged up close to the buildings in small groups, hoping to huddle and keep each other warm. This was quite miserable. The barns of the previous two nights were luxury resorts by comparison. I missed my cow.

The people of the town would not open their doors to us. But a few did. I was one of the lucky ones. I was permitted into a home where the people wore a friendly face and gave me some warm milk to drink.

We talked. At least we tried to talk. We used a combination of gestures and smatterings of German to communicate. I became the beneficiary of a large hunk of cheese, nearly a full loaf of black bread, plus a good-sized hunk of roast meat to boot.

I had not seen white bread since England, and even that had been graham bread not white. But I certainly wasn't complaining. This unexpected windfall made up for not having had a taste of that roast pig two nights back.

I put all that they had given me into my musette bag and thanked my lucky stars. In return, I gave them three bars of white soap, one pack of cigarettes and a chocolate bar, all originally from one of those Red Cross parcels we doled out when the Jerrys made us leave the Oflag. I would not soon forget that family's generosity.

After a cold night huddled against buildings outdoors, the Germans rounded us up. We moved on, but not before they checked each house to make sure none of us "accidentally" stayed behind.

After making another ten miles, we came upon a second town. It was a little larger than the first, but not by much. They stopped us beside an old abandoned brewery, where we were able to bed down for the night.

Please understand, when I say bed down, I don't mean in beds. But at least it wasn't outdoors, where we were exposed to the elements. Any relief from the winds was welcome. Plus, as we crowded into the various rooms, closets and alcoves, our combined body heat made quite a difference.

Next door to the brewery was some sort of official German headquarters. Cars, motorcycles, and bicycle messengers came and went almost constantly while we were there. I spotted a bicycle leaning against a post off to one side. I couldn't believe my eyes. Strapped to the handlebars was a small calibre automatic pistol.

I didn't even think. I lifted the holster flap, quickly removed the gun, and closed the holster back down again. *Now I had a gun!* Sweet as you please, I slipped back into the brewery and melted into the sea of Kriegies.

During the night, as I slept, one of the other officers, whose name I would rather forget, tried to remove from my musette bag some of the food that sweet family had given me the night before.

I sensed his presence and drew my knife, placing it firmly against his neck. Then I told the fellow in no uncertain terms that what he was doing was a sure-fire way to get himself killed.

I studied the man's face. He was little more than a kid. He had arrived at OFLAG 64 only days before the camp was dismantled and we pulled out. Green. *Hell, I probably had more time in the latrine than he had in the Army.*

I told the kid he should never steal from a man, not ever. He might have better luck asking.

So he did. He asked. He begged, with tears in his eyes. I felt pity for the man and gave him a tiny slice of bread, a nibble of cheese, and a small square of meat. I cut it all with my knife, so he would be sure to see how sharp it was. Sad.

The next morning we were given some bread and a cup of hot, ersatz coffee. This was a daily routine. Somehow or other, they managed to do it every day. We never got any real food, though. Hot ersatz coffee each morning. A little bread. That was it. The rest we had to scrounge on our own.

The next two days were uneventful. We slogged along. But never fast. Our guards were old. I'm guessing most were more than sixty years of age. Like us, they were getting more and more tired. Some were so weak they asked prisoners to carry their guns for them. The war was lost, and all they wanted was for it to be over so they could go home.

Finally, after many days of walking, we reached a large German training camp outside the city of Stargard. We were still inside Poland, but just barely. I would estimate we covered by foot somewhere in the neighborhood of one hundred and fifty miles in our long trek, maybe more. The German training camp was huge, but apparently no longer in use.

Here the column was halted. The Goons processed us one at a time in an adjoining field. They set up a number of small tables. Standing behind each table was a soldier. Our orders were to empty our pockets and our bags on the table, then register our name and our Kriegsgefangen number with the soldier standing behind it.

Ooops. This presented me with a bit of a problem. No way was I going to pass inspection with an automatic pistol in my bag. So I did the only sensible thing. I threw it away. There was a patch of tall grass beside the road and I tossed it in among the grass and weeds. *Damn it anyway! That thing might have come in handy.*

Soon it was my turn to be inspected. I emptied my pockets as ordered, as well as my musette bag. My silk map of France was folded like a handkerchief. It fell out on the table. The soldier ignored it, along with everything else. All he seemed to care about was my wallet. In it I had a couple of pictures. He turned each one over in turn to see if it was stamped properly. Approved pictures had to carry the stamp GEPRUFT OFLAG 64 on the backside. Mine did. "Gepruft" translates roughly to checked or approved.

While he did his little inspection, I stood with my hands in my pants pockets and half a smile on my face, like I was getting away with something.

All of a sudden, a German officer standing nearby started screaming at me.

"Nehmen sie die hände aus den taschen!"

I looked at him as if I did not understand what he was saying. He was yelling at me to remove my hands from my pockets. The more I stared dumbly at him, doing nothing, the louder he screamed.

"Nehmen sie die hände aus den taschen!"

Now one of their interpreters stepped over and translated. "Take your hands from the pockets!"

Of course, now my fun was over, and I did what I was told. But that contemptuous smile never left my face.

After everyone's meager belongings had been inspected and returned to us, they formed us back up into a column and marched us into the camp. It may have been February by now. I had lost all track of time.

We were housed in barracks. Not as nice as at OFLAG 64, but buildings nonetheless. There were cots but no mattresses. Nor were there blankets. The buildings were not heated. But the water was on and the toilets worked. That was a blessing. That evening we got a bread issue plus some hot soup. I called it mystery soup, as I had not a clue what was in it, perhaps some soggy pieces of potato.

We were only here overnight. The next morning we got hot ersatz coffee. After roll call, to take the daily count, we were marched to the railhead and loaded once more into those lousy, old forty-and-eights boxcars. We were once again going somewhere by rail.

We remained at the railhead until dusk. Once the sun set, the train pulled out of the yard. As before, we would travel only by night to avoid air attack.

Our trip lasted for more than two nights. During the daylight hours, we were kept in the cars while the train sat in some rail siding or yard. One of these sidings was near Berlin. There was no food or water for the entire trip.

Some hours into the third night, we stopped. This time we disembarked and were formed up into a sort of line. They marched us a few miles and we passed through the small German resort town of Luckenwalde. We were now some fifty miles south of Berlin.

Outside of town we passed a small lake with many cottages dotting its shore and straight into a POW camp.

This must be the place, I thought. Our new home.

FEBRUARY & MARCH 1945

The camp was Stalag III-A.

We were registered and assigned to barracks. These quarters were a little roomier than what we had lived in at OFLAG 64. Plus, the population of prisoners at this location was much more international. There were several barracks of British officers, several more of Polish officers, at least one or two of Norwegian officers and some French. The Germans were apparently gathering all of us in one place so that we would not fall into Russian hands, although more ominous rumors were circulating.

This was a large place. From my barracks, I could see across a large, unused sportsplatz. Beyond it was more barracks. From the guards we came to learn that there were several thousand more American GIs being held across the way. But we'd never know for sure, as a series of barbed wire fences prevented access to the sportsplatz or the compound beyond.

On a positive note, now that we were once again situated, we went back on regular German rations. But it wasn't much, and hunger continued to be a major facet of our lives. We were there at least ten days before so much as a Red Cross parcel reached our mouths. The Goons had apparently diverted a shipment intended for another camp to us.

In many ways, we reverted to the same type of existence we had left behind at OFLAG 64, but without a lot of our prior creature comforts or diversions. Our movements were much more restricted. Many of the luxuries we had previously enjoyed, like the "ITEM," like our theatre program, like our library — all gone. Conversation still revolved around the old subjects — hunger, the life back home, our next shower. In a word: our life became that much more miserable.

With a more international population of prisoners, we soon learned that not all Kriegies were treated the same. The Norwegians, for instance, had a somewhat different "arrangement" with their German captors than we Americans did. They received frequent parcels from home, far more than we ever did. They could also go home on "leave," giving their parole and later returning. The Germans even provided them with roundtrip travel. *What a deal.*

Don't get me wrong. Those "Norskis" were all nice guys. Every week or so they would cook up a great fish stew which was built around "fiskboller" sent from home. This fiskboller stuff was sort of like an American fish stick, only round. It translated roughly as "fish ball." I don't know what was in it. But the stuff was delicious, and they would always share it with us.

The Poles had long since organized a singing group from certain of their number. They performed for the other officer prisoners on more than one occasion, and I was privileged to be present for one of their performances.

Their singing was a cappella, and the music was beautiful. Through a series of traditional folk songs, the music told of the many years of suffering the Polish people had endured. Listening to the men sing, you could feel the misery. Haunting, at times. Even now, after all the many years that have gone by, it still runs through my mind. I shiver and want to cry.

By some miracle, the guys involved with the "Bird" operation had somehow managed to smuggle the radio and the hand-cranked generator past the inspection at Stargard. We were once again able to keep up with the progress of the war. I was once again able to keep better track of time.

Our internal structure, as I described it to you before, was still very much intact. A few cigarettes placed in the proper hands bought an opportunity for several officer details to get over to the enlisted men's compound. After several visits, a complete roster of men had been compiled and a number of provisional units organized.

This organizational effort began to unfold in late February. By mid-March, it was complete. As units were organized, the command structure was filled and officers assigned. If and when the stalag fell, we didn't want the enlisted men doing anything rash like storming the gates or scattering into the countryside.

We were confident the Russian Army would arrive any day now, and we intended to be ready for whatever came to pass. Along with many other young officers, I was temporarily placed in an unassigned officer's pool. I felt left out, but this soon would change.

Long about the same time, we learned of yet a third compound. It lay about a mile to the west of us and contained some fifteen thousand Russian soldiers taken prisoner by the Germans.

Each day, at dawn, large groups of these Russian soldiers were made to march out of their camp and set to work repairing rail lines, bridges, roads, and the like. That is how we learned of them.

After dark each day, these soldiers returned to their holding facility. Let me tell you. The Germans treated these men very badly. They received little food, even less than we did. Plus, their barracks were a wreck. Cement floors, which were always under water. No sanitation. Practically no furniture.

In addition to being systematically starved to death, the Russian prisoners were forced labor, working hard for hours on end. We heard that about fifty of them died each day.

Criminal.

12 APRIL 1945

When President Roosevelt died on 12 April and Truman took the helm, we knew about it almost immediately. Or rather, we knew about it the moment the BBC broadcast the news over the wireless.

We were shocked. Most of us said, "Who the hell is Truman?" We had been so busy concentrating on the war and on staying alive, few of us had kept up with politics. Hell, practically none of us Kriegies had even voted in the last election. That had been six months ago. *Who cares about politics when you're wondering where your next meal is going to come from?*

When the "official" news was given to us by the Germans, we exhibited little surprise, mostly remorse. Practically everyone already knew.

At about the same time, a rumor began to circulate. The word was that the German Commandant of our camp had been ordered to send us all to the gas chamber, rather than to allow the Russians the satisfaction of liberating us alive. This was normally done in the "entlausen" facility, substituting gas for water.

But the German CO was a gentleman of the old school. He was a Colonel, a Luftwaffe officer with service dating back to the First World War. He flatly refused.

Still, our existence was meager. Things continued as before — hunger, boredom, yearning for home. Our news link kept us informed. The Russian advance had slowed. They were amassing troops along the Oder River. But the river was at flood stage and they couldn't move forward, which is to say, in our direction.

The Oder River runs north and south through central Europe. It begins in the Czech Republic, flows through western Poland and, on present-day maps, defines part of the border between that country and Germany. The river passes some thirty-five miles east of Berlin. Our stalag was south and somewhat west of the city.

I knew a little something about crossing a river under fire, as I had undergone such an ordeal with my platoon back in France. Crossing a river under fire is bad enough. But trying to cross a *flooded* river under fire is a much more difficult thing. River banks are ill-defined and treacherous at flood stage, currents uncertain. To get armor across such a body of water would require a great deal of preparation. *But how much?* We didn't have much time. Survival was on our minds.

In the other direction, the Americans and the British were only about forty miles from Berlin. They had crossed the River Elbe and seemed to be headed our way. *Certainly they would be in Berlin any day now.*

Our reasoning made sense, even if it was wrong. Unbeknownst to us, Eisenhower would ultimately halt the Allied advance and leave Berlin to the Russians. Had we known the truth, it might have crushed our spirits.

Finally, beginning at dawn on 15 April, a strong, low-pitched rumble rolled in from the east. It sounded like an approaching line of thunderstorms. Only it did not stop. Instead, it grew louder and closer. It was the Russian advance. That evening, the Bird picked up the news from the BBC. The Russians were advancing on a front more than two hundred and forty miles long.

On the afternoon of 16 April, two fighters swooped down upon us from the sky and strafed the camp. Everybody scrambled for cover. Our compound took some hits. Bullets penetrated our barracks. But no one was injured.

Sounds from a ferocious battle were getting closer. It was our general opinion that the Germans would not fight over us. Right after the strafing, our guards all disappeared. *Now was our chance!*

Immediately, organized groups of officers began to make their way through the barbed wire, past the sportsplatz, and over to the enlisted men's compound. The idea was to take command of the men and to maintain order. The internal structure that had been so painstakingly put in place beforehand was now made fully operational.

By the next morning we were in charge of our own camp. Movement between the two compounds was uninhibited. A sharp eye was kept in case of another air attack. It was 17 April.

Not far beyond our gates there was all kinds of activity. A major firefight was building up just south and east of the stalag. The senior officers convened and agreed it would be smart to send out several patrols to try and make contact with the Russians. One of my former cubicle mates from OFLAG 64, a Captain, suggested I lead one of the patrols. I was not thrilled by the idea. But it's not like I could exactly up and disobey orders. I was, after all, cleared for duty and one of many in the unassigned officer pool.

They assigned me three Sergeants and the four of us set out to try and make contact. There was definitely some risk associated with this undertaking. We had no weapons and our uniforms were sketchy. I was wearing a Serbian hat, an Italian Army coat, a Royal Canadian Air Force tunic, and a British Army officer's shirt.

Fortunately, though, I had a small American flag sewn on the right shoulder of my field jacket. If we did make contact, that flag might just keep us alive. Maybe they would see the flag and quickly identify us as Americans.

We worked our way to the left, around the big fight. Then we moved cross-country scouting for Russians. We tried to stay out in the open, where we could be easily seen.

As we came out of a small wooded area and started across a field, five Russian armored scout cars came along the road on the far side of that same field. They spotted us immediately and wheeled left in our direction. I told the others to stop and to remain perfectly still. It was scary. *Would they shoot us first and ask questions later?*

I raised my hands above my head, instructed my Sergeants to do the same. Our breath was coming faster now.

"Americanski! Americanski!"

I shouted it, loud as I could. That was the nearest I could come to a word they might understand. "Americanski!"

The armored cars drew closer, guns raised. But they held their fire. The cars circled up around us. We remained motionless, arms still over our heads. We tried to communicate.

They and we took turns trying. English. French. Finally a cross between German and English. They seemed to understand what we were saying. We were from a nearby camp. We were American.

They wanted to know if any Russian prisoners were there at the same camp. I told them fifteen thousand. Their jaws dropped. Now the four of us crammed into two of their cars and off we went. They were taking us to their Command Post.

At the Russian Command Post, we were quickly interrogated by English speaking officers. The one who questioned me was a woman, Major Irina Nikolayena (I'm not sure of the spelling, but it is close). She was a big one, about six feet tall and must have weighed two hundred and twenty pounds, about fifty percent more than my present weight.

Within minutes, it seemed, we were on our way back to the stalag. We were no longer on foot. I was riding on the lead tank pointing the way, the others following close behind on two other tanks.

Contact was made with our senior Allied officer. My three Sergeants and I were held on to by the Russians and taken to a different Command Post where we were interrogated again, this time in much greater detail.

Again the interrogator was a woman, this time a Major. She was gracious, handed each of us a glass of brandy. This woman knew her stuff. She spoke six languages fluently.

That brandy might as well have been a sedative. Take a badly undernourished body, douse it with just the tiniest bit of alcohol and Bingo! — you're out cold. I fell asleep mid-question. How long I was out is anybody's guess. But I woke up still seated in the same chair.

By then the questioning was over, and it was back to Stalag III-A. I was walking to my barracks just as a small herd of horses was driven into the compound by the Russians. Four truckloads of potatoes were dumped in our compound as well. This was the Russians bringing us food.

The horses were killed and butchered, and a good-sized detail set to work peeling potatoes. *Hooray! We were going to eat!* That night we had a meal. Meat and potatoes, all cooked with congealed blood. Delicious.

THE ROAD TO WAR

The next morning started with a serving of ersatz coffee. Then we fell out into a formation of our Provisional Companies. We marched the short distance over to the Russian compound where we took our place beside a Company of Russian troops and listened to Marshall Ivan Stepanovich Konev deliver an impassioned tribute (in Russian) to the Russian POW's. I did not understand a single word. But I caught the drift. I later learned this man was widely renowned for his brutality against the Germans in combat. I don't know if any of that is true. Standing there, free at last, I was sure happy to see the man, no matter what war crimes he may or may not have committed.

When we returned to the compound after the speech, we found countless German women gathered around the gates. They were begging for American soldiers to come with them to their homes, come home, share their beds, stay with them.

Their plea was simple if disquieting . . . . better one American soldier each night now, than six or seven or more Russians later on. This was an unfortunate fact of war. Voluntary submission was better than gang rape.

Plus, it seemed that as soon as an American serviceman moved in with a German woman, the Russians would bypass her house. It didn't hurt that Americans were very highly regarded by most Russian soldiers.

These frontline Russians were hell-bent-for-leather type of men. Tough soldiers, well disciplined and orderly. In our presence, they generally treated civilians well. But these frontline soldiers would say to us, "We are okay. Those who follow are beasts." Thus the desperate pleas voiced by the German women.

The unit I had first made contact with now set up their Headquarters in Luckenwalde just outside the camp gates. I was able to determine that this was a recon unit attached to the Sixth Ukrainian Guards Rifle Division. It was commanded by Major General Georgi Vasilievich Ivanov.

Here I visited again with Major Irina Nikolayena and got another glass full of brandy. This time I did not drink it quite so quickly.

19 APRIL 1945

Again, because I was in a pool of unassigned officers, I was up for special duty. The next day, 19 April, I accompanied the unit commanded by the woman Major fluent in so many languages, and we moved north toward Berlin.

I knew they were serious about my participation, when they handed me a helmet and an automatic pistol. It wasn't much — maybe 7 mm. But it was the first weapon I had handled in a while.

I rode up front in one of their armored scout cars. It was a little larger than our American Jeep and had a turret at the rear with a machine-gun swivel mounted on top of it. I was impressed. This contraption — I'm not sure what they called it — was a great little assault vehicle, armored all the way around. It carried three men plus a driver.

As an American officer, I more or less became assistant commander of a small contingent of six such cars. Maybe that's an overstatement. In any case, my tactical suggestions were well received by the actual Lieutenant in charge. His name was Josef. I don't know his last name. He spoke English remarkably well. The driver's name was Viktor, and the other two guys were Vasili and Pavel.

Our armored caravan worked its way northwest, cleaning out small pockets of German strong points as we came upon them. Our mission, as I understood it, was to gather intell from prisoners we captured and to get that information back to their Regiment. The prisoners were turned over to the Ukrainian Rifle Troops.

Resistance was not strong, except when we ran into units of Hitler-Jugend, which is to say, Hitler Youth. These highly indoctrinated kids were all fired up and rather dangerous fanatics, even this late in the war. Most of them were not more than twelve or fifteen years old. But they were armed with automatic weapons and Panzerfausts. They fought ferociously. We killed them.

The Panzerfaust, by the way, was a German anti-tank weapon. It loosely translates as "armor fist." The thing was far superior to our American bazooka, though its range was somewhat shorter. It had a more powerful explosive charge than ours, and was simple to operate. A solid hit from a Panzerfaust could disable a tank. These things were the precursors to the modern RPG, rocket-propelled grenade launcher. Dangerous stuff. And these kids were armed to the teeth with them.

We got as far as the Teltow Canal before we ran into a strong point manned by Hitler-Jugend well dug in. Josef caught a bullet in the right shoulder. But it was not serious. His aid man bandaged him, and he continued to fight. By then I was becoming real good with the machine gun.

One of the kids fired a Panzerfaust, which hit one of our armored cars and overturned it. My driver turned into the kids' position, and I hosed them good with my machine gun. Blood flew everywhere. Josef dispatched a car to each of our two flanks and then the whole group poured out machine-gun fire on the lot of them.

My car was closest to the car that had been hit. I yelled to Pavel to take my machine gun. Then I dove out of the vehicle and ran to the overturned car. It was lying on its side.

I quickly checked the men. Only one was alive. But he too was wounded. That man was probably the gunner.

I pulled the wounded man out, dragged him behind a building, beyond the line of fire. Josef pulled the other cars back out of range of the Panzerfausts and we waited for the tanks to arrive. One of our number was in constant contact with their Regiment.

The tanks caught up with us within minutes. They let loose a couple of rounds into the strong point. The kids panicked and surrendered. The foot troops that accompanied the tanks took them prisoner. The position was ours.

At this point I had had enough. I couldn't take anymore killing, and certainly not of children. I bid goodbye to Josef and to my car mates. Then I made my way back to Luckenwalde. It was too far to walk so I hitched a ride. It didn't take long. An American-built General Motors 2 1/2 ton truck happened by. Josef had called Headquarters; the woman Major had dispatched a truck to pick me up. That said something.

Back at camp I found that the American Army had sent in an armored column to pick us up. It was now 22 April. One of my good friends commented that he was happy to see me alive. He had been afraid that I had been sent to my death with that last patrol. *Him and me both!*

Our troops were loading up as I arrived. Within hours, the column pulled out. Destination? The American lines some forty miles to the west. *Yes!*

I slept most of the way. I should imagine that many of us did. When I woke up, we had arrived at Hildesheim, home to a large airfield and well behind American lines. The airfield had been captured pretty much intact.

In no time at all, we were assigned to temporary barracks. Everybody rushed the showers. Everybody wanted to clean up at once. As they say, it was a zoo. As we exited the showers, we were sprayed down with something designed to kill lice. I'm guessing we all suffered the same problem. *But, boy, did it feel great to be clean again!*

We were directed to a large mess hall. Inside, it was set up cafeteria-style. At the beginning of the line stood a large sign.

TAKE ALL YOU WANT
BUT EAT ALL YOU TAKE!

We all knew our stomachs had shrunk to half their normal size. So the warning was understandable. — But I was hungry.

So I made a couple extra sandwiches — on <u>white</u> bread, by the way — and I stuck them in my pockets to smuggle out and eat later. I seriously doubt I was the only one. And, just for good measure, I snuck out an orange as well.

Actually, I don't think the mess hall crew really cared one way or the other what we took. So far as I know, not even those whose pockets were bulging with food were challenged at the door. All that good food smelled so wonderful, we really did not want to leave any of it behind.

And let me tell you something else. After so long without, that white bread tasted like angel food cake to my quivering tongue.

At Hildesheim, after our cleanup, we were issued new uniforms. Also, shoes and toilet articles. These uniforms were of the olive-drab wool variety, standard GI issue.

We were also issued a brand new musette bag to carry home our extra clothing and assorted other things we had collected along the way. Then we were processed as returned POW's.

The third day I was loaded onboard a C-47 along with about twenty other officers, and we were all flown to the city of Nancy in France. This was a rather exciting flight. The Douglas C-47 Skytrain — nicknamed "Dakota" (an acronym built on letters from "Douglas Aircraft Company Transport") — was a military transport based on the earlier Douglas DC-3 airliner. It is very safe in the air, with a cruising speed above one hundred and sixty miles per hour, and a very reliable aircraft. But this flight almost didn't turn out so well.

One of the returning POW's onboard was a former pilot. After we were in the air, he convinced the actual pilot to let him take over the controls. That's when the fun began.

This guy was some kind of nut. He flew that plane at about fifty to seventy-five feet above the ground for many miles. He scared the hell out of us, not to mention field after field of grazing cows. At times, I swear we were below the level of the treetops. Thank goodness, Nancy is perhaps three hundred miles southwest of Hildesheim, just inside France, a couple hours by air.

Once safely on the ground at Nancy, we were loaded onto trucks and transported across town to a railroad station. There we boarded railcars similar to our coaches back home. No forty-and-eights for us this time.

The train pulled out and we were taken fifty miles south, still in France, to the city of Épinal in the district famous for brandy. From there by truck to the site of a former manufacturing plant where we were temporarily housed in barracks once used by factory workers but now converted for military use.

This is where we would spend our time while we were being out-processed and orders were being cut. I decided to use my free time to explore the factory a bit. You know me. I love to go on walkabout.

No sooner had I set out on my mini-adventure, than I found a beautiful new set of Johansson Blocks in a mahogany case. I was stunned. Tools of the toolmaker. That set of blocks must have been worth five thousand dollars, a princely sum. I made room for it in my new musette bag.

Johansson Blocks, by the way, are precision-made gauge blocks. They are metal, and of varying size, and they can be combined to make up a length of any measure. At the time, machine shops the world-over used them as a measuring standard to ensure accuracy in the manufacturing of metal parts, from gun making to the machining of automobile parts. Very valuable.

Three days later, my orders were cut. I was taken, along with countless others, by truck convoy, on a long, cross-country trip to Camp Twenty Grand on the heights overlooking Le Havre, France. I was now fifty miles east of OMAHA BEACH and due south of Portsmouth, England, where this all began. Curious.

At Camp Twenty Grand, we were issued more personal gear, more underwear, more socks. We were given partial pay and offered leave of up to two weeks in France before going home. I met a guy there, who had been a machinist back in the world, and gave him the set of Johansson Blocks I had found. He couldn't believe his good fortune.

I also became acquainted with Lieutenant Albert Miller, Jr., a flamboyant New Yorker. He told me he was the son of Albert Miller, who was a big name in the hotel industry and operated the famous Warwick Hotel in New York City. Should I ever be in New York and need a room, all I need do was mention his father's name, and I would be taken care of. I stored that one away for future reference. The Warwick had been commissioned by none other than William Randolph Hearst himself.

Albert decided to take a week's leave and go to Paris. I opted to remain in Le Havre and be ready to ship out as quickly as possible. I missed my wife and my family.

My war had come to an end.

MAY 1945

The Germans surrendered on 8 May. It was time to go home.

The Army used a point system. Any soldier with enough "points" was eligible to be shipped home. I had more than enough points. On top of that, I was a Casual Officer and unassigned. It was homeward bound for me. *Hooray!*

A few days after the Germans surrendered, my orders were cut. I was hardly the only one. Hundreds, perhaps thousands now boarded trucks to be taken to the docks. Le Havre was on the coast. We would soon board a ship.

I was pleasantly surprised when our trucks unloaded dockside. The ship we were to take home was a converted luxury liner. It had been born Italian, the *Conte Grande*. When the U.S. captured it from the Italians and took it over as a troop ship, it was renamed the U.S.S. *Monticello*.

We pulled out of the harbor and took our place within a large convoy. This worried me a bit. *The war was over, right? No more submarine packs hunting down ships, right?*

We headed west. The *Monticello* was apparently not fast enough to travel alone, as the *Mauritania* had been when I first shipped to England. It was wider of beam and plowed along almost without a roll or pitch. Of course, we were traveling much farther south in the Atlantic, and the seas were calmer. That had been October; this was May.

The days at sea were clear and sunny. I spent most of my time just lounging on deck, enjoying the sun. It was great.

As some weeks had now passed since the German surrender, once we were well at sea, the convoy ran with lights. This was a first. Not since the war in Europe began more than five years ago had a convoy run with lights.

The war really was over. German U-boats were no longer prowling the oceans trying to sink us.

Eight or ten days after we left Le Havre, we pulled into New York harbor. I had lost about fifty dollars playing poker to pass the time. *But who the heck cared?*

As we passed by the Statue of Liberty standing there at the foot of Manhattan, my eyes teared and a great swelling of pride grew in my chest. I was home!

After we docked and the ship was unloaded, they directed us to a train. It carried us to Camp Kilmer outside New Brunswick, New Jersey. I found this curious in one respect. The camp was named for Joyce Kilmer, the soldier-poet of World War One fame. You may remember that I knew his son Christopher from my Fort Meade days, two years earlier. *Had it been two years?* It didn't seem possible.

At Camp Kilmer, men were processed for shipment to various camps around the country. I was sent to Fort Dix, New Jersey, where I received all my back pay, some fourteen months' worth. Orders were cut ordering me to report to the Army Ground and Service Forces Redistribution Station, Asheville, North Carolina, on 9 August 1945, some two months hence.

I smiled at the news. I had just been granted a sixty-three-day recuperation leave, as well as three days' travel time. Sixty-six days in all. *What to do?*

I put on my uniform, flagged a taxi for Trenton. From there, I boarded a train for Penn Station in New York City, no distance at all. I exited the station carrying my musette bag and walked slowly north on Sixth Avenue. *Boy, was it good to be home!*

Everybody I passed gave a quick sideways glance at my Service Ribbons. *Boy, did I feel proud.* Purple Heart. European-African-Middle Eastern Campaign Medal, with two Stars. Arrowhead (Beach Assault). Combat Infantryman Badge.

When I had gone far enough up Sixth Avenue, I walked over to the Warwick New York Hotel and asked for a room. The desk clerk told me that no room was available. I looked him in the eye, told him that Mr. Albert Miller had said if I mentioned his name something could be arranged. That got the man's attention.

He looked with envy at the strip of Service Ribbons proudly displayed on my chest, asked me to have a seat in the lobby. He'd see what he could do.

A few minutes later, he called me over. No, there was no room here at the Warwick. But if I was to go over to the Saint Regis Hotel, they were holding a room for me. I thanked him and walked over the few blocks. This was all of a four-minute walk.

When I stepped into the Saint Regis, the desk clerk greeted me and also looked over my ribbons. I signed in and he personally escorted me to a Penthouse Suite. I thought: *Oh, boy, this is going to cost.* But I was too tired to argue and anyway, I had a pocketful of cash from being paid.

So I thanked the man and made myself to home. Soft music on the radio, a shot of brandy, an expensive cigar, feet on the ottoman, telephone in my hand. I called Connie to tell her I was back.

Even as late as it was, she wanted to rush over across the bridge and join me. But I begged off. I told her how tired I was and that I would be home the very next day. By then I was already half in bed and fading fast.

Tomorrow I would see my wife.

5 JUNE 1945

Penthouse suite, Saint Regis Hotel, Fifth Avenue, three blocks south of Central Park, New York City, U.S.A.

Silk sheets, soft bedding, milled soap, cotton towels, hot shower.

I slept late that morning.

I called room service, ordered breakfast. Orange juice. Buttered toast with jam. Eggs. Bacon. Lots of — you guessed it — hot, black coffee. No ersatz for me.

When the waiter arrived at my door with the tray of food, he treated me like royalty. An hour later, when I went downstairs to check out, I thought: *Oh my, here it comes, the bill.*

I couldn't believe my eyes when the desk clerk handed it to me. My total charges came to two dollars and thirty-five cents! The desk clerk thanked me for having fought for him and for everybody else and wished me Godspeed.

I didn't even think to ask him what the two-dollar charge was for. Probably that telephone call. New York to New Jersey. Interstate telephone calls did not come cheap in those days.

I walked out the door, floating on air. I caught a subway that took me midtown to the Bus Station. From there I hopped a bus for Hackensack. Then it was through the Lincoln Tunnel and past the towns and villages I'd known all my life. What a ride!

I got off the bus at Essex Street, one block short of where Connie's folks lived. I knew she would be there waiting for me. My arrival was greeted with much joy.

From a distance of so many years, and in the context of a marriage that subsequently failed, it is hard to form my feelings into words. Our reunion was joyful, of course. But also awkward. I had been a prisoner of war for nearly one year. I had suffered every form of deprivation known to man, including the touch of a loving woman. So it took a while.

•

•

The next day the two of us went down to my parents' home, where I was again greeted with much joy.

Mom was mom, walking around with tears in her eyes and a big, proud smile on her face. Pop had greeted me with a bear hug and a few tears of his own, though he tried his level best to hide them from me. It was then that I found out the strangest thing.

A year ago, on the very day I was wounded, my father had a premonition. On the exact day, 13 June, he said to my mom, "Something's happened to Bill."

Within a day of him saying that, boils broke out on Pop's legs, right where my wounds were. Strange? Maybe not. Me and God were talking pretty regularly about then. Maybe this was His way of sending a message home to my folks that I was wounded but okay.

The father of one of Connie's friends — I'll call him Mr. G. — owned a hotel in New York's Catskill Mountains. He offered Connie and me a week's stay there at his hotel, no charge. I jumped at the offer.

Dad was willing to lend me his car, but gasoline was a bit of a problem. Strict wartime rationing was still in effect. The Catskills were more than a hundred miles away.

Fortunately, the folks had set aside some gas stamps for this very moment, in case I wanted to drive somewhere when I got home.

When we got to the hotel, we had an even bigger surprise. Mr. G. had arranged for us to have an unlimited number of truck gas-rationing stamps at our disposal. These stamps authorized many more gallons of fuel per stamp than those authorized for an ordinary car.

Now Connie and I were ready to roll!

9 AUGUST 1945

The summer months had flown by quickly. After a wonderful week of doing nothing in the Catskill Mountains, it was back home trying to reconnect with my former life. The balance of my recuperation leave seemed to be gone in no time at all.

There were of course lots of parties that summer, some with other guys from my old "gang." One by one, they all returned home from the war or other pursuits. My childhood gang of fifteen guys my age produced two Naval officers, two Army officers, three sergeants, three ordinary soldiers, and two sailors. I guess we were a patriotic bunch.

I was under orders to report to a Replacement Center in Asheville, North Carolina, on 9 August 1945. This worried me a bit, as the war in the Pacific continued to rage on. Depending on manpower requirements, I very well might yet be called up for that.

I left Hackensack by train on 6 August. After changing railroad lines twice, I finally arrived around noon at the Army Ground and Service Forces Redistribution Station in Asheville. *Surprise!* The "Station" was actually located in The Grove Park Inn, a luxury hotel set in the beautiful mountains. In peacetime, this place was known to be very expensive, certainly out of my league.

The lobby of the hotel took my breath away. It was immense. At either end of the lobby was a fireplace, equally immense. A five-foot-tall woman could easily stand upright inside the firebox of either one of those two fireplaces without ruining her hairdo, that's how large they were.

Outside, there were four tennis courts on the grounds, plus a swimming pool below the main level. It stood in full view of a very large terrace. Beyond them all, stretching from right to left as far as the eye could see: a grand golf course.

Connie was not due to arrive in Asheville for four more days. So I drew a set of golf clubs and some balls from the Service Club operation and set out on the course. I was rusty.

I had been introduced to the game at age sixteen. Developers had dredged the river bottom in an effort to make Hackensack a seaport. The sediment was used to fill in a large, low-lying riverside tract. The tract changed hands several times, eventually becoming a driving range.

As a boy, I worked at the driving range picking up balls, cutting grass, doing odd jobs. That's where I learned the game, from a former golf pro who, in his declining years, hung around the course. His name was Cyril Walker. Walker won the 1924 U.S. Open. It was played in Michigan, at Oakland Hills.

Cyril was a great teacher. But he was also an alcoholic. The man died of alcohol poisoning in 1948 in, of all places, our own Hackensack city jail.

But his death was still three years down the road. Today, right now in fact, here in August 1945, I was fumbling around out on the course like an amateur. I had forgotten most of what Walker had taught me.

Soon, though, I befriended a couple fellows who looked like they knew what they were doing and we played. These guys were paratroopers with stories to tell. Minutes later, we three were joined by an older man.

Unlike the three of us, this older fellow was dressed for the part — white stockings, white knickers, a regular white shirt, black bowtie, white cap. Obviously a gentleman golfer.

Well, as you can imagine, that gentleman golfer skunked us young guys badly. Boy, could he play! And, to add insult to our injury, the man carried only four clubs with him. That included his putter. We each carried an entire set.

Our nights were just as challenging as our days. Each night there was some sort of entertainment in that immense lobby. Refreshments too. But no booze. This was, after all, an Army installation, no matter how casual it looked. Whatever booze made it into that room was totally bootleg.

Then the big news hit. On 14 August 1945 Japan surrendered. The war was over. At last.

Connie had been with me the day Japan bombed Pearl Harbor. Now she was with me again on the day Japan gave it up.

Within an hour of the announcement, bootleggers pulled up under the roof of the hotel's coach entrance and started peddling their wares. There was no stopping the celebration now, regulations be damned. The vendors opened up their car doors and began selling booze by the quart, most of it bottled in Mason jars.

A man had three choices of what to buy from these dealers — Gin (white lightning distilled from corn), Bourbon (white lightning with a little syrup and coloring blended in), or Scotch (white lightning with a few drops of iodine added).

Whatever these moonshiners called it, we drank it. Whatever it was that we drank, it was strong. That night's scheduled activity in the lobby was well-oiled. No one went to bed sober.

Good fun was had by all that night but none less than me. Orders had already been cut ordering me to the China-Burma-India Theater. Now, with the war officially over, all such orders were rescinded.

•

•

On 23 August 1945, I was issued new orders. I was to report right away to Fort Dix, New Jersey, for separation. I arrived there the next day.

It was at Fort Dix that I signed into the Army Reserve. I was granted a terminal leave which extended until 7 November. This was an unexpected but happy development. It meant that my pay and allowances would remain uninterrupted until then.

Naturally, there continued to be a lot of parties during my terminal leave, as the rest of my old gang returned home from service. There were weddings, too. But I found I couldn't just sit around doing nothing for days on end.

Truth is, I went back to work at the Post Office even before my terminal leave formally ended. I found that the Post Office had promoted me three times while I was away in the Army.

My promotion to 1st Lieutenant finally caught up with me in early September. The documentation on my Purple Heart and Combat Infantryman Badge also caught up with me at about the same time. The paperwork on both had been put through within days of the events of 13 June 1944. But, because I had been listed as missing in action for so long, they both had been lost in a sea of red tape.

Of all my ribbons, I am most proud of that Combat Infantryman Badge. While it is true that the sum-total of my actual time in combat was relatively short — only a matter of days — the actions I was involved in had been fierce and almost constant.

The Combat Infantryman Badge is awarded to any soldier who is personally present, and under hostile fire, while serving in a unit of the Infantry or Special Forces that, at the time of his presence, was actively engaging the enemy in ground combat.

After I received my combat medals, I put them away and began what would be more than fifty years of trying to put those traumatic events behind me.

But I never really succeeded. In my declining years, I found myself looking at that badge I was so proud of more and more often. The Combat Infantryman Badge is actually quite beautiful. Let me describe it to you:

The badge is framed in silver and enamel. It consists of a three-inch-wide rectangular bar set in a field of infantry-blue. Superimposed on that field of blue is a Springfield Arsenal Musket, Model 1795. That model musket dates to an era just after our War of Independence.

Both the blue field and the musket are affixed to an elliptic oak-leaf wreath. That wreath symbolizes three things — steadfast character, strength, and loyalty. I would like to believe I possessed all three qualities.

I'm not sure anymore who said it, but there is truth in this adage:

To be born free is an accident.
To live free is a wonderful, God-given opportunity.
But to die free? That is an awesome responsibility.

EPILOGUE

William C. Frodsham died free. He died free in a nation he helped keep free.

After the war, William continued to serve his country in various capacities. Having signed into the Army Reserve, he was promptly assigned to a unit. Although it was designated as an Infantry Regiment, the regiment existed only on paper. In those days, there was no pay for reservists.

The reservists met in an old storefront on Banta Place off Central Avenue in downtown Hackensack. Army Headquarters assigned their Reserve Unit a Captain, who became their advisor. For several years they met downtown once a week, where they received instruction.

Eventually, Congress got off its duff (to use his exact words) and established a real reserve program, with pay and all. William was assigned to the 1018th Army Reserve Service Unit. Now the unit drilled in a new place, a building in the shipyards of Newark, New Jersey.

But then war came again, this time on the Korean Peninsula. America's involvement in that conflict began in the summer of 1950. Within days of the war's outbreak, William was called up for duty.

But it was only one day's duty. The Army was cataloguing its resources. The purpose of the call-up was for each man to take a physical examination. This William did, along with nearly six hundred other company-grade officers in the State of New Jersey.

The Army placed an immediate requisition for four hundred and fifty-two officers. The physical examination had eliminated only six of those who tested. Others who had already experienced hard service were also excused. This included William. The bulk of those ordered to active duty were recent graduates of college ROTC programs.

William thought this an unwise decision on the Army's part. Putting untried men in harm's way was not the proper approach. Why pass up all that proven experience? Why pass *him* up?

Not being asked to serve bothered him. His reserve unit was placed in the highest category for activation. They trained continuously but were never called. This bothered him even more. The man wanted to serve.

Finally, William applied for active duty. He specifically requested assignment to an Airborne Division, a unit of parachute infantry stationed at Fort Campbell, Kentucky. Perhaps he had fond memories of that brief stint in jump school back in Britain. Perhaps he had other motives.

Meanwhile, his father was working behind the scenes to prevent William from taking such a dangerous course of action. By then William was already a father, with a four-year-old son. His marriage to Connie had ended in divorce only six months before, in January 1950.

William's father was good friends with their local Congressman. The Congressman sat on the Armed Services Committee of the House of Representatives. Lo and behold, Bill's military records could not be "found."

The records did turn up again, several years later, after his fervor for war had died down. The Congressman had likely requested William's records at his father's request and stuck them in a desk drawer to be forgotten.

But maybe William's father was right to hold his son back. Maybe he thought his son was distraught over his recent divorce. In any case, before the war drew to a close in the summer of 1953, William had remarried. His marriage to his second wife, Joan, was consummated in October 1952. She died of natural causes six years later.

William was promoted to Captain in 1956. His new assignment was that of Troop Commander. The unit he commanded was staffed with a complete command structure, all its officers and sergeants. All it needed to be operational was a full complement of soldiers. Had William's unit been called up at full strength, he would have been responsible for more than six hundred men. Surely something to be proud of.

Captain Frodsham retired from the Army in May 1964. By then he had again remarried, this time to Dorothy Mae Humm, "Dottie" as she liked to be called. He and Dottie had two fine children, a son and a daughter, and he and his new wife remained together for the rest of their natural lives.

William tried his best to forget the worst parts of his war experience. But he never could.

Then came a day when he changed his mind. Instead of trying to forget, he tried to remember. He joined his Division's Association. He began corresponding with former brothers-in-arms. He began to write down his memories, not only to ease his mind but also to help his three children understand him better.

This very personal story is the product of that righteous effort.

APPENDIX

THE OFLAG 64 ITEM
JANUARY 1, 1945 ISSUE

(reprinted with permission by the Estate of Captain William C. Frodsham, Jr.)

The Oflag 64 Item

New Year's Edition

Peace in '45 Or Bust

"One ITEM is Worth 10,000 Pictures"

No. 15   Altburgund, Germany — January 1, 1945   Price: 50 Pfg

OFLAG NEWS IN BRIEF

● Thinking they might save some time, the camp bookbinders decided it would be best to print the book titles on the covers first, then cover the books.

It worked — but the covers ended up on the books upside down!

● A White House kriegy who has been in the bag two years received a formal invitation last month to graduation exercises in June, 1944.

● Ormond Roberts had been sweating out a letter for a long time. Mail call came and Robbie heard his name. He rushed over, quickly opened his letter and found that it was from a girl friend's pet puppy, Dixie. Roberts has been growling ever since.

● Question of the month: A new captain was heard to ask at the carpenter shop -- "Have you got a 2 ft. length of mahogany I could have?"

● Recently Barracks 6A was awakened in the middle of the night by a still unidentified voice that shouted, "Home, it's wonderful!"

● Rumor No. 3762: A new man came up to Room 28 wanting to see the stove on which 36 men could cook at one time!

● Jeff Rogers from Barracks 9A finally got a Red Cross box last month. He put the D-Bar in his jacket pocket and went to bed. Midnight passed. He was still awake with visions of D-bars parading before him, 1 a.m., 2 a.m. Still no sleep. Finally at 3 a.m. he could stand it no longer. He got up, ate his D-bar, and retired happily.

● Sidney Thal, Schubin trapeze artist, recently received a comforting letter from home. "Your next parcel will contain all clothes. We know you have plenty to eat."

Oflagites Greet New Year With Chilblains and Hope

Jeers Oust Old Year, Kriegies Salaam 1945

"It beats the hell outta me," said John Kriegie last night as the big clock in the White House knocked out 12 bells.

And with these words of wild celebration, John pulled the bed sack over his head and closed his eyes, while 1945 limped into Oflag 64 cursing its chilblains.

There were no tears among Altburgund's American colony at the departure of 1944.

For the older gefangeners it had been a year of great expectations that had misfired; for the younger generation it had been the year of the Great Shock.

(You know — "Hell's bells, Lieutenant, I figured on being wounded or killed, but I never even dreamed of being captured!")

The new year brought new hope — plenty of it.

John Kriegie awoke this morning from dreams of beefsteak, Scotch and Lana Turner with a new gleam in his eye.

"It won't be long now!" he shouted, diving for his ersatz coffee.

New Year's Message

By: Col. Paul R. Goode

"More than ever before, the coming year has a deep and far reaching significance for us all! Home and reunion with our loved ones — and once more taking our places as useful members of the armed forces of our country.

"Let us now, by our every action and thought prepare ourselves for that glorious day when being a "kriegie" is only a memory! Let us never forget we are Americans and constantly prepare ourselves spiritually, morally, mentally, and physically for what America may have in store for us! Let us be worthy of the uniform we wear!

"Thank you for your fine conduct and cooperation during the time I have been S. A. O. — and may 1945 bring nothing but happiness to you and yours."

New Year's Day Program

Today's New Year's Day program includes:

Catholic masses at 9:15 and 10:20 a.m.;

Midday feast of Red Cross meat, meat gravy, and a vegetable.

Special showing of "Room Service," produced by John Hannan, at 7:15 p. m. in the Little Theater.

SEE PAGE THREE FOR THE ITEM'S COMPREHENSIVE SURVEY OF OFLAG 64

The Oflag 64 Item

Published monthly by and for American officers temporarily detained in Offizierslager 64, Altburgund (Schubin), Germany.

Editor: 2nd Lt. Frank Diggs
Associate Editors: 1st Lt. Larry Phelan, 1st Lt. David Englander

News: 2nd Lt. Frank Hancock
2nd Lt. Howard Holder
1st Lt. Teddy Roggen
Capt. Charles Wilkinson
Wright Bryan, War Correspondent
Sports: 2nd Lt. Robert Cheatham
Art: 1st Lt. James Bickers, 2nd Lt. Alexander Ross

JANUARY 1, 1945

»» ITEMIZING ««

New Year's resolutions, in our opinion, are both futile and pointless, since they usually consist of a determination to do doggedly the things we don't want to do, and to give up those that make life bearable.

The one point in their favor is that they rarely outlive the first week in January — a week that could do with some asceticism anyway.

Reversing the conventional procedure, we would like to suggest the following list of SENSIBLE resolutions for the shining new year of 1945:

Resolved:
1. To eat ourselves into a state of gasping, glutted insensibility four or five times each day;
2. To catch up on all lost drinking time;
3. To exercise our charm (and what-not) on all females of the species within range;
4. To sleep (and what-not) until noon each day in a double Simmons Beauty-Rest;
5. To wear civilian clothes;
6. To accomplish the above and more at the earliest feasible date.

HAPPY NEW YEAR! L. P.

Signs of the Times

The kitchen and dining room staff, tin store personnel, cobbler, tailor and carpenter shop workers, teachers, greenhouse custodians, S-4 operators, canteen people, and all those who catch sweeping, scrubbing and carrying details with monotonous regularity, are all wondering these days how to go about resigning their commissions for a Pfc. rating, complete with weekly parcel.

Gal of The Month

Each month the ITEM reminds its readers that such things still exist. Our choice for January: Miss Marianne Simson, lovely German film starlet.

Kriegy Sketches

MAJOR KERMIT HANSEN

High on the list of Oflag 64's biggest operators is the camp's hardworking new adjutant: energetic, graying 27-year-old Major Kermit Hansen.

Hailing from Omaha, Major Hansen arrived here last September and was volunteered almost immediately for the important job of S-1.

Soon thereafter he became M. C. and one-man sparkplug for Bob Rankin's "Swingland," the director of the Sunday afternoon recorded program, and a leading light in the Glee Club.

His pre-kriegy career shows the same tendencies.

At the University of Nebraska, for instance, he was the Colonel of Cadets and honor graduate of the Class of '39.

Then, for two years, he energized Radio Station KOWH in Omaha as announcer, singer, script-

IN REQUIEM

1944

It's been a long tough year — just ask any kriegy who has spent 1944 at Oflag 64!

As time is measured in a German prison camp, it has been 12 months of rumors, hope, Red Cross boxes, endless bull sessions, study, writing and waiting.

More than anything else, 1944 was a succession of projects — attempts to make life liveable under the damndest of conditions.

For instance:

JANUARY, 1944, opened with a big beer-party program in the mess hall and saw the begining of the Promenade Walk project and iceskating operations.

FEBRUARY was highlighted by an all-camp poll, in which Oflagites collectively decided that the war would end in September, 1944.

MARCH saw the beginning of the 2-acre camp garden project and witnessed the Oflag's most ambitious stage production until then — "The Man Who Came To Dinner."

APRIL came with a flurry of trading on the newly-set up Mart, an impressive Easter program and a persistent rumor of mass repatriation to Sweden.

MAY brought "Three Men on a Horse" to the Oflag stage, the camp's first maternity case in the form of two kittens and the climax of the spring softball tournament.

JUNE saw the Oflag's first an-

(See REQUIEM, page six)

writer and program director.

In August of '41, he came on active service in the army as a 2nd Lieutenant, going overseas to Ireland in February of the next year.

Since then, he made the African landing in '42 and gradually rose through S-1, S-2, and S-3 staff jobs to become a battalion commander.

Then one night in France he crossed the Mosel river with some advance elements of his outfit and here he is.

As for Item A, Major Hansen says he definitely thinks the war will end — some day.

Page Three   THE OFLAG ITEM   Survey

The Saga of John Kriegy

Item Comprehensive Survey of Oflag 64 Shows that Average Kriegy Is 27, from N. Y., College-Trained, Food-Conscious, Efficient & Making the Best of It

ITEM news-sleuths last month combed the Oflag from White House to outhouse, peeting and prying into every twist and turn of kriegie operations to find what makes the camp tick.

Here's what they found.

Lieutenant John Average Kriegie of Oflag 64, sitting for his composite statistical portrait, reveals these facts about himself:

He is 27 years old. His home is in New York or Pennsylvania or Texas. He is half bachelor and half married (most men are like that).

He attended college but, more likely than not, left the academic halls without a degree.

His civilian occupation was that of student or salesman, clerk or businessman.

His favorite pastime, at which he is, through no fault of his own, in but poor practice, is eating.

Pastimes...

The occupation to which he devotes most time is thinking and talking and dreaming about food, preparing menus for future repasts and devising means of stretching Red Cross parcels, when available, to their ultimate maximum of nutrition, longevity and satisfaction. Otherwise he occupies his time with smoking, reading and all manner of housewifery with liberal schedules of educational classes, dramatic and musical entertainment, religious services and games (all indoor at this season, but in better weather and on more adequate diet including many athletic sports).

An over-all group picture of Oflag 64's population discloses abundant deviation from the average. The age of kriegies here ranges from the average of 27 down to a minimum of 19 (two officers) and up to a maximum of 52

(one officer). Of a total camp strength numbering 1035 when the tabulation was made, 650 came within the age group 23 to 26, inclusive.

Each of the 48 American states is represented in the camp population with numbers varying from New York's 106, Pennsylvania's 56 and Texas' 74 to Delaware's, Montana's, Rhode Island's, Utah's and Wyoming's 2 each. The District of Columbia claims 13 and Hawaii 3. Our Allied nations are represented as follows: France, 1; Morocco, 3; Algeria, 2; Tunisia, 2, and Canada, 1.

Married men in camp number 516.

A total of 643 Kriegies here have attended college, and more than 300 of them won degrees. There are 155 Bachelors of Science, including BS in Commerce and in various branches of engineering, and 105 Bachelors of Art. There are 49 M.D's and 14 Bachelors of Law, and 9 M.A.'s. There is a Ph. D. and LL. D. and such assorted degrees as B. B. A., Ph. B., B. E., B. S., M. S. C. M., J. D., B.B.S., D.D.S., B.D., and A.A. — not to mention R. F. D., P. D. Q., and W. P. A.

Professions...

It would take an I. B. M. machine and a flock of assorted forms to classify in detail the civilian occupations of Oflag 64, but the broad groups include 120 who were students, 98 clerks, 98 salesmen, and 89 in other fields of business. There are 46 professional soldiers in this collection of PoWs from a civilian army, 42 engineers, 36 farmers, 34 teachers, and 34 laborers, 19 doctors and 2 dentists; 5 professors, ministers and 2 priests; and 10 journalists (a journalist is a newspaper man with spots and a cane).

This by no means exhausts the catalog. Our kriegies include an explorer and a labor arbitrator, a forest ranger and an expediter (just that fellow in charge of mail and parcels), two bartenders and and a photolithographer, a professional fund raiser, a porcelain

enamelist, a fingerprint classifier, a calendar designer, a pro baseball player, a Boy Scout executive, a watchmaker, a marine inspector, a photo-statistician, a hatter (not yet used) a seaman, a U.S. Treasury investigator, a worsted cloth finisher, 6 ranchers and a horse trainer, a policeman, an artist, an actor, a patent attorney, and the Commandant of a Military School.

Camp Setup...

Under the command of Col. Paul B. Goode, Senior American Officer, a thoroughly organized staff supervises the internal administration of John Kriegie's camp. Col. George Millett is Executive Officer, Lt. Col. Max Gooler, assistant Executive officer, and Col. F. W. Drury, Inspector General.

Maj. Kermit Hansen is S-1, Lt. Col. James Alger S-2, Lt. Col. John Waters S-3, and Lt. Col. Louis Gershenow S-4, Capt. Floyd Burgeson is Medical Officer and Capt. Charles Gleeson is chaplain.

Two departments of the camp organization, the kitchen and mess under Lt. Col. William Martz and the tin store under Capt. Tony Lumpkin, dispense wise, too, and if available, that substance with which every Kriegie is preoccupied: FOOD.

Food...

The kitchen prepares for John Kriegie each day 550 liters of soup, 1056 pounds of potatoes, 1056 pounds of cabbage or turnips, as the case may be and 1464 liters of ersatz coffee. The camp's food-statistician might be able to figure how many ounces vessel the soup might float in a year, but Lt. Average Kriegie measures it by the tablespoonful. Other items from the German ration supplied to Oflag 64 include 1.26 ounces

(See SURVEY, Page Four)

Lt. Kriegy Served by Well-Equipped Hospital, Tailor Shop, Barber Service and 7,000 - Volume Library

SURVEY...

es per man per day of fresh uncooked meat (including bones), six one thousandths of an ounce of spice, two one-thousandths of an ounce of vinegar, and seven-tenths of an ounce of salt.

The total German ration, before boning and cooking, is 86 pounds per day. Food is served through 122 messes.

The short order cooking, serving twenty messes a day, handles between 40 and 60 culinary concoctions a day when Red Cross parcels are coming in regularly. Three hundred fifty cans are opened each day when parcels are available.

Col. Marta' assistant mess officers are Capt. George Lacey, Capt. Allan White, Lt. Robert Aschim and Lt. Len Farber. Capt. Joe Emerson is ration officer. Capt. Paul Miller. Lt. Fay Straight and Lt. Curtis Jones handle short order cooking.

The camp cooks are Sgt. D.C. Olson, who was a CCC cook before entering the army, Sgt. M. D. Massey, Pfc. J. Patton and Pvt. L. A. Annunziata who was master baker at Russo's Bakery, Brooklyn.

The K. P. staff includes Sgt. V. H. Byrd T/5 Alvarado, Pfc. V. Long and Pvts. J. Cedillo, M. Greenfield, J. B. Browning, W. E. Elkins, D. Kakae, D. McConnaughy and L. Gallis.

Parcel Store...

The parcel stores, handling Red Cross and private parcels, has an average of 300 - 400 customers a day during good times and 100 - 125 a day during bad times.

The tobacco store handles 12,000 cigarettes a day, 200 cigars and 100 packages of pipe tobacco.

In stock as of October 1 were 1,000,000 cigarettes (47 different brands), 12,000 cigars (23 brands) and 10,000 packages of pipe tobacco (37 brands).

Most popular brands are Camel cigarettes, El Roi-Tan cigars, and Sir Walter Raleigh pipe tobacco.

Stores are open 9:00 to 10:30 a. m. weekdays and 9:30 to 10:30 a. m. Sundays. The D-bar store is open only on Tuesdays.

Soup is available at all times (1 bar per man).

One Kriegie, applying for pipe tobacco and asked what brand, inquired, "What kind ya got?!!"

Another applied for 87 cigarettes.

Capt. Lumpkin has been head of the

entire tin store since June 6, 1943. Capt. Maynard Flies has the same record of service as head of the tobacco division and Capt. James Dicks as head of parcel issue.

Assistants in the tobacco division are Lt. Robert Wick, Lt. Vic Laughlin and Lt. Gabriel Gever, and in the parcel issue Lt. Royal Lee, Lt. Nelson Tavy and Lt. Harry Schultz.

Lt. LeRoy Ihrie handles incoming books; Lt. Francis Noonan and Lt. Milton Jellison are in charge of the D-bar and private food stores, and W.O. Austin Knapp of the kitchen tin store. Lt. Amon G. Carter is private package operator and Lt. Tom Morse is bookkeeper and auditor.

Health...

Lt. Average Kriegie's health is constantly watched by a medical staff of which Capt. Floyd Burgeson is head. Capt. Robert Blatherwick is assistant medical officer and Capt. Eben Bergman administrative officer. Lt. Harry Abrahams is camp sanitator, and a staff of 13 orderlies under 1st Sgt. Butler do the kitchen and sanitation work of the hospital.

When Lt. Kriegie requires hospitalization, there are 22 beds available of which 12 to 15 are usually occupied. Facilities are adequate for handling general ailments and minor surgery. More serious surgical cases go to Wollstein, where Lt. James Godfrey is U.S. medical representative and Polish surgeons are available.

For minor ailments not requiring hospitalization, Lt. Kriegie goes to sick call, where, on the average, 20 of his fellow kriegies appear each day. Most frequently recurring cases are those of the upper respiratory tract, skin ailments, minor cuts and bruises, with occasional cases of stomach trouble.

Capt. Burgeson emphasized to Lt. Kriegie that worry and depression cause a large percentage of the camp's ailments. He tells Lt. Kriegie to keep busy and practice personal hygiene and he is likely to stay well.

Capt. John Thornquist, dental officer, aided by W. O. Roger Cannon, voluntary dental assistant, keeps an eye on J. A. Kriegie's teeth and treats the most urgent cases.

Tailor Shop...

Lt. Kriegie is no Beau Brummel, but he stands inspection every Saturday and "Appel" twice a day, and the climate of Oflag 64 calls for the warmest available clothing. So Lt. Kriegie devotes much time to procuring, swapping, mending, and washing his meagre wardrobe. In this he receives considerable help from the camp's established services.

Headed by Lt. Verris Hubbel and three aides — Lts. Donald Rockwell, Delbert Dorman and Selwyn Goodman, the camp tailor shop repairs anything that's repairable except long-handled underwear.

(Sidelight on Kriegie life: most frequently needed uniform repairs are on "the seat of the pants.")

With three American sewing machines and one iron, the tailor shop has altered more than 2,000 pairs of trousers and as many shirts since November, 1943. The tailor shop also makes costumes, including feminine ones, which Lt. Kriegie wears in his theatrical productions. Lt. Hubbel says the most fun is making false breasts and hip pads for female impersonators and that the oddest garment tailored in Oflag 64 was a bullet costume for use in "You Can't Take It With You."

The camp pressing service under Capts. Warren Walters and Dalton Medlen leaves Lt. Kriegie with no excuse for not having at least his Sunday-go-to-meeting trousers properly creased. Pressing 20 pairs of pants a day with one electric iron is the job of this service, which has handled almost 3,000 pairs since last May.

Lt. Kriegie's shoes (more than 2,000 pairs since July) are repaired in the cobbler shop under Lt. Ormond Roberts. Assisting him are Lts. Art Bryant and Henry Desmond.

With limited and antiquated equipment consisting of a German sanding and buffing machine and a Polish leather sewing machine, the shop turns out proper American repair jobs to the number of 10 to 15 pairs daily.

Like the tailors, the Kriegie cobblers also design and manufacture costume

(See SURVEY, Page Five)

Gnome Bookbindery Keeps Over-age Books Circulating

SURVEY...

properties for the camp theater — items like dancing slippers, pumps, and sandals.

Lt. Roberts offers J. A. one important bit of advice "Keep your shoes off the hot stove ('Who said that stove was hot?') if you don't want the soles to crack and leave you barefooted."

Barber Shop...

When Lt. Kriegie needs a haircut (or rather when his turn comes according to a carefully arranged schedule), he goes to the barber shop presided over by Lt. John Monks. Pfc. Serda, who is in direct charge of the five barber chairs, is a graduate of a barber's school.

The shop was started by two British enlisted men who owned clippers but whose other equipment was crude. The shop is now supplied with white coats, mirrors and sterilizing equipment—everything but the manicure girl and shoeshine boy.

Each barber gives 15 haircuts a day and the shop has 350 customers a week, giving each Oflagite a chance to get his hair cut every 21 days.

When Lt. Kriegie has completed his

cooking and his housekeeping, he falls back on the camp educational, library and religious services, and on games and that old stand-by, the bull-session, to occupy his time.

Library...

A library of 7,000 volumes managed by Capt. Marion Parrot caters to his varied reading tastes. More than 250 books are withdrawn each day.

Most popular classification is fiction, but the library has well patronized sections of Travel, Essays, Biography, Verse, Drama, Psychology, Art, Religion, Sciences, History and Languages.

On a "reserve" list are most popular works, such as "Arundel" by Kenneth Roberts, "Canal Town" by Samuel Hopkins Adams, and "Lee's Lieutenants" by Dr. Douglas Freeman. There are 35 copies of Lloyd Douglas' "The Robe."

The library was built up from a nucleus of 1,000 volumes to its present size by generous contributions of the YMCA and by individual gifts. More than 400 copies of the paperbound "Armed Services Editions" and the British "Penguin" books also have helped supply the demand for reading matter.

A spacious, well-lighted reading room

was recently added to the library through the use of Red Cross boxes and the ingenuity of Lou Otterbein and others.

Gnomerie...

A great help in keeping Lt. Kriegie's favorite volumes in circulation is the bookbinding shop superintended by Lt. Donald Lussenden and staffed by Lts. Harry Hauschild, William Hanson, and Vernon Paulson — all without previous experience in bookbinding, but learning fast in the school of practical work. For bookbinding material they use wax paper from cigarette cartons and binding tape from old Red Cross boxes. A book trimming machine obtained from a German blacksmith shop, hammer, wooden clamps, a sewing frame and needles are the principal tools of this shop. More than 600 books have been salvaged and restored to circulation.

"Westerns," detective stories, and historical novels come into the shop most frequently.

More than 30 officers have applied to learn bookbinding as a hobby and Lt. Lussenden hopes that eventually he may provide facilities for them.

(See SURVEY, Page Six)

John Kriegy's Temporary Home...

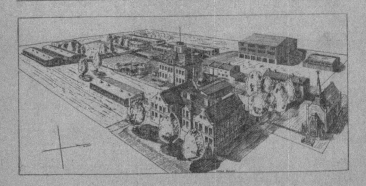

Page Six   THE OFLAG ITEM   Survey

15-6

J.K. Gets Homegrown Education, Entertainment, News

SURVEY...

Education...

If Lt. Kriegie wants to study any of more than 80 subjects, from elementary English to advanced psychology he may attend the "Altburgund Academy" supervised by Capt. Hubert Eldridge, an educator of 22 years experience. The curriculum and faculty were listed in detail in the December 1 ITEM. More than 850 students are enrolled. Special lectures open to all kriegies frequently supplement the regular curriculum.

Lt. Kriegie's spiritual welfare is the concern of chaplains who conduct two services each Sunday for Protestants and daily masses for Catholics. The religious program also includes semi-weekly Bible classes and twice-a-month communion services for Protestants, and evening prayer service and a course in Christian Apologetics for Catholics.

Theater...

All entertainment for Lt. Kriegie is under supervision of the Theater Group which meets regularly, selects plays and appoints producers for each. The group has presented eight 3-act plays, all former Broadway hits, seven one-act plays, eight musical revues, about a dozen Swingland programs, two operatic recitals, and one original 3-act musical comedy.

The backstage group, under Lt. Lou Otlerbein constructed the stage, seating stands, 35 stage sets and hundreds of props.

In better weather when Red Cross parcels were more numerous, Lt. Kriegie participated in an active athletic program. Now he gets his exercise by walking and his favorite sports are cribbage, poker, bridge and chess.

Publications...

Lt. Kriegie gets his news from publications edited by Lt. Frank Diggs, News Officer, under supervision of the S-2, Lt. Col. James Alger. The Daily

Gedruckt: Oflag 64, Abteilung I d.
Druck: Willi Kricks, Altburgund

New Year's Sonnet

(Written to the loveliest girl in the world — who won't like it a bit)

I dream as only captive man can dream
Of life as lived in days that went before;
Of scrambled eggs and shortcakes thick with cream,
And onion soup and lobster Thermidor;
Of roasted beef and chops and T-bone steaks,
And turkey breast and golden leg or wing,
Of sausage, maple syrup, buckwheat cakes,
And chickens, broiled or fried or à la King.
I dwell on rolls or buns for days and days,
Hot cornbread, biscuits, Philadelphia scrapple,
Asparagus in cream or Hollandaise,
And deep-dish pies — mince, huckleberry, apple;
I long for buttered, creamy oyster stew,
And now and then, my pet, I long for you.

— Larry Phelan

Bulletin staff includes Lt. Diggs, editor; Lt. Seymour Bollen, chief translator; Lt. Ken Goddard, art editor; Lt. David Englander, feature editor; Lt. Tom Magee, printer; Lt. Charles Poaz, cartographer. Wright Bryan, Sunday editor; and Lts. Martin Smith, Carl Hansen and Ed Spicher, translators.

The OFLAG 64 ITEM staff includes Lt. Diggs, editor, and Lt. Larry Phelan, Lt. David Englander, Lt. Frank Hancock, Lt. Howard Holder, Lt. Teddy Roggen, Capt. Charles Wilkinson, Lt. Robert Cheatham, Lt. James Bickers, Lt. Alexander Ross and War Correspondent Wright Bryan.

Mail...

Of course the most important news to Lt. Kriegie is news from family and home. He gets this through the mail officer, Capt. Robert Schultz, and his assistant, Lt. Robert Henry.

Lt. Kriegie's allowance of outgoing mail is three letters and four cards a month. Protected personnel are allowed double this amount, while order-

ties are allowed two letters and four cards.

Letters from home average about 100 days in reaching Oflag 64. One took 467 days and the speed record is held by a letter to Lt. Amon Carter which reached here 14 days after it was written.

Incoming mail totals about 350 letters a day which works out to an average of about one letter every three days for the entire Oflag population, but old kriegies average about 15 letters a month.

All in all, John Average Kriegy has set up an efficient and well-run American camp within the barbed wire. He only wishes it were about 3000 miles due West from Altburgund.

REQUIEM...

(Continued from Page Two)

anniversary and other historic events being celebrated on the 6th, with all-star ball games, feasting, a special show and near-hysteria.

JULY was the month of the big carnival and "horse race" on Independence Day, mass sunbathing, Sol Levy's Variety Show and major gambling operations at the "Bloody Gut."

AUGUST brought a flood of new kriegies who all made bets with their elders that the war would be over in three weeks — or at the most three months, by Gawd.

SEPTEMBER brought the big all-camp track meet, the ITEM'S famed beauty contest, and big G-2 operations throughout the Oflag on whether the war would last out the fall.

OCTOBER was the first month of the Shortage and the Big Freeze, when a short, brisk fall sports program died.

NOVEMBER was the month of the camp's first all-original musical show, "Full Swing," the birth of "Altburgund Academy" as a full-scale camp education program, and a decline to the ersatz miniature golf craze.

DECEMBER killed all hopes of peace in '44, brought Red Cross parcels into the Oflag scene once more, and saw 1100 kriegies digging in for winter, emerging only long enough for the camp's classic Christmas feast last week. And here it is 1945.

F. D.